TALKING OF CHARLOTTE

E. A. Dineley

OTHER WORKS BY E.A. DINELEY

A Year and a Day (a poem available from the author)

The Death of Lyndon Wilder and the Consequences There Of and *Castle Orchard* (novels published by Constable and Robinson)

The Tale of Westcott Park and *North Rivenhead*

TALKING OF CHARLOTTE

VOLUME I

A companion to the diaries of Charlotte
Grove of Ferne House, between
the years 1811 and 1826

E.A. DINELEY

Copyright © E.A. Dineley 2023

All rights reserved.

Paperback ISBN: 979-8-36835-169-8
Hardback ISBN: 979-8-36835-223-7

The 1828 diary images on the front and back cover are reproduced by courtesy of the Wiltshire & Swindon History Centre (1641/157).

For the people of Berwick St John, past, present and future.

Introduction

The late Desmond Hawkins published a version of the Grove diaries, the work of four diarists from the same family, in 1995. It was he who unearthed them from the Grove family papers when he was researching his book on Agnes Grove, the wife of Walter Grove, Charlotte Grove's great-nephew. There being a vast amount of material, Desmond Hawkins produced only a portion of Charlotte's journals in his book. In their entirety they cover the period 1811 to 1858. Another small publication, which my husband unexpectedly produced from our bookshelves, was given to my husband by Desmond Hawkins in 1997. It is a transcription of Charlotte's brother Tom's journal of a tour to Scotland in 1818. In just a few lines it enlightened me on various matters that had puzzled me.

John Lane and his cousin, the late Valerie Lane Kay, are descended from the Lane family, once tenants of Upper and Lower Bridmore, Berwick St John. Their research into their ancestry led them to the Grove diaries. They painstakingly transcribed the whole of Charlotte's diaries and produced them in four handsome volumes, which are available from Claret Jug Publications. Without them I would never have begun to write my companions to these diaries, as aids to getting a better understanding of them. I should like to emphasise nothing can beat the real thing. I have picked my way through the diaries, drawing out what I find most relevant to Charlotte's family life, her social life and her relationship to Berwick St John. I am also indebted to John Lane for much additional information on the people who inhabited this area, rich and poor, two hundred years ago. In these companions, I reflect on the things that enlarge our knowledge of the period, what has altered and, surprisingly, what has stayed the same. I identify houses and places. I discuss the wider world when Charlotte bothers to mention it. My slant upon it is personal. Another person, settling to the same task, would have made a different selection; their comments would have differed from mine. I was born at Waterloo Farm, Motcombe, and brought up in Maiden Bradley. I have lived at Woodlands (Woolens to Charlotte), since 1969, when I married Francis Dineley, so I am familiar with the places that were familiar to Charlotte. Francis has lived here all his life, his grandmother arriving in 1909, so he has been able to provide me with all sorts of background knowledge. Our son Perin farms the land once farmed by Charles Foot.

I have added the odd comma, dash or full stop to quotes from Charlotte's diaries to make things intelligible. I have chosen to start each entry with the day and the month, in contrast to the manuscript, in which the day of the week is included. Charlotte did not spell with any accuracy, and unfortunately neither do I. Charlotte refers to Ferne both with and without an E. Charlotte was also a fanatical, illogical and erratic underliner. Reproducing it accurately is more than patience can manage, and it has been decided the text is better read without the distraction. Here is an example from the year 1814 and another from 1839:

'My little nephews *very* *much* *admired*. John talked about living upon A very spare D*iet* denominated *Love*.'

'We had a *delightful* *musical* treat & a very pleasant evening – the ladies were par*ticular*ly a*greea*ble (Mr Reads playing on the Piano Forte was difficult but not *h*armonious in my opinion).'

She has also, as I suspect was convention of the time, written Mr and Mrs with a superscript 'r' and 'rs' respectively, but for ease of reading I have not reproduced that when quoting her diaries. It does not matter too much. This is not a scholarly work. You must refer to John Lane and his cousin for that.

Spelling mistakes could be hers but sometimes they may be mine: I am grateful to Pen Milburn, Angela Bridges, Ralph Perry Robinson and Samantha Friesenbruch for their endeavours to rectify this and any other anomalies. They have all lived or now live in Berwick St John.

The diaries themselves are kept in the Wiltshire Archives. You may view them one by one. When John and Val saw them, they were at Trowbridge bundled into two cardboard boxes. They asked to have them put on to microfilm and from that their labours commenced.

The Groves of Ferne during the period 1811–1826

> Thomas Grove, born 1758. (His sisters were Aunt Chafin Grove of Zeals House and Aunt Grove of Netherhampton. Neither had children.)
> Charlotte Pilfold, born 1764, his wife. (She had two brothers, John, a captain in the Navy, and James. They both had Pilfold children. One sister was Mrs Jackson, married to Rev Gilbert Jackson, Rector of Donhead St Mary, parents of six sons and two daughters. The other sister was Lady Shelley, wife of Sir Timothy. They were parents of the poet Percy Bysshe, four daughters and a second son.)

> Charlotte was their eldest child, born 1783.
> Thomas, born 1783, married Henrietta Farquharson. No children. Two children with second wife.
> John, born 1784, married Jean Fraser. Seven children.
> Emma, born 1788, married John Horsey Waddington. Seven children.

William, born 1790, married Frances Grove. No children.
Harriet, born 1791, married William Helyar. Twelve children.
George, born 1793, married Charlotte Eyre. No children.
Charles, born 1794, married Elizabeth Hopkins. Six daughters.

Lots of these children – the Grove grandchildren, Charlotte's nephews and nieces – were born after 1826, and they make their appearances one by one throughout the diaries.

Charlotte Grove

Charles Bowles, a friend of the Grove family, was the brother of the poet William Bowles. As boys they lived at Barton Hill House, now the boarding house for Shaftesbury School. He wrote a book called *Hundred of Chalke*, which he published in 1830, three years after Charlotte Grove married the Rector of Berwick St John. It is a description of various villages, including ours. He starts the chapter headed Berwick St John in this manner: 'In pursuance of the plan I had prescribed to myself, I now enter the Vale of Chalke, the most sequestered and unfrequented district of this county.' He also says, 'The roads in the vale are impassable for any other four-wheel carriages than those used for husbandry purposes, and are suited only for a *sure footed* horse. Husbandry is, however, well understood, and the improved turnip system is generally pursued here.' With this fine introduction, we may enter Charlotte's Berwick St John.

Daughter of Thomas Grove and his wife, Charlotte née Pilfold, Charlotte was born in 1783, the year Britain finally recognised America as an independent state, daughter of Thomas Grove of Fernc. We need to have an idea of her brothers and sisters, the comings and goings of whom are her main concern. She is the eldest, but Thomas was born in the same year. In 1810 they were both twenty-seven, Charlotte on February 10th but Tom not until Christmas Day. He is already married to Henrietta Farquharson. John is twenty-six, training to be a doctor, I presume in London as he lives in Lincoln's Inn Fields. After that, the Groves' next three babies died as infants. Emma is twenty-two, married to John Horsey Waddington when she was seventeen and at this date is already a mother. William is twenty. He is in the Navy. Harriet was a year younger than him, so she is nineteen in 1810. Her diary, in 1809, says, *'Joy Joy Joy William Dear Dear William's come home'* and then *'William is so altered I should not have known him anywhere'*. This is hardly surprising as he had been in the Navy, in the East Indies, for the last seven years, since he was twelve. Marianne had been a year younger than Harriet but died when her dress caught fire, at the age of thirteen. George is seventeen. He was in the Merchant Navy. Charles is sixteen, in the Royal Navy. His ship was HMS BELLEROPHON, to which Napoleon surrendered after Waterloo, in 1815. His dislike of his profession is such that he, like George, gives it up. There is talk of his training to be a physician and he starts to learn Greek but by the time Charlotte is writing in 1811, he is at Oxford, preparing to be ordained. Louisa, the youngest, dies at fourteen, of whooping cough. Her death makes heart-rending reading in Harriet's diary, which precedes Charlotte's.

Charlotte started her diary in 1811. She lived until 1860, recording her life day to day, though some of her journals are missing. The earliest journals are devoted to her family and their social life. As she gets older, she becomes increasingly involved in the lives of the modest inhabitants not only of Berwick St John but also of Ludwell, Milkwell and the Donheads. I start where she starts, a woman of nearly twenty-eight. She says she bought her pocket book in Salisbury. Her parents tease her because the keeping of a pocket book is considered an occupation for an old maid. By twenty-eight you would have been considered past your best.

The Groves lived for two years at Tollard Royal whilst a new Ferne House was being built, I believe in what was the Rectory, so this is where she is. She describes them always walking. You can think of their clothes, early 19th century, much as depicted in a Jane Austen adaptation for the cinema or the television, the inconvenience of long gowns to the ankles and high waists, the men with very high collars and tight neck cloths.

1811

This first journal is one that I looked at. It is made of red leather with a folding flap. Inside it says it is 'The Complete Pocketbook or Gentleman's & Tradesman's Daily Journal for the Year of our Lord 1811'. It is laid out like an account book, but Charlotte wrote straight across the two pages and over the columns for £, s and d.

January 5th *'My Brothers John George & Charles walked to Aunt Jacksons & slept there. The former lost his hat on Win Green & the good humoured noisy George tied A Hdf. over his head.'* A man was never without his hat or a woman her bonnet. Mrs Jackson was Mrs Grove's sister, married to Gilbert Jackson, Rector of Donhead St Mary, so they were walking from Tollard Royal to Shute House, then the Rectory for Donhead St Mary. In Charlotte's day, it was known as Upper Donhead as opposed to Lower Donhead, now Donhead St Andrew.

January 7th *'My Sister & Self walked to Fern with My Father. A very disagreeable Walk. The Wind blew so I was stiff The whole Evening. The new Kitchen is A delightful Room & I like The grand Staircase.'*

To visualise the Ferne House then being built, think of the Old Rectory, Berwick St John. It has a central door and a window on each side. Ferne, which Charlotte spells with no final E, was similar but with two windows on each side, so that much bigger. It had a triangular pediment at the top which the Rectory does not have. The Rectory was built by the Rev Thomas Boys, Rector of Berwick St John when Charlotte commences her diary, so it cannot have been much older than Ferne.

Charlotte was not too precious. I get a feel of her tramping about our countryside here, on this occasion with her old school friend, Helen Tregonwell, in late January. *'I stumbled about in Pattens, thought I had broke a leg, stuck in the Mud and Helen hung in a Hedge like A Petticoat hung out to dry.'* At the same time, she is aware of her own position, and while visiting Bath complains a *'Gentleman impertinently wished to get acquainted with Me.'*

When it was too wet to walk they played *'battledore'* indoors. There was a game called Dumb Crambo, similar to charades: a word to be guessed from a mime. Later Charlotte becomes obsessed with chess. The family reads aloud to each other in the evening and always attend church on Sundays. If the weather is too bad, Mr Grove reads prayers at home.

January 9th *'We went to Mrs Gordons & over Ashcombe Hill in A Cart, were fearful the bottom of it would come out. Mrs Benett dined with Us & accompanied Us to the Shaston Ball, not many People & very freezing Cold.'* There were significant Benetts at Pythouse, but they also had cousins living in Berwick. Mrs Benett was probably one of the latter. There was more dancing to be had with the Gordons at Wincombe.

Charlotte is anxious for Harriet to marry William Helyar, the heir to Coker Court, but he was living in the meantime at Sedgehill in what we know as Hayes House. She makes various veiled references to this – *'on our return found Mr H Helyar at Tollard. A disappointment. H thought it was Billy'* and *'We saw Mr J Helyars servant at the Cottage, Harriet knew the Livery directly.'* Henry was one of William's brothers and John Helyar was his uncle, the Rector at Tollard Royal.

Mr Grove and George had been to London. On the 16th, *'George came home to Dinner & My Father just as We were set down at the Table. The little Man ties his cravat so well since he has been to Town that He looks quite smart.'* Charlotte was devoted to her father but affectionately refers to him as 'the little man'. On the 21st, *'My dearest of Brothers George left us to join His Ship.'* On the same day they drink to William's health: *'it being His Birthday & He of Age this Day.'*

January 24th *'The King is better. I hope He will be well before the Regency takes place.'* This is a reference to George III, who became insane. His eldest son was not entirely approved of. The Regency did not take place until 1820.

On the last day of January they hear Miss Laura Arundell is going to be married to *'A Mr Weld'*. This would unite two large Catholic, land-owning families, the Arundells of Wardour and the Welds of Lulworth Castle, both of whom have managed to stay in place until this day, though the Arundells no longer live in New Wardour Castle. As there were enormous restrictions placed on Catholics during this period, this is extra remarkable.

February 1st *'Charles Jackson and Hugh Helyar called. The Former has charming manners. The latter very shy indeed.'* The Jacksons had eleven or twelve children, of which Charles was the second. Hugh was another of William Helyar's brothers.

On the 5th, when eldest brother Tom is visiting with Mr Fraser, Charlotte says, with underlinings, obviously shocked, *'They called Mr Percival a Methodist.'* Mr Percival was Prime Minister at this time. A Miss F Benett came to stay, apparently a Catholic. In all my studies of Charlotte's diaries this is the only time I have found her to be mocking and unpleasant, so it quite pains me to include the entry. On Friday February 8th, *'The fair Catholic fasted. H & I took her blowing her nose for some of her devotions. H thought she was whipping herself.'* The *'took her'* as used here means interpreted. Miss Benett was the daughter of the late Rector of Donhead St Andrew, which makes her Catholic leanings strange. She would be a first cousin of John Benett of Pythouse. Many of Miss Benett's six siblings are mentioned by Charlotte.

February 9th *'My Father hunted so late, that We did not dine till 7 o'clock & it made Us very sleepy.'* At this period, they probably dined somewhere between three and five.

On the 11th they move out of their bedroom to make room for the Waddington family: Charlotte's married sister, Emma, her husband, John, and their three children, *'my dear little niece & two beautiful nephews'*. These are Emma, who is four, John, two, and George, born in 1810. The 14th is the Waddington's sixth wedding anniversary. *'The Servants drank Punch on the occasion & were very merry.'*

Mrs Grove wins a quarter of a lottery ticket of twenty-five pounds, a reasonable amount of money then. Charlotte *'finished making pink roses for our Bath expedition'*.

February 20th *'Dyed our Crape Gowns & made A fine dirty Room of it'*. It would be interesting to know how they did it and what they used.

February 24th *'Went to Church in the morning. It rained on our return. Waddington assisted me down the Hill having My Pattens on – obliged to run home as fast as We could as it rained quite hard.'* Pattens were a sort of metal overshoe, most often worn by the poor than the gentry.

They hope the Waddingtons will come to live at *'Woodcots'*. John Waddington owned a property of this name that I believe likely to be Woodcuts at Sixpenny Handley. Charlotte much regrets their departure; they return to their own bedroom.

February 27th *'My Father thinks the colour of whited brown Paper very pretty for one of the Rooms at Fern'*. Charlotte agrees and thinks she would like a gown of the same colour.

They visit Bath. *'In a Bustle packing up. A great event to Us Rusticks.'* I am interested they make no attempt to do the London season. In fact, the Groves, though large fish in this immediate locality, were not particularly grand. They are entertained at Wardour, Pythouse and at all the other places of similar standing, as well as having friends and relations in the Donheads. They do not go to Longleat or Wilton House. They arrive in Bath on the 1st of March and proceed to balls, concerts and theatres ad lib and do lots and lots of walking, so much so Charlotte complains of *'tired muscles very much with walking'*. They have a great-aunt there, Aunt Rudge. *'The old Aunt quite lame – The Servants run up & down the Room with Her. She looked like A Corpse.'*

I get a feel of Bath life. They go to the places one would expect, the Pump Room, the Circus, the Crescent, *'walked up Lansdown', 'walked to Prior Park'*, and of course the Assembly Rooms. There were two of these, the Upper, which can be seen to this day, and the Lower. The Upper Rooms opened in 1771, according to Wikipedia, and the Lower ones since demolished. Charlotte danced in both. Charlotte says, *'went to the Ball in the Lower Rooms'*, this being 1811. Getting a partner for dancing could be haphazard, as the master of ceremonies, at this time Mr King, could bring a man up to be introduced to you. Charlotte says, *'went to the ball – danced with a vulgar partner'*. The weather played a part *'Mrs Groves took Us to the Rooms – being wet no chance of getting into A Cotillion'*. This I take it because an indoors occupation was preferable to walking and shopping. *'We went to the Ball But did not dance.'* I am reminded of the heroine in *Northanger Abbey*, but things could be better. This is indeed the Bath as depicted by Jane Austen. On the 18th, *'In the Evening to Mrs Jekylls Rout stupid enough, to the Ball afterwards which We liked. I danced before tea with Mr Willoughby afterwards with a Gentleman introduced by Mr King.'* (Stupid was used where we would say dull or boring.) The word rout confuses me. A rout is a disorderly flight after a defeat in battle, so how does it also come to mean a formal gathering, usually in the evening? I suppose a rout has morphed into the modern smartish drinks party. Charlotte obviously thought them a dull form of entertainment. She preferred to dine or dance. *'Went to Dr Hayworths Rout. I did not like it at all. The Ice the best thing there.'*

March 25th *'Went to the Upper Rooms. Mr King introduced Me to A Mr Scott A very gentlemanlike Man with whom I danced Country dances before Tea & he is engaged as My Partner for Cotillons.'* At this period, no connotation seems to be put on dancing with the same man throughout the entertainment. On the other hand, in *Northanger Abbey*, written about twelve years earlier, Jane Austen makes a point of Miss Thorpe saying she must not dance more than twice with James Moreland, so I cannot get to the bottom of it. Charlotte does remark on Harriet dancing *'all the evening'* with a Mr Cratton who is *'rather struck with her'*. I wonder if William Helyar is happy to leave Harriet to all the temptations of Bath society, but I cannot see he pursues her very ardently. They sometimes spent the morning practising cotillions: Charlotte spells them any way but thus. *'Fagging about our Cotillons in the morning, disappointed in the Evening. A stupid hot Ball, danced Country Dances with Mr Ross.' 'Practised in the morning & danced Cotillons in the Evening. My Partner Mr Scott many young Ladies wished to be introduced to him.'* Charlotte had many partners during their stay, not always satisfactory.

They spend time with Mrs J Helyar. *'Call on the Helyars. Mr Harry Helyar there. We walked to Sydney Gardens & got into the Swing. Mr H Helyar left Us in the Labyrinth with His Nephew.'* Harry was, I think, one of William's brothers, as he had one called Henry. Mr and Mrs J Helyar, you may remember, were William's aunt and uncle. The twelve acres of Sydney Gardens were laid out in 1795. I do not know if they have a labyrinth now, I shall have to go and look, but they obviously had things to amuse. Jane Austen lived at 4, Sydney Place.

Charlotte does not say where they were living or whether *'Aunt Chafin'*, with whom they were staying, had a house in Bath or took one for a month or so. They went to church in what Charlotte refers to as Margarets. Whilst in Bath *'Poor Miss Randolph died of a decline'*. I sometimes wonder if a decline amounted to anorexia.

April 2nd *'We went to the Lower Rooms. I am nearly tired of Dancing. A Mr Thomas My Partner Mrs Merrick nearly lamed me in the morning.'*

April 4th *'We tried to persuade Mr H Helyar to dance Cotillons but he would not however We made up Our Set after Tea.'*

April 5th *'Aunt Jackson had another Son heard it the 1st of April.'*

April 6th *'Left Bath sorry to part with My Aunt Chafin. We read Shakespeare in the Carriage – met Mr William Helyar & Mr Wake close to Sedgehill. Found My dear Parents quite well on our return to Tollard & my dear friend Helen Tregonwell with them.'*

April 7th *'Mr Elwin called, Those naughty Girls did not call me down stairs chusing to have that agreeable Man all to themselves – We had a very pleasant Conversation after Dinner against Atheism.*' Charlotte's cousin Bysshe Shelley had been expelled from Oxford, on March 25th, for failing to deny writing a pamphlet entitled 'The Necessity of Atheism'.

Mr Hamilton, the architect, is sending the plasterers into Ferne.

On April 12th, Charlotte reports on little George Waddington having the whooping cough. She then says, *'Ld. Wellington has driven Massina out of Portugal'.* The withdrawal of the French from Portugal into Spain actually happened on April 5th. She mentions this again on the 24th, so this possibly accounts for the time the news took to arrive in greater detail. Britain had been at war, first with the French revolutionary army and then with Napoleon, on and off but mostly on, since 1793. The years 1808 to 1814 were spent in turning the French out of Spain and Portugal.

April 13th *'Fox the Newfoundland Dog walked with us.'*

On the 14th, *'Went to Church in the Evening. Knelt too devoutly in the wrong Place. Helen and My Mother laughed at Me & the little Man looked as grave as A Judge.'*

April 15th *'Harriet & I staid at Home purposely to receive Mr John Helyar & he did not call on Us – My mother & Helen met the impolite Man on Ashcombe Hill & He was highly flattered by our attention proud enough I make no doubt.'*

Charlotte does not ride but Mrs Grove does. *'My Mother rode & Myrtle was rather frisky.'*

April 26th *'We walked to Ash Grove. Helen descried three Villains lurking behind A hedge which forced Us to a hasty retreat & in as quick A manner as Wellington drove Massena from Portugal.'*

Charlotte is reading *The Mysteries of Udolpho*, which is just what Catherine Morland is reading in Northanger Abbey – Jane Austen making fun of it.

Visits to Ferne were frequent. Charlotte calls the intervening ascents and descents between Tollard and Berwick the Alps. Even in May, *'A thorough wet Day, were glad when We got safe over the Alps without being blown over.'*

May 12th *'Byshe Shelley is returned home.'* He and Harriet had been youthful sweethearts. Mrs Grove and Shelley's mother were sisters. Harriet's journals for 1809 and 1810 make many references to him, later crossed out, but now she seems much more interested in William Helyar, though he does not often make an appearance. The church-going Groves would have not approved of atheism.

May 13th *'Tom came over to see us with a Budget of Grievances.'* Tom, married to Henrietta Farquharson, was usually sunny and amusing, so this is out of character. The entry is concluded with the words, *'My Mother frightened with some Mice in her Cupboard.'*

They visit the Stills who lived at Clouds. The present 'Clouds', a much later building, was the creation of the Wyndhams. Eileen Fisher-Row, whom many people will remember living at Ansty, was married to a Still of this same family. He died young. One of his two daughters lives at Hindon, but as far as I know there are none bearing the name of Still in the area now.

May 15th *'Harriet & myself walked to Fern…on our return got wet through & went to Bed. Mr Tregonwell came to Dinner & slept here – entertained Us talking of our income (my Sister & Me).'* Charlotte is amused by this because as girls their only income would have been pocket money given them by their father. All their brothers, except the eldest, were expected to have careers. Mr Grove would have to find money for the girls if they married; a young woman of their social standing was not expected to come to the altar empty handed.

May 18th *'We walked out in the evening & played our Flageolets to the Cows whilst They were milked. My Father saw Us & laughed at Us.'* A flageolet is a wooden instrument something like a recorder. Charlotte does not mention playing one of these again, so maybe only the cows benefited.

May 20th *'Received before Breakfast A Kind Note & Present of A Gown from Tom & Henrietta. The latter has invited Harriet & Myself to go with her to Col Pleydells Ball next Wednesday.'* This gown would have been a piece of cloth of the correct length to be made up into a gown, rather than the finished article. It would have been possible to buy ready-made clothes, but the Groves were unlikely to have done so.

Tom and Henrietta were at Lyttleton, a house still to be seen in Blandford St Mary, now divided into flats. It is difficult, at times, to work out where Tom was living while he waited to inherit Ferne from his father. It is a recurrent theme through Charlotte's diaries. Littleton, as it seems to be spelt now – though I see the road nearby is spelt with a Y – was a Farquharson property. Tom's brother-in-law was a famous master of foxhounds, J.J. Farquharson.

The ball was at Blandford. The following day they walk into Blandford *'to see Col Pleydell & Officers on Parade & heard their Band play.'* Britain teemed with soldiers at this period owing to the Napoleonic wars.

May 24th *'We returned to Tollard. Coming through Blandford Our Horses frightened by the Military band. Went into the Inn till they had done playing.'*

On the 25th, *'My father walked after Dinner with Harriet & me & told Us the names of some Herbs Shrubs &c. We had A dissertation on fair people & Brunettes my Mother & Self against My Father & Harriet.'* As we have no image of Charlotte, I wonder what category she came under.

May 26th *'The weather so intensely hot We shall for the future walk after tea.'* Tea was taken sometime after dinner, dinner at this period probably round about four o'clock. *'Mr Mrs Warren & the Plaisterer dined here. I hope it will induce the latter to keep sober.'* They would have dined with the servants. We do not know where the builders who built Ferne came from or where they lived whilst doing so. Mr Hamilton, the architect, was in charge, though builders and architects were not so clearly defined as they are now. The Warrens are not otherwise mentioned, so we do not know who they were.

May 27th *'Mrs White the Millers Wife at Critchell brought to bed of three Girls. My father gave them A £1 note on the occasion.'* Unfortunately, we do not hear if they survived. As there was a shortage of gold owing to the French Revolutionary War, one pound bank notes were issued in 1805. They were hand-written.

On the 29th, they go off to Cranborne. Charlotte at this period talks of St Barbe. *'He is very good tempered & particularly civil to the ladies.'* I have to turn to Desmond Hawkins to find out who these people are. Mr Tregonwell is Lewis Dymoke Grosvenor Tregonwell no less, the father of Charlotte's friend Helen, and St Barbe is her brother. They were the children of his first wife. He later married Henrietta Portman of Bryanston, which would explain the frequent Portman presence. Where Tregonwell built his new house is now the centre of Bournemouth, and he is viewed as the founding father of the town. He built the new house as a summer residence for his second wife who had become depressed after the death of her second child from an accidental overdose of medicine. There is a slightly odd-looking statue of Tregonwell in Bournemouth, a little too odd to describe. His house in Cranborne was Cranborne Lodge, as opposed to Cranborne Manor, which, then and now, belonged to the Salisburys.

May 30th *'A party of Pleasure to Bourne Cliff, Mr Tregonwells new House, dined on cold meat in the house…St Barbe walked through A Brook 8 times to help Us over. Mrs Portman & The Miss Williams's met us at Bourne. The Sea Shore there beautiful. Returned in the evening.'*

June 1st *We came home. St Barbe gave Us a beautiful Nosegay. My Father rode to Fern. The building has proceeded very fast this week.'*

There is an early reference to the odd history of Ashcombe. In June, they hear Mr Arundell is going to let it to Mr Paul Methuen, the Methuens being the family from Corsham Court.

There is much to-ing and fro-ing of visits. The Penruddockes from Compton Chamberlayne stay with them. The Arundells from Wardour call. Walter Long, their relation, *'commanded the Hindon Troop at the review'*.

June 14th *'we are in hopes of an insurrection in France'*, that is an uprising against Napoleon.

Mr Grove wakes in the night, having heard someone trying to get through the drawing room window. He opened the bedroom window and frightened him away. The next night precautions are taken. *'We barricaded the Doors &c – & put Cybele in the Passage fearful lest the Thieves should come again.'* Cybele is one of the family dogs.

At Ferne, *'Mr Towsey came to cut the Arms & could not do it. My Father sent to Mr Hyscock of Blandford'*. In the photograph of the 1811 Ferne, this coat of arms is clearly visible, central above the top story windows. Francis says it was still there in the much-enlarged later version of the house.

June 18th *'We went to Fern in the Phaeton – the New Garden Wall is measured out.'* This is no doubt a bit of Charlotte's Ferne that is still there.

June 19th *'Went first to Fern where I lost my near sighted Glass.'* My image of Charlotte shifts a little – she was short-sighted. She finds it a few days later.

They stay at Netherhampton, the home of her father's unmarried sister, Aunt Grove. You can see this pretty house from the road if you come down from Salisbury racecourse and branch right as towards Odstock. It is set back on your left, and it has a distinctive shape, the central block higher than the sides.

June 22nd *'Dined at Close Gate with Our old Uncle & Aunt. The former quite facetious.'* This Salisbury property was later inhabited by John. The aunt and uncle I think are a great-aunt and -uncle, but they are not explained. Charlotte then says, *'Walked into the Cathedral & saw my Uncle Longs Monument by Flaxman, the most elegant one there.'* Flaxman (1755–1826) was a leading sculptor of the period. They return two days later.

Mrs Grove is seeing someone about furniture for Ferne. *'Harriet & Myself walked in the HayField. She impudently threw me on the Haycocks.'* As I have read through these diaries many times, I see Charlotte was at her most frivolous when she still had Harriet as a companion.

June 28th *'Walked in the Evening with my Father & Harriet to Rushmore. The little Man rather frisky. We were obliged to keep him in order.'*

On July 1st, *'Mr Foots son of the Barick Farm met with an accident – his left hand was blown off. Particularly unfortunate as he is a lawyer.'* I cannot see why being a lawyer made it more than ordinarily unfortunate, unless he was left handed.

I shall take this moment to divert from the diaries in order to outline the farming families of the parish, though we learn more about them later. This is the first mention of the Foots, who were farming Manor – or Berwick – Farm. Charlotte is casual in the spelling of Berwick, first Barick, sometimes Barrick, then settles to Berwick. In older documents, I have seen it spelt Barwick. According to Bowles, the Foots had been two hundred years in Berwick by the time of his writing. There are monuments to them in the south transept of the church, and thirty-two of them are mentioned in the Rev Mr Goodchild's list of monumental inscriptions compiled in 1920.

When I came here in 1969, Dolly Foot lived on the Cross. She had a grandson called Gerald who used to ask Francis for a cottage, as Berwick was the natural home of the Foot family. Bunty Hall, married into a longstanding Berwick farming family, tells me Dolly Foot was the mother of Phil Foot, who lived in the ex-police house at the bottom of Elcombe Lane, Alvediston. His children were Gerald and Gill. It occurred to me later that as he of the diaries, Charles Foot of Manor Farm, left no male heir and nor did his brother Samuel, a lawyer, from whom did the modern-day Foots descend? There was also Stephen Foot, not known to be of the same family as Charles and Samuel, who owned no property and was of a different social background, but regularly featured in the diaries, especially the later ones, as parish clerk and a player of the bass viol. He had one son, James. I applied to John Lane, who immediately enlightened me. That one son, James, a carpenter, married Anna Lathey in 1856 and had a son, William, a gardener, who married Catherine Brickwood in 1886. They had a son, Reginald, who married Dorothy Burt and lived in Water Street. They were the parents of Philip (Phil) Foot and the grandparents of Gerald and Gill. Apart from John Lane himself, they are the only people I can tie in as direct descendants of someone living in Berwick St John at the time Charlotte Grove was writing her diaries.

Bowles – whose writing I find extremely confusing, so I may not have got it all right – says the parish of Berwick St John was about 3578 acres. He states it is made up of 'the ancient freehold estates called Easton Farm, Cotties or Cothayes, Upton, Upper and Lower Bridmore, Ashcombe and Rushmore, and the farm called Berwick Farm, anciently held by lease of the lord of the manor, but now converted to a freehold.' Manor Farm was usually referred to as Berwick Farm, but Bowles is clear they were one and the same. Dairy House Farm and Cross Farm are not mentioned, so basically the farming land was divided between Upton, the two Bridmores, Berwick Farm, with Ashcombe and Rushmore on the perimeter. Mr John Lush was Thomas Grove's tenant at Upton but had some property of his own in the parish.

Cothays (Cuttis, where Judy Bell, a resident, kept her cow) is described as an ancient freehold estate. Monks, which are the two fields on from the Halls' dairy, belonged to Henry Foot, who obtained them via his wife, who was her brother James Foot's heir. The Foots must have intermarried. Berwick Farm was being farmed by this Henry Foot, who died in 1820, and then by his fourth son, Charles. The two Bridmores, Lord Rivers owning Upper Bridmore and Thomas Grove owning Lower Bridmore, were farmed by the Lane family, whose descendants have so painstakingly transcribed and published Charlotte's diaries. Some properties were leased for the duration of three lives. This was certainly the case for Berwick Farm. Mr Lush also owned Vincent's and Gould's. I do not know where these places are, but the names all appear in the Rev Goodchild's (Rector of Berwick 1899–1933) manuscripts. He copied documents relating to the village in the 17th century. In the parish register pertaining to the 18th century, one Samuel Foot married Anne Bright of Berwick St John in 1729. Lisle Gould, daughter of Josiah and Jane Gould, was born here in 1768. She married Samuel Foot (I assume not the same one) in 1786. Their son was baptised on 22nd December 1790. Both mother and child were buried in the January of 1791. In 1655, there were living here a Vincent, a Bright, a Monke/Munke, a

Gould, a Foote and then Lucus, Scamell and Sanger. Names of places linger on, but they are fluid. They disappear or are overridden. A prime example is Woodlands. I was confused because Charlotte never referred to Woodlands but she often walked via Woolens when returning from Norrington. At a chance meeting I had with Angela Bridges, she told me she had been talking to Mrs Dobbs, daughter of the late Joe and Molly Scammell, long-time resident here, who mentioned Woolens. *Where was that? Do you mean Woodlands?* Mrs Dobbs then said they always called it Woolens. I fumbled through the Goodchild papers for the hundredth time. He writes clearly Woollands and also Woodlands. Back in the 17th century, it seems to be Wollens. When old Mrs Dineley built this house in 1936, perhaps to clear up confusion, perhaps not liking Woodlands because there is no wood, she called it Whitesheet. Francis changed it back so that it agreed with the ordnance survey map.

Bowles talks of the monument to Samuel Foot in the south transept. He had been a solicitor in Sherborne, dying in 1792, so of a previous generation. In the grounds of one of the boarding houses attached to Sherborne School is an amazing building, the interior decorated from top to bottom with shells. I was asked to photograph it by the Dorset Gardens Trust, who assured me, at the time, it was created by this Samuel Foot. Since then, I have heard there is another contender. Bowles says that Samuel Foot, having been successful, 'retired to his native place, and having purchased of a Mr Barrett, the house at the east end of the parish, he enlarged the same and died there'. The likely candidate for this house must be the Priory, though it is never mentioned by any name in the diaries until the end of Charlotte's life. Francis and the Halls tell me it was Townsend Farm, but I get no mention of a Townsend Farm. In the tythe redemption map of 1840, there is a mention of Townsend Field but not farm. Samuel Foot was born in 1704. He wrote a will in 1784, eight years before he died. His first wife was Mary Gundry. She must have been a widow, because he leaves a little money to her son and daughter. He leaves property to his present wife and money to his nephews and nieces. He seems to have had no children of his own. He leaves to his brother Joseph 'the house and orchard with the lease of ground called Clarks…which I purchased of Cecelia James and John her son in Berwick St John.' Joseph was also to have 'the rick and staddle that stands in the said orchard with the stones that appurts thereto belonging…' Francis says Clarks was where Enid Winston's house now stands, Highfields. The Henry Foot farming Berwick Farm was Samuel's nephew and his 'residuary legatee', inheriting all his possessions not mentioned otherwise. This Henry, obviously the most favoured nephew, was also his executor.

Bowles, in his piece on Easton Farm, all one until the advent of Norman and Bryan Follet, tells us how this ground belonged to the manor of Easton Basset in Donhead St Andrew, which explains the oddity of the east side of Water Street, until rectified, being in Donhead. At one time, if as a bride you lived on that side but wished to be married in Berwick church, you had to take up at least pretend residence on the west side for the requisite number of months. In our copy of *Hundred of Chalke*, we have an extra paper by Rev William Goodchild dated 1920. He says the mansion at Easton was near the chapel (meaning the long-departed chapel that gives Chapel Farm its name) but was pulled down in 1643 and the materials used to build the present house, which must be the farmhouse that was until recently the farmhouse for Easton Farm. Bowles gives the date as 1658. Nigel Follet, whose family have farmed here for several generations, told me at one time this house had a storey added to it. At one end of it but not at the other, the thatch of an older roof can be observed under the later roof, which does seem more than curious. I now return to Charlotte.

July 2nd *'A Thunder Storm, My Mother hid herself in the Cellar – Mr Lushes eldest Son came to talk to my Father about Woodcots.'* This was Waddington's property, which I have mentioned as probably being Woodcuts in Handley.

July 4th *'We received A large Pacquet from William. He is now A first Lieutenant on board The Hecate Frigate º & they are going to take the*

Island of Java.' This turned out to be a major disaster for William, which we will come to shortly. On the 7th, she copies some of William's letter for her *'Uncle Pilfold'*. Mrs Grove had two brothers who feature in the diaries, John and James. John was a captain in the Navy and had been at Trafalgar, so I reckon he is the likely one to want news of William. I am thinking of adopting Charlotte's spelling of packet.

Some of Charlotte's entries ring home to us folk with dogs. *'Harriet & myself walked in the Evening to Rushmore. Rover went with Us obliged to lead him by tyeing A pocket hdf. over him or he would have hunted the Deer.'* This must be one of the oldest popular names for a dog, whereas Cybele is a Roman goddess.

July 8th *'The Miss Benetts of Norton came to Us… They think This cottage in situation like Their Cousins at Barick.'* Do they refer to the Priory, though not named as such? People had an odd notion of a cottage, anything smaller than a mansion. I have a book by Robert Moody, *Mr Benett of Wiltshire*, about John Benett of Pythouse. He makes mention of James Bennett, two Ns and two Ts, of Berwick St John, who was a distant cousin, a watchmaker and silversmith, living in Salisbury, of which he was elected mayor in 1825 when he was twenty-eight. The Bennetts of our war memorial have two Ns and two Ts. The exact connection I do not know, but they were cousins. The Miss Benetts of Norton (Norton Bavant) were definitely Pythouse Benetts, the unmarried sisters of John Benett. They were learned. Etheldred studied geology and supplied a catalogue of fossils for Hoare's *Modern Wiltshire*. It is said she was given a doctorate in civil law by St Petersburg; they thought she was a man. In those days, women were not accepted in scholarly societies. Anna was an amateur botanist. Charlotte goes walking with Miss Anna. They see the church *'in which is A Knight Templar & also seeing King John's Palace'*.

July 11th *'The Miss Benetts left Us – The Antiquarian A good creature But very Talkative.'*

A few days later they walk to Ferne and sit down in the stone quarry in the wood. They walk to Ferne most days, recording the progress of the building step by step, as any of us know who have been in that situation. They eat the fruit in the gardens there. *'They have painted The Attics at Fern so badly with The White Paint, that it will not last not having put any lead in it.'* In those days you were careful not to inhabit newly painted rooms until quite dry because of the lead in the paint.

July 14th *'Read in the Newspaper Col Sergison's death.'* In Charlotte's journals this is the only reference to Col Sergison. She had stayed some time with her uncle, Captain Pilfold, who had hoped, I have somewhere read, she might marry this widower, who was a friend of his.

July 15th *'We went to Fern – St Swithin's & it rained A little. We walked with My Father & Mother to the Farmers new enclosure of Fern Park – Mr Wilkins came to see Thomas the Bailiff who had caught A Chill drinking cold Beer when he was hot.'* This was obviously deemed a very dangerous practice. I assume Charlotte refers to Thomas Shere, but the use of his Christian name is unusual, so I am left with a question mark.

July 16th *'We then went to Fern. The house does not appear to proceed much. The Windows are come.'* It seems strange to have painted the attics before putting in the windows.

July 18th *'In the Evening surprised by the arrival of My Aunt Grove. Edwards bounced into the Room & announced her.'* Edwards was their butler.

July 19th *'A Dog ran away with a Chicken just as the Cook was going to truss it. Her & Mr Whatley had a run in consequence.'*

On the 21st *'My good Aunt in A fright about her taxes.'*

On the 24th, they go off to Netherhampton in order to go to Salisbury races. These included a ball and a supper. Charlotte dances with *'Mr Locke & Mr C Penruuddocke'*. On the 27th, they go on to Compton Chamberlayne, the seat of the Penruddockes.

On the 28th, *'Only 50 minutes in Church. Dr Poole was so very rapid.'* We 21st-century members of the congregation would not feel so very short changed with fifty minutes.

They then return to Netherhampton: *'We all walked in the Evening in Wilton Park & saw Lady Pembrokes Cottage.'* The Groves were once stewards of the Pembrokes. Though they do not associate with them, Lord Pembroke is applied to in times of trouble.

Charlotte and Harriet go on to Zeals at the beginning of August to stay a few days with Aunt Chafin, their father's other sister, who had married a family connection, William Chafin Grove. As I grew up at Maiden Bradley, I was familiar with Zeals House – known as Black Dogs, Zeals, owing to the two lead dogs on the gate pillars that could be seen before they altered the road to give access to the new A303. The black dogs are of course the Talbot dogs of the Grove heraldic crest, as in our pub. There were no Chafin Groves there when I was young, but there was a Mrs Troyte Bullock, who had certainly married a descendant. I went to the odd party in the house. It is now one of those unfortunate places that frequently changes hands, the mysterious owners locked behind their park walls. *'My Aunt Chafin received Us most cordially & kissed both of Us…Harriet & Myself walked in the wood after dinner – & played Chess in the Evening which put Us in A heat.'*

August 3rd *'A wet Evening & of course rather dull As We did not read & got very tired of Work.'* Though Charlotte does not say so, Aunt Grove is the preferred aunt. This one obviously sets them down to a great deal of sewing.

August 4th *'Went to Church at Mere, in the great lumbering coach. Mr Carwithers preached very well & gave Us an excellent Sermon.'*

Aunt Chafin shows them a portfolio of her drawings and gives them two. They begin to teach her to play chess but *'She did not seem in the least interested about it.'* Aunt Grove comes to join them. *'Her Sister treats her very rudely We think.'* Mr Martin and Mr Carwithers come to dinner: *'A silent Party at first, But the latter talked a great deal at last.'* They now start to teach Aunt Grove chess. They walk up Castle Hill in Mere and see *'Barkers Hill, Donhead Cliffs, Knoyle and Shaftesbury'*.

Bypassing Ferne, they accompany both aunts back to Netherhampton. *'We saw Fern at A distance & met Mr Beckfords Dwarf.'* They must have broken their journey in the vicinity of Fonthill. Mr Beckford's dwarf had a cottage and a garden especially made for him. I will talk of Beckford a bit later on.

From Netherhampton, they walk into Salisbury. Charlotte says, *'We saw the Wild Beasts'* and then *'The Zebra is a beautiful Animal.'* I never heard there was a zoo in Salisbury. It was probably a travelling menagerie of some sort. Photography makes us familiar with much of the world of which our ancestors could only guess at from books or would have no understanding.

August 15th *'We went to see Wilton House – Mr Merrick gave us much information. The statues &c more interesting to me than ever on that account.'* Mr and Mrs Merrick were friends of Aunt Grove.

August 17th *'We came to Bishopstone; Found our Friends the Bromleys quite well. Mr John & Charles Louder with them. The House reminds me of a Welch Inn.'* I do not know Bishopstone well enough to identify this, but Mr Bromley was the Rural Dean. During their stay, they take an evening walk *'to the upper Mill'* where they are *'treated with Beer & Cyder by the Miller'*. This somewhat affects Mr Bromley, who is *'A little elevated after Supper…subdued at last.'* Having supper indicates the hour of dinner was early, three or four o'clock.

They proceed to Cranbourne, as Charlotte spells it, on the 21st, to stay with the Tregonwells at Cranborne Lodge. Mrs and Miss Portman are there. *'Mr Tregonwell & St Barbe came home from Bourne in the evening.'*

August 23rd *'We hunted after Gypsies to have Our Fortunes told. Miss W Portman dressed up as A married Lady Likely to increase her Family. But unluckily we did not meet with Them. Mrs Smith tumbled which made Us all laugh.'* I have a sense of Charlotte and Harriet running a little wild, free from the constraints of parental authority. Gypsies were usually to be avoided.

The following evening, they go to Cranborne Fair. Charlotte says she and St Barbe *'lead the Way coming home in the Dark through the Shrubbery. We had some Fun. Mrs T. gave H & myself Fairings.'* A fairing was some trifling object bought at a fair.

On the 25th, Peregrine Bingham dines with them and *'played & sung to Us with great taste and expression'*. He was one of the two sons of Mr and Mrs Bingham. The following day they *'called on Mrs Bingham by appointment to hear her Son play on the Flute. The Poet walked to Ringwood and forgot it…Mrs B came to make apologies for her absent Son. He himself came in the Evening in the best manner He could with His Flute – (Mrs Smart & Niece of the Party of disappointed Ladies).'* I came across a reference to Peregrine Bingham in *The Journal of Thomas Moore*. Thomas Moore was an Irish poet and a significant composer of sheet music, the 'pop idol' of the period. Though he was hailed as 'the first poet of the age', he is now little known. He could often be persuaded to sing after dinner, his own Irish Melodies, reducing the tender hearted to tears, ladies rushing from the room overcome with emotion. He met young Bingham in the company of Bingham's uncle, William Bowles, another poet, who at one time was curate in East Knoyle. Moore says, 'Bingham clever and talkative…Sung in the evening; so did Mr Bingham, some of Burn's and of mine, with a good deal of spirit.' This was in 1824. Peregrine Bingham's father, another Peregrine, becomes Rector of Berwick St John in 1817 (succeeding Mr Boys), so they feature in the journals extensively from then on. Mrs Bingham was a sister of Charles and William Bowles.

The Binghams were from Binghams Melcombe. I have already mentioned the musical son. The Rev Peregrine Bingham had been a chaplain in the Navy, serving under Thomas Hardy, whose references to him, in various letters, indicate considerable irritation at his never being on board ship when he should have been. He was, I believe, on board the *Victory* at the blockade of Toulon, but went home before Trafalgar.

On August 29th, they return to Tollard. *'The Phaeton sent for Us with A pr. of Horses in it.'*

August 30th *'We called on Mrs Cooke. Miss Cooke is A very pretty Crop.'* Mrs Cooke was the widow of Captain John Cooke, who was killed commanding the Bellerophon at Trafalgar. You can see his monument in Donhead St Andrew Church, complete with a poem by William Bowles. A crop, very short hair, was something I know women did have at this period but I rarely see illustrated. The Cookes lived at Donhead Lodge and their daughter was Louisa. For a man to have had his hair cropped had radical connotation. It was all to do with not having your hair powdered, as the powder was made from flour and thus you were depriving the poor, the flour needed for bread. It was also a sign of being a Jacobin. Charles James Fox had his hair cropped, but I would say by this date powdering was on the wane and probably the associated connotation of cropped hair too.

Ferne now does look just about ready. Charlotte remarks on the *'Two Tent Beds'* being in *'our room'* and the following day *'Placed Our Beds to Our Satisfaction.'* I imagine from this she and Harriet share a room. They see *'The Marble Chimney Piece for the Dining Room.'*

September 3rd *'My Father went into the Garden & eat A great many Nuts. (naughty little Man).'*

September 5th *'The grates arrived from Bristol & two of the Doors from Town.'* Town meant London, but one would have thought they could have been acquired closer or just made by the estate carpenter.

They see the comet on the 6th and again on the 9th, walking up the hill especially. On the 9th, William Helyar dines with them after shooting with John. He returns to Sedgehill the next day.

September 16th *'The Man is putting up The Kitchen Grate & Smoke Jack.'* A smoke jack was a rotating spit for roasting meat. It was driven by the hot air rising from the fire, turning a fan up the chimney.

September 17th *'Wagons going off. Bustle and confusion sending Our things to Fern.'*

September 21st *'We got in The New House at Fern to Our great joy. May the Owners of this charming Mansion enjoy years of happiness within these Walls...we made an excellent Dinner upon Cold Roast Beef.'*

On the 23rd, her brother John gets a black eye out hunting, *'which made this Beau fear he should not look so well at the races.'* The following day, the 24th, they go off to Rood Ashton. This belonged to their cousins, the Longs. The house was built in 1808 to replace an earlier house, so it was quite new. It was added to in the 1930s and became huge. A servants' wing, rescued, is all that is left of it now. It is in the vicinity of Chippenham, where they attend the races. *'Lady Arundell and Miss Jones accompanied Us in the Barouche. We laughed & talked the whole time.'* Afterwards there was a ball. Charlotte names her partners as Captain Langham RN, Walter Long and Lord Arundell. Miss Jones was Lady Arundell's sister. They do pretty much the same the next day, with the addition of a concert. On the 27th they dine at Corsham Court, the seat of the Methuens, but return to Rood Ashton in the evening. The entertainment when not dancing was *'commerce'*, which they played with real money but not high stakes. They go home on the 30th.

Charlotte talked of *'building castles in the air'* both for Harriet and John. By today's standards, Harriet hardly seems to have seen William Helyar. We do not know if they were permitted to correspond. She had corresponded with Shelley, but there was the excuse that they were cousins. On October 1st, John and Charles go to Sedgehill to shoot with William Helyar and bring him back to Ferne the following day. *'He danced with Harriet in the Evening & I have hopes that what I wish may happen.'* Charlotte shows not the smallest signs of jealousy.

October 2nd *'Our Castles have A good Foundation. Harriet check-mated by W.H.'* Later in the day he *'drove Harriet out in his curricle.'* A curricle was a two-wheeled vehicle drawn by a pair of horses. The owner would drive it himself. It all seems very sudden to me. It may have been the first time this young couple were alone together. It was fashionable to have the smallest possible man or boy, known as a tiger, to sit up behind, ready to jump down and hold the horses' heads when they came to a halt. It was very much the sports car of the era.

On October 3rd, they were visited by *'The Miss Benetts of Barick.'* I again wonder where they lived; the Priory, then anonymous, was still the most likely. I think of the Samuel Foot who acquired 'the house at the east end of the parish' in the previous century. A few days later, they admire the Miss Benetts' piano forte. There are not many houses in Berwick that could have boasted a piano and also pleasure grounds, mentioned later.

October 5th *'Walked round the Plantation alone – I like my future Brother better every day.'* Though Charlotte expresses every joy at Harriet's marriage, she will lose her chief companion. Harriet is twenty, eight years younger than Charlotte. William Helyar is twenty-three.

On the 8th, *'two of the Columns in the Hall taken down, now it looks perfectly beautiful.'* In Desmond Hawkins' book, there is a picture of the hall at Ferne, complete with columns, but Francis says these were the columns of the house enlarged by Charlotte's nephew in the early 1850s. When Ferne was demolished, he bought the columns. Some of them now adorn the Priory swimming pool.

Their social life continues unabated. Charlotte plays the piano, Miss Wyndham plays the harp, they dance, Lady Arundell and her sister sing, as does Louisa Cooke. It was an asset in Georgian society to be able to entertain. Edward Bingham, Peregrine's brother, stays a night and goes out hunting with Mr Grove, *'riding before the Hounds the Whole way'*. This was not and is not hunting etiquette. He was in the Navy. Is there not some saying about sailors and horses?

They go to London accompanied by William Helyar, to whom the sisters read all the way. They dine and sleep at Halford Bridge. In London, they are visited by Charlotte's uncle, I take it Timothy Shelley. He tells them of *'odd circumstances'*. I surmise that this is talk of Bysshe Shelley, expelled from Oxford that March. According to Desmond Hawkins, Tom Grove invited Shelley to Cwm Ellen, Tom's property in Wales, at this juncture, which Shelley accepted.

October 31st *'Harriet measured for Fatima's – wishes to have them large enough. Provident certainly.'* I have not got to the bottom of what a Fatima refers to, but I suppose Harriet had pregnancy in mind.

'My father looked at Harriets Wedding Clothes & admired the White Satin Pelisse.' White was not considered a necessity for a wedding, but

the idea of it was creeping in. At the end of Jane Austen's *Emma*, one of the characters complains of the wedding, no white satin.

On November 14th, Harriet is married. Charlotte is one of the bridesmaids with Helen Tregonwell, cousin Fanny Jackson and little Emma Waddington. Otherwise, *'Aunt Jackson and C. Bennet came'*. Weddings were not the great 'do' of nowadays, but were these the sole congregation? *'Dr Jackson performed the Ceremony.'* I suspect this was in Donhead St Andrew Church, or Lower Donhead, as the house at Ferne is in that parish, but Dr Jackson, Harriet's uncle, was Rector of Donhead St Mary.

Charlotte still tends to refer to William Helyar as Mr Wm Helyar but sometimes as *'my brother'* and occasionally as *'Billy'*, but the latter on a frivolous note. A week after the wedding, *'Mr & Mrs Wm Helyar came – I was delighted to see my Sister Harriet again.'* While waiting to inherit Coker Court, William Helyar occupied what is now called Hayes House at Sedgehill, so this was Harriet's initial home in her married life. Charlotte stays there often for quite protracted periods when Harriet was waiting to produce her innumerable offspring.

Miss C Benett is showing further signs of becoming a Catholic. November 18th *'I had a conversation with C Bennett. She appears very nonsensical & foolish.'* We can see what Charlotte thinks of Catholicism.

Ashcombe is a place to be considered, intriguing long before the advent of Madonna or even Cecil Beaton. It had been built by a Robert Barber sometime after 1686, 'mansion house, stables, and offices, and resided here until his death in 1740', according to Bowles. His only child, a daughter, Anne, married a Wyndham and their only child, also Anne, married an Arundell. Bowles says when this Arundell inherited Wardour in 1814, he sold a lot of property to pay off 'heavy encumbrances' attached to the Wardour estate, including Ashcombe, which was purchased by Thomas Grove the younger, who shortly afterwards 'pulled down the mansion house, and converted part of the stables into a farm house and farm offices'. In fact, Thomas Grove, Charlotte's eldest brother, did not actually buy Ashcombe at all; the sale fell through, and that was not until the April of 1815. According to a memorandum to which Bowles refers, written by the Rector, Mr Boys, it was then let to Paul Methuen, Esq, but we know from Charlotte it was let to the Methuens by the Arundells in June of 1811, prior to the Groves' attempt to purchase it. On December 13th 1813, *'I walk with My Father to see the new Road he is making up Ashcombe Hill.'*

This was the route that goes from Higher Berrycourt up the downs in the direction of Win Green. We used to assume this was to link Ashcombe with Ferne, but this was not so, as in 1811 the Groves had nothing to do with Ashcombe. The Stancombs, some time ago, endeavoured to prevent this old track being reclassified as a 'Boat', that is a 'byway open to all traffic'. To achieve this, it was necessary to prove it was not a right of way for four-wheeled vehicles. Francis spoke for them but the case was lost. If only we had had Charlotte's pocket book, we could have proved it was a private road built by Thomas Grove with no right of way over it at all.

Higher Berrycourt seems to have been the home farm for Ferne. When Charlotte refers to the farm, I believe it to be Higher Berrycourt and the bailiff Thomas Shere. Goodchild copied a list of property that paid tythe to the Rector in 1840, at that time Richard Downes. Thomas Shere is listed as a tenant of Thomas Grove but it also lists fields, including Ferne Park, Thomas had 'in hand' that he farmed himself. It is unlikely Mr Grove farmed without a bailiff.

Charlotte describes the protracted labour of Mrs Shere, whom they call on at the farm. It starts on December 6th but on the 7th, *'Mr Wilkins says Mrs Shere will do very well & that She was not in labour.'* On the 7th, *'Mrs Shere in great danger, brought to bed of A still born Son that had been dead A week.'* Childbirth was a hazardous business.

Walks are described. The Glove, Milkwell and Clay Lanes are frequently mentioned as a particular route. We know about Milkwell, but Clay Lane must be the lane running back towards Ferne from Milkwell. The Glove, now Arundell Farm, was the coaching inn on what is described as the Turnpike Road, now the A30. The coach road as we know it had been abandoned in 1786 in favour of this lower road, but if you walk along it now you can still spot the milestones informing you of the distance to Hyde Park Corner. There are also milestones to be spotted on the A30. The Glove was quite an establishment, with balls held. On the 16th, *'In the Evening went to the Glove Ball – We met A great many of Our Neighbours there. I danced every Dance.'* Charlotte mentions her father going to dine there with one of her brothers. Colin Smart, whose father-in-law lives in the house, tells me the dining room has a sprung floor, a floor designed for dancing.

Her friend Helen Tregonwell is often staying at Ferne. They walk and play chess. Charlotte was obsessed with chess. It seems her family could get tired of it. *'Helen and I played Chess… & the Gentlemen pelted Us with Oyster Shells to prevent Our finishing Our Game.'*

On the 17th of December, they receive very bad news from her brother William in the Navy, *'he has undergone A Court Martial instead of being promoted at the taking of Batavia & acquiring £3000 Prize Money as We hoped & expected.'* A few days later her brother Charles arrives and *'cheered us all in regard to William.'*

Desmond Hawkins explains this incident. William, who had been in the Navy just prior to his tenth birthday, was accused of 'behaving in a cruel and oppressive manner to the company of HMS *Hecate*.'

Charles also *'entertained Us with his account of Bysshe Shelley'*. It was in this month that Shelley eloped with Harriet Westbrook. It is said it was in part reaction to his failed romance with Harriet Grove.

On the 24th, *'The Fox hounds at Wardour. The Gentlemen hunted & Charles fell three times.'* Charlotte says he was not hurt but felt a little unwell the following evening, Christmas Day.

The year 1811 draws to a close. They go to stay with her eldest brother at Blandford and come home on December 29th. *'The roads very slippery over the Downs & Ashcombe Hill.'* Despite what Charles Bowles says about the state of the roads, they still ventured boldly out.

In a note at the end of the year, Charlotte remarks, *'Our good King being ill The Prince of Wales was appointed Regent – & as he ought kept in his fathers Ministers.'* The Prince of Wales, in opposition to his father, supported the Whigs, who had expected to gain office as soon as he was Regent, but he disappointed them.

Beneath this she writes, *'sorry to hear Byshe was expelled Oxford for writing to the Bishops on Atheism.'* Oxford and Cambridge were primarily designed for the training of the clergy, so this was a disastrous move on the part of the young Shelley. The universities were of course also useful for wealthy young men to meet their peers.

Charlotte also says she paid £3 11s 0d for Harriet's stays. I have wondered for the necessity of stays when the gowns were 'Empire', so no waist, but they still seemed to have them.

1812

Charlotte makes a list at the start of this year of what she took to Bath, which includes *'2 pr Stays'*. I note white is the predominant colour for her gowns, morning and evening. She has two coloured morning gowns as opposed to six white ones and four white evening gowns, two coloured. She has one satin dress but does not say the colour. She also takes no less than eighteen pocket handkerchiefs. This whole list is fascinating, what with green veils, tippets, twelve frills, a velvet pelisse and also a silk one, let alone the bonnets and shoes, black kid and buff Grecian.

January 1st *'New years Gifts & The Compliments of the Season past at Breakfast time.'* Nowadays we have exhausted our present giving by Christmas, but my half Italian grandchildren get presents on January 6th.

On the 2nd, Harriet comes to Ferne to take Charlotte and Helen Tregonwell, who is visiting them, to Sedgehill: *'my Mother rather low at our leaving Her'*. Their social life continues. They dine at Pythouse and the Stills dine with them. They attend church at *'Knoyle'* where Mr Ogle was Rector. *'Ghost Stories at Night.'*

January 7th *'We walked round the Plantation, & afterwards dined at The Ogles. Fanny Still & Mr Wake there. Mrs Ogle played & sang to Us most delightfully. We danced afterwards. Mr Ogle very facetious.'* Mr Wake was a curate, according to Hawkins. A Dr Wake was Rector at East Knoyle until his death in 1796, so it seems likely there was a connection.

On the 9th, Mrs Grove arrives with various brothers *'& Miss F Benett in the Barouche. Helen & myself much grieved as they took Us home with Them from the pleasantest Visit I ever paid in My Life.'*

They make up for it the next day. Their cousin Charles Jackson dines with them and they dance afterwards. *'The Fern Band played to Us.'* I imagine this to be made up of various servants. I know Daniel, the footman, could produce some music.

January 11th *'A letter from Mrs Cooke to inform William he must appear before the board of Admiralty – He was rather in the Dumps But recovered his spirits afterwards.'* He leaves for London the next day and returns on the 19th. Mrs Cooke writing might seem strange, but I assume it had to do with her late husband's high naval connections. William was dismissed the service, but Charlotte does not comment on this.

'My Father told Helen at Chess & She beat Me.' There is much indignant underlining. On the following day, Helen *'beat Me owing to having General Grove on her right Hand'.*

They dine with the Gordons, who lived at Wincombe. *'Came home very safely though A dark Night.'* It was customary to rely on the moon when dining out as the lamps on the carriages could do little.

Charlotte stays at Lyttleton, the seat of the Farquharsons, the family into which her brother Tom had married. Mr Phelips, of Montecute, is one of the party. They pay morning visits, play whist and go to the ball at Blandford. *'Not A very good Ball, A rare fault. Too Many Gentlemen.'*

In February they have a visit from Laetitia Popham, the Pophams old family friend from Bagborough in Somerset. Charlotte sometimes calls her Miss Popham and sometimes Laetitia. They go off together to stay at Sedgehill. I feel Charlotte's delight in saying, *'Miss P likes my new Brother very much.'*

They go to a dance at Pythouse and *'returned home about four o'clock in the Morning'.* They go home to Ferne the following day and begin to read *'The Scottish Chiefs'* lent them by Mrs Benett, *'But went to Bed early, being all fatigued with our late gaieties.'*

On February 9th she visits Mrs Shere, who she reports as *'rather better.'* The Rector, Mr Boys, churched her. This was originally, I believe, to thank for a safe delivery, hardly the case with Mrs Shere. It seemed to have got muddled in peoples' minds as to its actual purpose.

February 8th *'My Mother rode out on her Welch Poney.'*

Sometimes the Rector and his wife dine at Ferne: *'good sort of People But rather prosing'*. On another occasion the Rector leaves *'A Train of Oil on the Hall Floor, no good addition to it'*. This sounds a rather modern and certainly inexplicable accident.

February 14th *'Mr & Mrs JH Waddington have been married 7 years (May They continue as happy as They have hitherto been.) We all drank their Healths after Dinner.'*

Charlotte remarks her brother William *'becoming very polite under The tuition of Laetitia Popham'*. I wonder if being continuously on a battle ship from the age of twelve until the age of twenty leaves a young man a little unsuited to female company.

Ferne never seems quite finished. February 17th *'The scaffolding so erected, we can not go down the best staircase.'* They still have plenty of visitors, including aunts. Charlotte has taught Miss Popham to play chess and they read out Fielding's *Amelia* amongst other books.

On March 9th, they get the information they must have been waiting for. *'A Letter from Ld Pembroke saying William is reinstated in the Navy, but at the bottom of the List of Lieutenants.'* Lord Pembroke had obviously been asked to use his influence and he had achieved what was required, but it would mean William would have a very long wait to get promotion.

March 10th *'Laetitia & I took A nice walk together, climbing Hedges, & getting over Gates: My Father had some Elm Trees transplanted & put in close to the House. Laetitia found a curious Fossil near the Stone Quarry.'*

The next day, *'Miss F. Benett & her Brother George called upon Us. The Catholic would not eat any Luncheon.'* Charlotte did not seem to mind the Arundells being Catholic; I think she disliked the idea of a person becoming one. It seems Frances and Catherine Benett were drawn to Catholicism. The question of lunch arises again, who had it and when.

They go to Sedgehill and meet William Helyar's parents. Of his father, Charlotte says, *'very odd, & made fine Speeches to Laetitia & Me'*.

March 17th *'Mr George Benett dined here. Report says he is A Methodist, he looks like one certainly.'* I wonder how one has to look to look like a Methodist. It was perfectly normal to view any aberration from the Church of England with the deepest suspicion. These children of Dr John Benett, Rector of Donhead St Andrew, who had died in 1808, seem disinclined to take the conventional route expected of the offspring of a Church of England clergyman.

The year goes on much the same, walking with her father to the farm, nearly sticking in the mud, walking on Win Green and admiring *'My father's beautiful flock of sheep'* that were grazing the park. There is chess, whist, battledore, cribbage, reading, visitors etc. There is the odd impromptu dance at Ferne, music supplied by Daniel. Charlotte and her aunt *'traced out the old Road that led to the House formerly.'* They visit Mrs Shere and Charlotte remarks on *'A new Entrance to the Farm House'*. Charles comes home on the 19th *'being the Oxford Vacation'*. A regular visitor is Mr Easton, a clergyman, who has a son in the Navy. Harriet comes to stay while her husband is in London with his father. She and Charlotte soon start their games of chess. At one moment Harriet was not well and Mr Wilkins came to see her. He *'says that She is doing very well'*. I surmise Harriet is at the start of her fourteen pregnancies.

Charlotte's cousin, Elizabeth Shelley, sister of the poet, stays for some time. Born in 1794, she is seventeen, the same age as Charles. She had published some poetry with her brother, who was two years older than her, the previous year. None of Shelley's sisters married. Charlotte says, *'She is in the highest Spirits'*. She rides out with Charlotte's brothers. Elizabeth is obviously lively. *'A Wet Day again I am sorry to say. Politicks Our Topic of Conversation. Elizabeth as usual permitted her Tongue its full office.'* On another occasion, *'Elizabeth not quite well Before Dinner. She* had An Hysterical Laugh.' A Helyar relative *'is dangerously ill in A Frenzy Fever'*. One can sort of imagine these things.

Charlotte sometimes talks of Amy. She has a discussion with him about potatoes, but I now see he is the gardener, probably the head gardener. Later I find he was parish clerk and ran the Sunday school. Charlotte is visiting him in Berwick years later. Of all her brothers, Tom and Charles were interested in gardening. Charles returns to Oxford on April 10th.

Another person now referred to and frequently visited is Oldy, I think at some stage a nurse or nanny to the Groves. Her actual name was Mary Marchant.

They call on Miss Benett in Berwick, who was out, but *'We walked all over her Pleasure Grounds.'*

April 13th *'In the evening under the tuition of My Mother & Fanny We learnt Quadrille.'* Fanny was Fanny Jackson. This was a fashionable card game played in pairs with a deck of forty cards, the eights, nines and tens removed. It is of course also a dance. Arundells, Benetts, Jacksons, Cookes and *'Miss Charlotte Lipscombe'* come and go. Miss Lipscombe stays with the Cookes, Mrs Cooke being her aunt.

On April 20th, *'Dear William left Us to join the Primrose Sloop off the Downs – He gave me A Cameo Broach.'*

Charlotte has an invitation from Aunt Chafin to stay in Bath. On the 21st, *'Elizabeth & I left Fern with very great Regret.'* They do not sound particularly enthusiastic. *'Went as far as Warminster in the Phaeton. There We were met by Mrs Parkers Carriage and proceeded to Bath in it.'* On the return journey, they leave at ten in the morning and get home at six. It could all be done in a day. A phaeton seems a term to have covered any privately owned carriage.

April 23rd *'I was entertained by seeing Mrs Williams A Woman of fifty dance Cotillions.'* According to Wikipedia, 'the cotillion kept all the dancers in almost perpetual motion', so I suppose it was not considered suitable for such an old lady.

On April 25th and 28th they go to the play. *'Saw Betty perform Orestes & extremely well he did it'* and *'Betty performed Rolla & inimitably well.'* Betty was William Betty who, as a boy, was known as the Young Roscius, having been the child prodigy of the era. He played Hamlet and other such parts with adult casts, though there were some dissenting voices from those who would have preferred him not to do so. Roscius was a Roman actor of such talent that his name became synonymous with great performers. Betty was a grown-up twenty-two by the time Charlotte saw him in Bath. She goes on to say, *'returned home afterwards, having on A coloured Gown did not go to Lady Nugents Rout which I did not at all regret'*. This is a little eye-opener into the period. White seems to have been essential for a formal occasion. I had assumed white was for the younger, unmarried woman. Charlotte is twenty-nine but, being unmarried, did she keep having to wear white forever? I spend hours looking at early 19th-century miniatures, and once asked a dealer why all the women were in white. I was told they were painted when they got engaged so they were wearing their best. I was not convinced at the time, but perhaps it was so.

They know plenty of people in Bath and are well entertained with balls and parties, but I get the feeling Charlotte has little enthusiasm for it all. They do not ardently practise cotillions, nor does she always bother to name her partners. She sees plenty of Elizabeth, but they are not both staying with Aunt Grove. At a ball she is partnered by Admiral Linois, *'to whom E. & Myself spoke French'*. To speak French was obviously a part of their education, but it seems they would have had very little chance to use it. Charlotte's visits to London are rare enough, and she never goes abroad at all.

May 5th *'I staid at Home in the Evening & walked with Miss Stephens, instead of going to the nasty Old Routs.'* She was ever watchful for the eccentric or the absurd. Mrs Parker *'had A Wreath of Flowers on, like The Queen of May'*. The same lady *'danced to the Ladies in the Columbine Style'*.

On the 9th, they went to walk in Sydney Gardens but were caught in the rain *'& obliged to return Home in Chairs'*. The sedan chair was a feature of Bath, carried by two men.

May 11th *'Went with Mrs C Grove & chose The Furniture for the Library at Ferne.'* Ferne suddenly gets an E at the end of it. *'Called on Elizabeth & spent the Morning with Her.'*

May 12th *'Mr Percival Chancellor of the Exchequer was shot dead going to The House of Commons in the lobby.'* The chancellor of the exchequer was the equivalent of prime minister then. He is our only prime minister to have been assassinated. I have read he was shot in mistake for somebody else. People cheered in the street on hearing the news and congratulated the perpetrator. I suppose the mentality of the Internet troll has, depressingly, always been around. Mr Percival, who I do not think an evil character, left a widow and eleven children. The government gave them a pension, but a greater sum was raised by the populace for the widow and the family of the assassin, who was hanged. I believe it was the idea Percival was a Methodist that had made him unpopular.

May 15th *'Took leave of My dear Cousin, with the greatest Regret.'* Elizabeth, twelve years younger than Charlotte, must have endeared herself. I had the impression Charlotte slightly disapproved of her when she first arrived at Ferne.

They return to Ferne the next day. *'I was delighted to see my Dear Parents & to be Home again.'*

On the 18th, *'In the Evening being Whit Monday the L. Donhead Club came up, & their Band played Us some very pretty tunes.'*

May 19th *'a fine warm Rain, We called upon The Bride & Bridegroom Mr & Mrs Kneller, I think that Jacky shows a good taste in his Wife. She is a very pretty elegant Brown Woman.'* Godfrey John Kneller was known as Jacky. The Knellers were descended from the artist of that name and lived at Donhead Hall. They soon dine at Ferne. *'In the Evening They both sung to us.'*

Charlotte goes to stay with Harriet on the 23rd, where she is much annoyed by her brother-in-law's capacity to win their games of chess.

'Billy played Chess with Me in the evening & I am ashamed to say beat Me every game.' This is a recurring event. Otherwise, they are as social as ever. They sit outdoors and read the *'Persian Tales'*. They take the usual long walks, on one occasion *'round by Semley Common.'* On another day, *'I walked in the evening with Wm. to My Fathers Farm.'* Mr Grove had a farm at Sedgehill. Her sister and brother-in-law fall asleep after dinner on which Charlotte comments that she gets on with her book.

She goes home on June 2nd and remarks on their new carriage arriving at Ferne but *'with no arms on it'*. She is of course referring to the coat of arms. Was this a mistake or an economy?

A man called Hyscock is planting potatoes in some ground her father has lent to the poor on the 3rd. It seems late, to me, to be putting them in, but John Lane, whose expertise can be relied on for information beyond family trees and historical references, assures me it is not too late in the south.

June 6th *'We all went into the garden & hunted The Snails off The Fruit Trees. After Tea My Father & I walked as far as His new Road.'*

The next day Charlotte pronounces that *'Helen has decided properly in regard to Capt. Markland.'* She does marry him, so I assume this was her acceptance. Captain Markland was a post captain in the Navy.

While visiting the Farquharsons at Langton, Charlotte and her father play whist against Mr and Mrs Farquharson, winning eighteen shillings. I think this the only mention of playing for serious money, this amount being quite a bit more than a working man's weekly wage, which was probably about ten to fifteen shillings.

June 12th *'J Snook put up the curtains in the Library.'* The following day *'my Mother & Self busily employed cleaning the Old Family Pictures.'* They seem rather slow at getting everything complete at Ferne, nine months since they had moved in. Eventually the pictures are hung in the dining room.

Mrs Shere looks well, but then there is some little doubt. She is to stay in bed for a week and they lend her *The Mysteries of Udolpho*. They often walk over the farm, reporting on *'my father's Wheat field'*. Harriet's husband has the whooping cough, but it has not prevented them from coming to dinner. Charlotte's youngest sister Louisa had died of this aged fourteen.

Charlotte is reading out loud *Sense and Sensibility* and underlines *'one of the best novels'*. Her brother Charles is down from Oxford for the long vacation. He had to go as far as Shaftesbury to buy silk stockings, which at this period were only worn for evening wear. He and Charlotte walk together, on one occasion *'Both of us in Pattens'*. Charlotte underlines this, so it probably indicates the fact they were not usually worn by men who did not have troublesome long garments to keep out of the mud.

On the 27th, Charlotte and Charles go to Preshaw, the Hampshire home of their Long cousins, to attend Winchester races. *'Walters alterations There are very good.'* These were done by Nash in 1810, so two years earlier. The Longs sold the house in 1898, and in 1986 developers bought it and divided it up. The land has been retained by the Pelly family.

'We saw little Ellen, Lady Marys youngest child. The Eldest too ill & unfortunate looking to be seen.' Lady Mary was Walter Long's wife, but what was the matter with the poor child?

George joins them and Charlotte goes on the race course with her two brothers, *'Lady Mary not chusing To take more than one Lady with Her.'* I can see Charlotte thought this rude. Afterwards they went to the ball and danced until three in the morning. Each day of the races were followed by balls, the next one going until five. They go home on July 3rd: *'George in high Spirits in again breathing his Native Air he said.'*

She walks with her mother to Berricourt Cottage, where the shepherd's children are ill with scarlet fever.

July 30th *'Lady Arundell her Mother & another Lady called here – her Ladyship dressed in A yellow Pelisse & Bonnett with Pink Roses & Brown & yellow Columbine Boots.'* Charlotte, with many underlinings, obviously thought this way over the top. A pelisse was a type of fitted overcoat, originally borrowed from the short fur-lined jacket worn by light cavalry regiments but soon altered and adapted by the whims of fashion.

They are shortly off to Netherhampton to do the Salisbury races and balls.

George has designs on Louisa Cooke, because the brothers are always off to Donhead Lodge, and Charlotte says, after an evening walk there and staying to supper, *'Success attend George.'* She follows his courtship closely. *'George very alert with his partner'* and *'George in the highest glee.'* They really are extremely social, dinners, dances and suppers and visitors, particularly the Helyars, all the time. They also spend time at Sedgehill. On the 24th, *'For a Wonder My Brothers staid An Evening at Home.'* They next go to Littleton, the Farquharsons, to attend the Blandford races. One of the balls does not end until six in the morning. It concluded with the 'Boulanger', a country dance in which partners were changed all the time. Mrs Bennet mentions it in *Pride and Prejudice* when describing the frequency of Mr Bingley's dancing with Jane.

August 11th *'Mr J Helyar called at Pythouse & saw the little Boy – thinks the same as We do of A certain likeness.'* Charlotte was not much of a gossip, but this is surely a hint of something irregular in the Benett family. John Benett's sons were John, born in 1808, and Thomas, born this year, 1812, but not till December, so it was John to which she was referring. John Helyar was Rector of Tollard Royal and an uncle of William.

John Helyar intends to make *'A Spectatorial Garden at Tollard'*. The Larmer Tree gardens were laid out by General Pit Rivers in 1880, but I wonder what was in the vicinity already.

August 15th *'Mr Hugh Hellyer having but one Coat, came down into the Library whilst it was brushed in his Night Gown. A ring at The Bell he thought it Lady Arundell & leaped out of the Window over The Flower Pots &c. It proved to be Mr J Ogle.'* He was Rector of East Knoyle. Mr H Helyar also *'had A design of making his Aunt tipsey'*. This was at Sedgehill, where Charlotte has gone to await the arrival of Harriet's first child.

August 17th *'Good News of Ld. Wellingtons Victory.'* Wellington defeated the French at Salamanca on July 22nd and entered Madrid on August 12th. It sounds as if Charlotte is referring to the battle, so it brings home how long news took to travel when only a sailing ship could bring it.

August 18th *'After dinner My Mother & Wm. rode through Summer Leaze. Harriet & I had A comfortable Chat with The Nurse, Agnes Selwood, & looked at An old Chair that Wm. had when He was A little Boy.'*

August 24th *'At five O'clock in The Morning Harriet was taken ill & brought to bed of A fine Boy, A little after 8 o'clock. Thank God She had as good & safe A Labour as possible. I saw The Baby dressed & had him in My Lap as soon as He was born.'*

The next day, *'My Sister continually looking at & admiring Her little Baby. Mr Wake dined here, & privately baptised The Child by The Name of William Hawker.'* Babies were often baptised soon after birth to ensure they could be buried in consecrated ground should they die. They were required to have a more formal church Christening later on.

August 27th *'Harriet sat up two Hours & eat some boiled Mutton, & turnips for Dinner.'*

On September 6th, *'We put cuffs on My Little Nephew or he would have scratched his eyes out.'*

On the 7th, Harriet comes downstairs to the drawing room. The next day, *'We sent out all ways to find out A Woman & Child fit for Our purpose.'*

On the 9th, *'A Woman, & her Love Child came. Little Wm. After A little hesitation took the Breast. The Child sucked Harriet very well.'* I was confused by this. They seem to swap babies for the purposes of suckling. The following day, her in-laws arrive with another wet nurse and her child, so the first one is sent away. I think the wet nurse was there as a back-up. Perhaps there was some problem with the feeding. *'Wm. very anxious about his little Boy.'*

Charlotte says of William's father: *'Mr Helyar very odd. He drinks a great deal.'*

On the 15th, her mother fetches her in the phaeton and takes her home. John has come home but George has returned to his ship.

The rounds of visits continue. They have a dance at Ferne. *'Mr & Mrs Boys were Partners.'* It is apparent that husband and wife dancing together was not the thing, in fact it was a bit ridiculous.

September 17th *'The Pointers ran away with two or three Joints from The Breakfast Table.'* This says as much about what you ate at breakfast as it does about the pointers.

September 22nd *'The Ladies called at Pythouse. Mrs Crofts & the Miss Benetts of Norton there. Miss Kneller as pleasant as ever – My Brothers quite delighted with Her.'* Miss Kneller was probably Mr Kneller's sister Sophia, according to John Lane, aged sixteen.

On the 25th, *'At Home with only My two Brothers, Daddy Mummy & I.'* I was surprised at this early use of Mummy and Daddy.

On the 27th, *'We went to Berwick Church, Mr Boyes treated Us with some of his excellent Fruit afterwards.'* I wonder about the Rectory garden and if Mr Boyes had hot houses.

Charlotte is as keen on chess as ever, but William Helyar seems to win every time he is her opponent.

Tom and his wife Henrietta arrive from Wales where Tom has an estate, Cwm Ellen. Tom is high sheriff there.

In October, they are reading *'Miss Edgeworth's Tales'*.

Charlotte gives a hint of her brother John's romance. She says, *'John is fond of Air.'* This is a reference to one of the Miss Eyres of New House, Redlynch. George returns on the 20th, and on 22nd October, Charlotte goes with her brothers to Netherhampton from whence they attend a ball and concert in Salisbury. *'We met Mrs Eyre & two of her Daughters.'* She does not say if it was the right daughter from John's point of view. Charles takes the coach back to Oxford.

There are many little impromptu dances at Ferne, usually attended by Miss Cooke and Miss Lypscomb. The young Groves, particularly the male ones, are always dining at Donhead Lodge. Eventually, on the 26th, *'Mrs Miss Cooke & Miss Lypscomb dined here. Alas! The last Day of the Lovers being together before The Voyage to China.'* George was in the Merchant Navy and probably in no financial position to marry, but was it Louisa Cooke or Charlotte Lipscombe who he fancied? I think the former. He and John leave the next day.

William, who is now twenty-two, has to go to the hospital at Deal *'having The Rheumatism very bad'*. I think this was something from which Naval officers suffered, but he does seem very young.

On the last day of the month, *'In My Walk I met Mrs Cooke upon Her Poney Perseverance.'*

There is a great deal of coming and going of the two aunts, not necessarily together. November 5th *'My Aunt & I called upon Mrs Shere & afterwards walked to Bericourt Cottage. We should have stuck in the Mud had it not been for the politeness of Our Bailiff.'*

Charlotte's father gives his harriers *'to old Mr Helyar'*.

On November 8th, *'We went to Berwick Church – Mr Boys gave Us rather A long Sermon for so cold A Day.'* This makes me think how lucky we are with the current heating in the church. It is hard to visualise the interior of the church as Charlotte knew it, because it was rebuilt in the 1860s after her death.

The Methuens, now renting Ashcombe from the Arundells, dine at Ferne: *'very pleasant Neighbours I think'*.

November 9th *'My Father & I took it by turns to read out Shakepears Play of King John.'*

They have above seventy for their Harvest Home. The countryside teemed with people working the fields.

November 14th *'We went to Cattistock & found My Brother & Sister quite well.'* This obviously refers to Tom and Henrietta. It is sometimes difficult to tell where they are living, but it was usually some place attached to the Farquharsons.

November 21st *'Mr Wooldridge of the Glove died very suddenly being thrown from his Horse.'*

November 22nd *'Poor Mrs Wooldridge is left A distressed Widow with seven Children.'*

A few days later they dine at Ashcombe. *'Miss Mildmay Mrs P Methuen's sister there. They are the largest young Women I almost ever saw – We got Home safe over the Alps as I call Ashcombe hill.'*

Elizabeth Shelley sends them a present of painted china and card racks. Their new chairs arrive from Bristol, black horsehair with mahogany backs.

On the 29th, *'Mr Boys shewed us a Document In The Parish Register, which ascertains My Fathers possession of The North Chancel of Berwick Church.'* Seeing how long the Groves had been at Ferne, it seems strange this was only now being asserted. Ferne House itself was and is in Donhead. Certain parts of the church were attached to land, the owners responsible for the upkeep, hence the Grove and Hamilton memorials in our church being in the north transept, which they were said to *'possess'*, and the Foots, similarly, owners of Manor Farm, in the south transept. Mark Dineley's hatchment hangs in the south transept for the same reason.

November 30th *'We went to Whatcombe – Lady Amelia, Mr Dillon Mr Trenchard & Mr Snow of our Party there – Cornelia & Mary at Weymouth.'* Whatcombe was the home of the Pleydells, a large, handsome house north of Winterbourne Whitchurch. It stayed in the same family, one way or another, until sold to become a school for 'maladjusted boys' in the 1960s, but it is now back in private hands. It was built in the early 1750s, so it was comparatively young when Charlotte is staying there. It is Grade II listed. She *'played a game of Chess with Louisa & defeated Her'*. She does the same with Emma the following day and with Margaretta the next. There were obviously lots of Pleydell girls. The *'gentlemen hunted with Mr Chafins Hounds'*. They return home on December 3rd.

December 6th *'My Father would not permit me to go to Church, My Cold being bad.'*

On December 10th, William comes home, looking thin *'But his Rheumatism is better.'*

They are prevented from going to Aunt Grove at Netherhampton by the threat of snow *'& have lost this chance of seeing The inimitable Mrs Jordon'*. She was not only a famous actress but the mistress of George

III's third son, the Duke of Clarence, later William IV, by whom she had ten children.

The following day, Charlotte remarks on *'Glorious News from Russia. They are daily beating The French & Buonaparte is retreating.'* Remember, we are in the winter of 1812, and this is the retreat from Moscow, so you can think *War and Peace*. Eleven days later she regrets *'Buonaparte's'* safe arrival in Paris.

It is too cold to go to church. She describes walking through Brook Water to what she spells as Whetsum Cross. Her brother Charles arrives from Oxford, having travelled all night in an open gig. There are more impromptu little dances at Ferne after dinner. They give away Christmas dinners to the poor people. Mrs Eyre and the four Miss Eyres come to stay. *'Mrs Eyre said what looks well in favour of Somebody.'* Charlotte is full of hope for John. *'The Miss Eyres sung Viva Enrico to us.'* Her last entry for 1812 is *'May what I particularly wish the end of this year come to pass.'*

The end papers for this year list *'clump shoes – sloppers'*, which I think quite explain themselves. Otherwise there are shifts and night shifts, four night caps, cambric and dimity petticoats, cravats and frills and a flannel bed-gown. Dimity was a sheer cotton fabric with raised stripes or checks. For her sister's nursery she bought *'caricature prints'*. Charlotte also records how many turns round the garden will make three miles.

There was a housemaid called Betty Stretch. She goes to work for Harriet and is replaced by *'Jane'*. Charlotte pays Betty Stretch for three letters. She had paid *'Bean Pere'* on Charlotte's behalf. Who or what was Bean Pere? This predates postage stamps. You paid for your letter on receipt. They visit Elizabeth Stretch. I think of the war memorial… Walter Stretch. Is this the same family a hundred years on? John Lane, who has documented this family, thinks it most likely.

1813

The start of 1813 is much taken up with John's ultimately unsatisfactory courtship with Miss Eyre. *'I hope to have A new Sister in Law before The end of this year.'* Of the numerous Eyre daughters, Miss Eyre would have been the eldest, Harriet. Mrs Eyre was an aunt of Charlotte's friend Laetitia Popham.

January 2nd *'Mrs & Miss Eyres left Us. We are invited to New House. Things put on A promising Appearance.'* On the 9th, Mr Grove goes to Newhouse and on the 11th Charlotte goes with her brothers. They all go to a concert and ball in Salisbury accompanied by the Eyres, but on a further visit to Redlynch things suddenly go wrong.

January 20th *'the old Eyre gave us a cool Reception'.*

On the 21st, *'A Thunder bolt upon us all. John looked the Picture of Woe. Mr Popham went home. Mr & Mrs Shucburgh dined with us. The Old Lady went to Bed with A violent Head ach.'* I suppose that is one way of dodging an awkward social occasion.

On the 22nd, *'We took A Frosty Flight from Newhouse.'*

They return home via Netherhampton and the aunts. *'My Aunts and Us talked over the Behaviour of A certain Lady.'*

January 23rd *'My Father planned A nice Scheme, Miss Kneller to be Cupids Messenger – We retuned home and could talk But on One Topic the whole evening.'*

January 24th *'I received A Note from Miss Eyre which looks favourable.'*

On the 26th, John rides to Salisbury, *'But was disappointed in meeting Miss Eyre. Miss Kneller is strenuous in the cause.'* The next day John writes to Miss Eyre himself, but it must have been to no avail. They had become so very intimate with the Eyres it was obviously a most distressing, let alone an embarrassing, incident. Charlotte says, at the end of the month, *'My Brother I hope will soon get over it.'*

February 1st *'Tom called, & did John much good by his high spirits.'*

On February 6th, John gives her a brooch, set in pearls, containing his hair. At this period there was a vogue for miniatures or other small articles of jewellery to contain hair, laid out in immaculate twists or curls. John, I feel, appreciates his sister's affectionate support. He is soon off to London on the coach, presumably to continue his medical studies. He is then preoccupied with trying to get into St Bartholomew's.

I was intrigued by this whole incident, so I looked up Newhouse on the Internet. It is a Jacobean house built in a Y shape, apparently to symbolise the Trinity. The Eyres bought it in 1633, adding two wings in the 18th century. They married into the Matcham family and they are still there. The Matchams were connections of Lord Nelson's. His daughter by Lady Hamilton spent much of her childhood at Newhouse, where her crib is to be seen. I note you can now have your wedding in this house, which the Groves might consider ironic. (In 2021, I see this house on the market for the first time.)

There are still constant visits to Mrs Shere. Her health is a great point of concern, but she is obviously a favourite. On February 10th, which happens to be Charlotte's thirtieth birthday, Mrs Shere has another stillborn son.

February 22nd *'A Bustle in the House in the Evening The Library Chimney being on Fire – Edwards Susan & one or two more sat up all Night.'* Mr and Mrs Still and their daughter Fanny and Miss Arundell are staying at the time. On the 24th, *'Fanny Still sang to us – & Our Band played.'*

The year goes on as usual, walking, dining, visiting, Arundells, Gordons, Knellers, Pophams, Mr Easton, hunting, various relations.

It was not always a pleasure. When Mr Kneller came of age, *'we dined there. A dull stupid party. We did not come home till 3 in the morning.'* Stupid meant boring in those days. The next day she writes *'rather fatigued with Our gaieties.'*

February 17th *'John wrote Us word there is A Vacancy in St Bartholomews. I hope He will get in.'*

Mr Easton took the service in Berwick on March 7th and told them Louis XVIII was going to live at Wardour. I never heard that he did. He had come to live in England in 1809. Mr Easton took the services here and there when required as he had no 'living' of his own. Charlotte wishes *'some rich person'* would give him a good one. Church livings were bought and sold by individuals or, like ours, university colleges. They allocated parsons to have the living, which varied considerably in the amount of income to be derived from them. The Rosses' house is called Tythe House because the tythe barn stood there, where the tythes were collected from the parish. Berwick St John also had glebe land that belonged to the church, the rector farming this for himself. When Charlotte is later married to Richard Downes, there are many references to this.

There is an odd entry at the end of the month. *'We went to Berwick Church & met Mr George Gra'eme at the end of the Park coming to call upon Us – Helen as usual builds Castles in the Air, I bet with Her half A Crown & I wish I may lose it.'* Was this a potential suitor for Charlotte?

At the beginning of March, *'We are once more Our charming little Trio.'*

They go on comfortably through March, viewing her father's lambs, walking, and reading aloud in the evenings as was their custom. They sometimes walk on the *'sand walk'*, probably when it was wet. Where was it?

March 13th *'We walked to the Glove – My Mother frightened by the sight of some Soldiers, however We were nobly guarded by the Miss Foots in Front.'* This may have been a recruiting party. They roamed about endeavouring to entice young men to join the ranks, regiments being constantly depleted by the war in Spain and Portugal. A lot of alcohol was involved but, unlike the Navy where the press gang operated, you could not be forcibly detained.

March 24th *'My Fathers Tenants dined with Him – We had not his agreeable Company till Tea-Time. The Rug My Mother worked, put down in The Library.'* In their own way, they were quite industrious.

They make a short visit to Sedgehill. *'Little William was very good-humoured I had A Visitor in My Bed-Room.'*

April 2nd *'I accompanied My Aunt, & Mother to Wardour, Miss Arundell was kind enough to show Us the Atticks, of which there are 18.'*

April 4th was a Sunday. *'Mr Easton did the Duty & afterwards dined with Us – The Ship his Son is in, has taken A Prize.'* Any reader of the novels of Patrick O'Brian will know about this. If a Naval ship captured an enemy ship, it was sold to the government and its value divided, in proportion, amongst the officers and the crew, so even the lowliest got a share.

They make a trip to London, starting out from Netherhampton. They dine at Stockbridge and sleep at Murrell Green. They get to London on April 14th and go straight to John. *'William here, John grown quite fat & looking very well.'* On the 16th, *'We left John's House & arrived at Clay Hall where We found Emma & Waddington with Their four lovely Children, quite well. I like the Place very well.'* Clay Hall is a district of Ilford, in the borough of Redbridge, deriving its name from a manor house once standing there. Wikipedia suggests the house was pulled down in the middle of the 18th century and replaced by a farmhouse, but it seems likely the Waddingtons were renting it in 1813. It would presumably have been rural then. The two places that are mentioned nearby, a gothic house and a village, are not quite decipherable in the original manuscript, but they also walk to Bennington, and there is a Bennington Road in Ilford. I do not know where they were living prior to this, but John Lane suggests Little Park, Gosport.

After leaving the Waddingtons, they spend a few days in London and go to Drury Lane. *'A beautiful Theatre But very bad Performers.'* They call on Sir William and Lady Fraser: *'We saw 9 of their daughters, two being at school.'* They go to *'Hefe's Exhibition of Water Colours'*. I suspect she means Heaphy, which is of interest to me as I have a watercolour of my own by this artist, of a girl carrying a sheaf of corn on her head. Heaphy went out to Spain in 1813 and made a painting of Wellington, his generals and his staff in the Pyrenees. This painting is lost but an engraving was made, and in the National Portrait Gallery you can see many of the beautiful preparatory sketches he did of Wellington and various officers. I also have one of the engravings.

They visit Astleys, the Circus.

May 4th *'Left Town, dined at Bagshot upon its famous Mutton. Slept at Basingstoke.'* I cannot say I associate Bagshot with mutton. The following day they dine at Salisbury, make a call and get home in the evening.

May 6th *'I walked into the Garden & into the Poultry yard. We dined at half past three, & walked in the Evening.'* The time of dining at this period seems to have varied. I suspect country hours were earlier than town.

On May 15th, Charlotte remarks that her father *'has been very generous to me'* and we are reminded that an unmarried woman had to rely on her family for every penny.

There are references to *'Lushes Cottage'*, but I don't know where it was. John Lush was farming Upton.

May 19th *'Mr & Mrs Boys dined with Us. The former rather overcome with Wine.'*

The Groves have lots of dogs. On June 1st, *'We took a Walk in the Evening – Pigeon the little Puppy very troublesome.'*

June 4th *'Harriet came to fetch me to Sedgehill, with Her little Boy.'*

June 5th *'We were called up in the Morning. Harriet being unexpectedly in labour & brought to Bed of A 7-months Child – A very little Boy.'*

Again, a wet nurse arrives with a baby a fortnight old. I am confused by the wet nurse business because I had assumed wet nurses' own babies were older and left behind somewhere, but from these accounts it seems the wet nurse must have fed both babies. Harriet's new baby is called

Carey. It is interesting that such a premature baby, at that time, could survive. Various Helyar relatives arrive *'and thought Carey The least Baby They had ever seen'*.

They were forever occupied with agriculture. On the 9th, Charlotte walks out with her brother-in-law *'and saw His new Cart Horse in the Plough'*.

On June 15th, Charlotte is still at Sedgehill. *'At night Carlos scratching made Us think there was A Thief, & Wm. Sallied down stairs armed (with the Poker).'* This always seems to have been the instrument for tackling burglars.

They are haymaking. John Helyar, William's uncle and Rector of Sedgehill, was not always popular. He took away two of William's mowers, but Charlotte's father sent him six of his. Of course, the mowing was done by hand.

On the 18th, the wet nurse goes home. What happened to the baby then? Had the wet nurse only been there in case Harriet failed to feed the baby herself? Harriet comes downstairs on the 28th. On July 4th, she is churched.

'Mr John Helyar called, rather more fire than ice in his composition. He had quite A dispute with Mrs Helyar.'

Charlotte returns home. On July 12th she remarks on Mr C Bowles dining with them, which brings him, and his *Hundred of Chalke,* suddenly to life. Mr Arundell and Lady Mary are staying with them and entertain them by singing *'most delightfully indeed.'* On Sunday, they all go to their respective churches, the Arundells to Wardour and the Groves to Berwick.

July 21st *'Charles & Myself went to Netherhampton in the Phaeton He being the Charioteer.'* They go to the races. Charlotte remarks on the Eyre family being there, Eyre carefully underlined, and also *'Mr G Gra'eme'*, about whom Laetitia Popham had teased Charlotte.

Later they go to the Blandford races, and by August 18th are back at Netherhampton. They hear Catalani sing in the cathedral. There are further concerts and a ball in which Charlotte is pleased to announce she danced every dance.

The Arundells often stay. *'The Miss Arundells walked to Ashcombe. I & Miss Catherine strolled about – the Air on the Hill being too keen for Her.'*

At the end of August, they return to Netherhampton and from there visit Marwell and Preshaw. These places belonged to their Long relatives.

August 31st *'We all went to see Marwell, the House My Uncle Long is building.'* The original house was built around 1320. According to the Internet, it was rebuilt in 1816, but we can see from the diaries it was started earlier. At one time it was owned by Sir Henry Seymour, brother of the Lord Protector. One of these Longs was an eminent surgeon at St Bartholomew's.

The rest of the year goes on as usual. At Donhead Hall, where lived the Knellers, Charlotte was impressed with *'A fine set of Plate at Dinner time'.*

John gets jaundice and Charles and his friend Mr Green go to *'Shaston Fair'.*

They go to Coker Court, Harriet's future home. The purpose of the visit was the Christening of the two little Helyar boys, William and Carey, celebrated with a ball. They go to see Montacute, belonging to the Phelips while they are at Coker, and spend a couple of nights at Zeals on their way home.

Though they went about and were very social, Charlotte's refrain is always one of pleasure at being at home alone with her parents: *'Our comfortable Trio'.*

October 30th *'My Mothers application to the Duke of Richmond successful.'* I wonder what this was about.

The Waddingtons arrive with their four children. November 5th *'We walked out and showed little John His Pony, A present from His Uncle Thomas.'* They are soon joined by the Helyars and their boys.

November 13th *'I had A very pleasant Walk with My two Sisters, We called at Wardour & were not admitted – which pleased Us all.'* The etiquette of visiting is very mysterious. They were on the friendliest terms with the

Arundells, and why call if you had no wish to be admitted? Three days later, various Arundells were calling at Ferne, as usual.

Tom's wife Henrietta is often poorly. November 28th *'Tom had A good Game of Romps with the Children. He left Us to Our sincere Regrets.'* The fact that Tom, the heir, had no children of his own, is never referred to, but I cannot help thinking it was on their minds.

The games of chess are incessant, each win or loss carefully recorded.

December 13th *'I walked with My Father to see the new Road he is making up Ashcombe Hill.'*

On the 19th, *'Mr Easton dined here, A dissertation on Ghosts. Mr E rather believes in Them.'* Charlotte is obviously not going to have any truck with superstition, even if endorsed by a clergyman.

On the 22nd, *'Harriet & I called on Mrs Shere. Wm. the groom went to old Amy's being rather in an odd way.'* It would be of interest if Charlotte had expanded on this. I assume being sent to old Amy was a benign treatment for some sort of mental health break down. In what one takes to be a harsher age, it is pleasant to find no references to the workhouse or an asylum. Charlotte talks of Amy or old Amy as being a gardener. His sister was Sarah Pinnock, running a school.

Various members of the family come and go. Tom walks all the way from Lyttleton, near Blandford, dines, spends the night and goes off again the next day.

They are entertained at Christmas by carol singers. Hymn singing was not a part of the Church of England service until sanctioned in 1822. The Methodists had hymns. Carols were viewed rather as folk songs and were certainly not sung in church. If you examine the dates so handily given in our nice new hymn books, you will find lots of hymns written in the early 19th century, but the music is Victorian, so we do not know to what music they were originally sung. 'Amazing Grace' was written by a reformed slaver by the name of John Newton (1725–1807). In the film about William Wilberforce, who did have a good singing voice, he sings 'Amazing Grace' in Whites, the gentlemen's club, an unlikely scenario, especially as the music was adapted from a folk song in 1952.

The mummers also pay a Christmas visit to Ferne, I suppose acting some little play.

Charlotte makes a note: *'This year ended with good News from Our Armies & The Allies, Buonaparte is rather on the Decline of His Power I am in hopes.'* The battle of Vitoria had been won, an occasion famous for the French having to retreat in such haste that the British were able to help themselves to all their baggage, including King Joseph's silver chamber pot. This article was secured by the 14th Light Dragoons and can still be seen at the barracks at Tidworth. Officers are expected to drink from it on mess nights.

The journal concludes with the usual list of expenses, mostly whilst she was away, gloves, silk stockings and getting things washed. The list includes books for the Waddington children, *'Dame Trudge & her Comical Parrot'*, *'Dame Trot & Her Comical Cat'* and *'Little Jenny Wren & Cock Robin'* for Emma, John and George respectively. Charlotte bought *'half hundred needles'* and also black silk and white silk, presumably sewing thread, as she had half an ounce of each, so purchased by weight.

1814

The January of 1814 was a hard one. January 5th *'It snowed very much. Very comfortable We found it round Our Fireside In the Evening.'*

On the 10th, *'I walked out with The aid of Snow Shoes. William Our Groom being much better returned to Us.'* A few weeks with old Amy had done the trick.

Charles, now twenty, has been at home for the vacation. Like his brothers, he spends a lot of time with Mrs Cooke and her daughter. Charles, prior to returning to Oxford, *'went to Donhead Lodge to take leave of its fair Inhabitants'.*

January 19th *'A great deal more Snow – I was obliged to change My Bed-Room. The Chimney smoked so much.'*

The snow was too deep for the mail coach to get through, the equivalent of the postman not turning up.

On the 25th, *'I walked with My Father to the Sheep Fold. The Icicles on the Hedge look like the most beautiful cut Glass.'* I remember such icicles from my childhood. The modern icicle seems less spectacular.

January 29th *'It continues wet, with a few Snow Storms. The Allied army are got to Lyons, the middle of France & met with great success.'*

There is no proper thaw until February 6th.

February 9th *'My father went in the Morning to Cranbourne & settled some Business relative to the marriage of Capt. Markland with Miss Tregonwell.'*

Mr Farquharson's hounds meet at Ansty, Mr Grove going out with them on his new horse.

Harriet arrives with her two boys. On the 22nd, *'We walked out & little Wm. was very much pleased running among the Lambs – he was quite A young Shepherd.'*

Despite the coming and going of wet nurses, Harriet feeds the child herself on February 25th. Charlotte says, *'Harriet weaned little Carey by My Fathers orders.'* Carey had been born at the beginning of June the previous year.

Harriet sends Helen Tregonwell a present of *'A Wedding Night Cap'*. I wonder how this differed from an ordinary night cap; I suppose it was more fancy. Everyone wore one, children and all.

March 1st *'This Month came in like a Lion. I hope it will go out like a lamb.'* For how many centuries have we been saying this?

Charlotte goes to Bath to stay with her Chafin Grove aunt. She has a great-aunt there on her mother's side. *'I accompanied My dear Aunt Rudge to Miss Rodgers party.'* Charlotte is very social, what between dances, the theatre (often bad, *'A miserable Performance written by a gentleman of this Place'*), shopping and paying calls, though there is still more snow. She notes the day Helen is married. After the custom of the day, she does not attend.

Sometimes things went wrong. March 22nd *'I called on Miss Augusta Robinson & was ushered into A Room full of Strangers, being A Lady of the same Name But quite unlike My Friend.'*

The following day she *'had the pleasure of meeting My dear Friend Miss Robertson & walked with Her in the Crescent Fields'.*

April 1st *'Arrived at My own dear Home just as the Family were seated at Dinner – Capt. & Mrs Markland here & Charles.'* Thus she refers to her newly married friend and is immediately defeated by the captain in two games of chess.

April 2nd *'Surprised at A circumstance that happened'.* A typical Charlotte mystery pronouncement, no explanation given.

Her sister Emma Waddington has another son, Thomas Grove.

Charles *'worked very hard in the flower garden with Amy'*. Charlotte takes a walk *'by Lushes cottage'*. This cottage is often mentioned as is the *'ruined cottage'*, but it is hard to say where they were.

April 9th *'The Allies are in Paris & Buonaparte in A bad way'*, and the next day, *'The glorious News that Buonaparte has surrendered Himself Coward as He is.'* Charlotte was nothing if not partisan. *'Mr J Helyar dined here. I enjoyed talking with Him on this joyful News.'*

As late as April 13th they are still hunting, this time at *'Knoyle Summer lea's'*. Charlotte is staying at Sedgehill. *'We went to Wardour & partook of A hot Luncheon at Fern.'* I am interested in the mention of luncheon. Generally breakfast was late and dinner early. The Groves seem to dine around three or four, so there was not much time for lunch. From my general reading, it seems if anyone took lunch it was not much more than a snack, so I suppose the consumption of a *'hot Luncheon'* was worthy of a mention.

April 21st *'Lady Mary & Mr Arundell are gone to Paris, with the French Royal Family.'*

On the 25th, *'Just as We had done Dinner My eldest Brother arrived from Wales – He was so agreeable that We sat up till 12 o'clock.'* He goes away the next day with the sister of Susan, a servant at Ferne, who is to work for Henrietta. Tom had property in Wales but he never took up permanent residence there. I expect it was considered too out of the way.

They had started reading a novel of Madame d'Arblay (Fanny Burney) with enthusiasm, but a few days later, *'Mde. D'Arblays Novel such stuff that We cannot finish it.'*

May 6th *'An unexpected Visit from Mr Chafin Grove, Who dined with Us. Manoeuvring necessary sometimes.'* I take this to be a nephew of Aunt Chafin Grove's late husband. As they had no children, Zeals passed to his nephews. There must have been something awkward about the situation.

Mr Grove has a violent attack of rheumatism in his shoulder and they are obliged to send for Mr Wilkins.

May 10th *'Buonaparte is retired to the Island of Elba.'* On the following day, *'Ld. Wellington is at Paris.'*

May 15th *'My Mother & I paid A long Visit at Upper Donhead Parsonage & then went to the Evening Church there – The Curate Mr Mills rather tedious.'* This visit would be to the Jacksons, Mrs Jackson one of Mrs Grove's sisters. She had the curious name of Bathia. The parsonage was what we know as Shute House.

May 16th *'In the Garden-House Edwards showed Us an Effigy the Work people have made of Buonaparte.'* I suppose a garden-house to be some sort of potting shed, unless it was a summer house. It is not mentioned elsewhere.

They are brought an estimate of Ashcombe on May 22nd. This is the earliest hint the Groves are interested in purchasing Ashcombe. Charlotte sometimes spells it as two words.

They spend a night at Netherhampton and shop in Salisbury *'& very cold it was'*. I don't know why we are ever surprised by the weather, as it is obvious it was as unpredictable then as it is now.

May 26th *'I had some conversation with Old Amy – The Effigy of Buonaparte was brought into the Passage & We went to see it.'*

May 30th *'My dear Father left us, on his journey to Town, accompanied by Edwards in the Phaeton.'* They probably took the coach, as they were in London in time for a letter from John to arrive at Ferne by the next day. The postal service was extra efficient when horses were used.

May 31st *'John sent Us A very droll letter about My Father Who is safely arrived in Town.'* I feel London was not Mr Grove's natural element, but they are a delightfully affectionate family. He returns on June 5th *'to Our very great joy'.*

June 8th *'It is still very cold.'*

On the 9th, *'The Emperor of Russia, King of Prussia & General Blucher are arrived in London on A Visit to the Prince Regent.'* These exotic foreigners, our allies, caused a huge stir in London, it being the rage to tear about trying to get a glimpse of them. I seem to remember the emperor caused offence by going to stay with his sister, declining the invitation of the Prince Regent. Most people had never seen a Russian, let alone an emperor.

June 10th *'A report of the Duke of Wellington being assassinated which I sincerely hope is not true.'* It certainly was not true. He did not die until 1852.

On June 11th, *'A Dinner on account of the Peace given to Our Work People. Miss Jackson Fanny & Arabella came. The Effigy of Buonaparte burnt upon White Sheet Hill. My Cousins & I went to see it, escorted Home by Mr Lush & Lane.'* With the formality of the period, Charlotte refers to her eldest female cousin as Miss Jackson. Lane was the tenant at Upper and Lower Bridmore. We still burn Guy Fawkes, but it has not crossed our modern minds to burn Napoleon.

June 17th *'In the Evening We took A pleasant Walk On the New Road to Ashcombe.'*

On the 21st, *'After Dinner I went out, & met with two poor Travellers, & their Child, going to Penzance in Cornwall. I collected A Subscription for Them & They slept at the Glove Inn.'*

Charlotte's Jackson cousins or her aunts are frequent visitors, but when they are gone she often comments on the pleasures of her quiet domestic life alone with her parents. *'We returned to Our own sociable hours & way of passing Our time.'*

They are told by Mrs Boys that Mr Simpson, her new neighbour, shoots with a long bow. I cannot think of the Rectory as exactly having a neighbour.

June 27th *'Charles arrived from Oxford for the long Vacation – He has been to Portsmouth to see the Allied Sovereigns, after Their having visited Oxford – I walked in the Garden with Him, & We had A great deal of conversation with the Gardiner about Plants.'*

On the next day, *'Charles very busy in the Flower Garden – In the Evening I walked with Him till it was dark – The 2nd Day of My Fathers Sheep shearing.'* Charles was definitely the gardener of the family. I see him as not at all suited to the Naval career he gave up.

At the end of the month, Tom and Henrietta arrive with *'The two Miss Frasers'*. On July 1st, they all go to pay a morning visit at Sedgehill. They go *'in My Brothers Barouchette, & The Phaeton'*. My book on carriages makes no mention of the former vehicle, but a barouche was a four-wheeled low carriage with a hood at the back, a driver's seat and a dickey. They use the same vehicles to get to church. There is talk of walking to Ferne wall. The only wall we can think of is at the bottom of the park.

The Helyars come to stay for a few days. Charlotte comments on little William being very fond of her but also that he *'is grown rather shy'*. Carey *'is much improved'*.

July 12th *'My Mother took Me to Sedgehill. In the Evening I helped to make the Hay.'*

On the following day, *'Mrs J Helyar Mrs Amsinck Lady Parker & Miss S Still rode up to the Door whilst We were dressing for Dinner.'* Charlotte then underlines something about Susan Still's donkey, which is sadly illegible. There is quite a mention of donkeys. Francis read somewhere these beasts were a rarity in Britain until the Peninsular War, at which juncture officers brought them home from Spain and Portugal.

Mrs J Helyar then spends the day with them. She and Charlotte play no less than seven games of chess. The following day they play another five.

In the middle of the month, they go to Lyttleton to stay with the Farquharsons and later to Netherhampton. *'My Aunt Groves Servants give Her much trouble.'*

They stop at Compton on the way home. Charlotte reports, *'Mrs Penruddocke is grown very thin with Her vegetable Diet.'* People got the same notions then as now.

At home, in August, they have the Penruddockes, Gordons (from Wincombe) and Marklands either to dine or to stay, and then Charles drives his sister in the phaeton to Lyttleton for the races. *'Thomas went with Mr Farquharson & Party to the Agriculture Society at Blandford.'*

They go to the balls. *'I danced every Dance.'* They are chaperoned by Mrs Farquharson. Though Charlotte is now thirty-one, her unmarried status does not qualify her as independent. Sometimes, at home or while visiting, she is relegated to playing the piano while younger members of the party do the dancing.

They then stay at Compton for the Salisbury races. Charlotte makes bets with Mr Vincent and Mr Hetley, most of which she wins, but she does not say how much they were for. She mentions other men, Walter Long and William Wyndham, staying and dining, Mr Douglas, Mr Tinney and Mr Walter Earle. *'Mr D. wanted to frighten Me out of taking Snuff.'* I find this an interesting comment. Queen Charlotte was an inveterate taker of snuff. Peninsular War officers talk of smoking cigars. Mr Grove, we know, smoked a pipe. There was the universal clay pipe, bits of which frequently come to light in our own landscape, but what percentage of the poor could have afforded tobacco? Peter Compton's father, old Jack Compton, told me he used to smoke the 'withy-wind' or bindweed, as we call it. Somehow, I did not expect Charlotte to be taking snuff. In what way was Mr Douglas warning her off it?

On August 22nd, Charlotte returns to Ferne to find *'My dear Brother George arrived'*.

The following day, she visits Sedgehill with the three Miss Wyndhams of Salisbury who are staying with them. *'Found Wm Helyar & My Brothers rather heated with the wine They had drank yesterday at Stour Head.'*

At the end of August, there are veiled references to Ashcombe. On the 28th, *'Mr Barnard & My Brother Helyar called at Fern & upon Mr G South Who was like Orator Mum in his answers relative to Ashcombe.'* Mr South was a relative by marriage of Mrs Grove. He lived at Charlton and acted as land agent or lawyer for the Groves. I do not know who Mr Barnard was, but it is apparent Ashcombe is on the market at this time. Orator Mum was a nickname given to an Irish lawyer who was too nervous to speak when first appearing in court.

In September, Charlotte goes to Langton for the Christening of *'Little Frederick'*, a Farquharson son. In the evening, they play *'Speculation'* and the following day there are fireworks. The Chinese Drum was spoilt, but *'The Catherine Wheels beautiful'*.

Back at Ferne, they have a whole string of visitors. William comes home. They play a round game called Snip Snap Snorum. John is back courting, this time a Fraser, one of the eleven daughters of Sir William Fraser. Her mother was a Farquharson. On the 20th, *'My little nephews very much admired. John talked about living upon A very spare Diet denominated Love.'* His *'Drawing Room Furniture'* arrives from Lincoln's Inn Fields, where he has been living, so is his medical training complete?

September 27th *'Wm. received A letter from the Admiralty appointing Him to the Hope Sloop.'* A sloop was rather a small battle ship with a single gun deck. I expect William thought himself lucky to get any place, following his disgrace.

There are all sorts of entertainments and impromptu dances and family visits. Daniel plays the violin and Charlotte's mother the tambourine so they may dance. September 28th *'Mrs Kneller came in the Morning. The rest of her Party to Dinner. My brothers entertained with the different display of the young Ladies.'*

On September 30th, *'The Statues put up on The Staircase'* so the embellishment of Ferne is still going on.

The harvest has been good: October 1st *'My Father has made A great many Wheat & Barley Ricks.'*

October 2nd *'My Brothers went to Lyttleton to fetch My eldest Brother & They all five dined here.'*

William now joins his ship at Portsmouth. Charlotte goes with her parents to stay with the Longs at Hall Place. I think of the Longs at Preshaw, and I am not sure of Hall Place. They see Marwell: *'The Building is gothic & very much got on since I saw it last.'*

October 8th *'We walked to Westbury to call on Lady Gage – We saw the Bust of Buonaparte & other Statuary brought from abroad, by Capt. Gage RN.'* Captain Gage had a distinguished career in the Navy, but I have failed in finding out if Westbury was a house or the town or where everyone had got to. I have other resources than the Internet, the latter sometimes useful and sometimes not. In this case I am defeated by Lady Gaga and the zoo.

On the 14th back at Ferne, *'Mr & Mrs Boys dined here – We had two card Tables in the Evening, Mrs E Long played at Quadrille & enjoyed it very much.'*

At Sedgehill, where her mother takes her on the 17th as Harriet is about to produce another baby, Charlotte practises waltzing. I have read this dance was made fashionable by Alexander, Emperor of Russia, performing it at Almack's, the exclusive London club, during the famous visit of the Allied Sovereigns. However, waltzing had many detractors. As late as 1816 in *The Times*, 'We remark with pain that the indecent foreign dance called the waltz was introduced at the English Court on Friday last…it is quite sufficient to cast one's eyes on the voluptuous intertwining of the limbs and close compressure on the bodies in their dance, to see that it is indeed far removed from the modest reserve which has hitherto been considered distinctive of English females.' At this period, as far as I can make out from contemporary prints, the couples held each other by the arms at shoulder height, but perhaps I misinterpret them. I thought the close embrace came later, but it was all too much for *The Times*. A German traveller to Paris in 1804 said, 'the waltz…is quite new & has become one of the vulgar fashions since the war, like smoking.' Who remembers Mary Sparkes and Jimmy Wills dancing away with such expertise in our hall, waltzes and quicksteps?

William Helyar often dines out, leaving *'A pleasant Trio of Ladies at Home'*. Caroline Helyar was with them.

Harriet has a daughter on October 26th named Agnes Grove. Charlotte is a godmother. There seems to have been no complications and there is no mention of wet nurses.

On October 30th, *'Mrs J Helyar called – Caroline & Myself ran out of the way of Morning Visitors.'*

November 3rd *'My Mother called & spent A long Morning here – (A shocking Elopement of Sir H Mildmay with Lady Roseberry his Sister in Law).'*

George Follet brought the hounds up from Coker Court to Ferne.

On November 10th, William, Charlotte's brother-in-law, breakfast at Ferne and hunt in Berwick Coombe. He gets in plenty of hunting while the hounds are at Ferne. The 14th is his and Harriet's third wedding anniversary…a baby a year. Harriet comes downstairs. There is still lots of chess, and Charlotte is more often than not defeated by her brother-in-law. *'I played Chess with Wm. & think I play worse & worse.'*

She does not go home until December 3rd. William, Harriet and the children return with her. Two days later she, and Harriet take little William to Hook Farm: *'Mr & Mrs Strickland at Home'.*

On the 9th, Charles arrives from Oxford. *'He has lately been at Clay Hall, & gives A very good account of the Waddingtons.'*

Charlotte, on the 13th, reads *'Roseberrys Divorce Sr. H. Mildmay is to pay £15000.'* The general idea was that a wife was the property of her husband, so if you stole her you had to pay. I think if you multiply the sum by fifty you get an idea of what the figure would be today, something like seven hundred and fifty thousand pounds.

December 20th *'Capt. Donaldson has got George appointed to the Rose East Indiaman.'* He leaves the next day.

Christmas Day is Tom's thirty-first birthday. *'We were waked by the Christmas Carols early in The Morning.'* Not quite when we expect them. They were entertained the day after Christmas by singers from Berwick, Upper and Lower Donhead.

Charles has Oxford friends staying, Mr Earle and Mr Pit. Charlotte goes to a dance at Pythouse with them but *'owing to the fineness of the young Oxonians, We did not arrive till the first Course was almost finished.'*

*

The end papers of the 1814 journal record a bet for 2s 6d Charlotte has with Fanny Still on who Mr Strickland will marry. *'I say Miss Catherine Arundell, she says Miss Laura Arundell.'* John Lane tells me neither.

There are notes about the length of material required to make a dress – two and a half yards. Frills should be three quarters wider than the gown. I wonder about these frills because they are often mentioned as a separate item. I remember Miss Bradbury, who was born in 1914, telling me her grandmother would unpick the frill on the hem of her dress and sew on a clean one, it being the part that touched the ground and got dirty. This meant only the frill need be washed. Charlotte buys seven yards of narrow silk and six yards of wide for making dresses and records how much a Miss Blagrove charges for making them, 7s 6d and a lot more for making a pelisse, 3s 10d. Ten shillings was spent on cleaning. Five and a half yards was needed as half edging for two tippets. For the information of those under the age of fifty, a yard is a little less than a metre. As for the money, one no longer equates with the other. If, as a child, you had a ten-shilling note, it was riches: now it is 50p.

Charlotte had brown long gloves and yellow French gloves this year, black pins and miles of satin ribbon.

She makes a note of *Pride and Prejudice* and also *Patience and Perseverance* the latter being, I think, an early title for *Sense and Sensibility*.

1815

On January 3rd, Captain Markland *'sent his Poodle Dog as A present to my Father.'* It is called Azor. Winter sports continue, hunting with Mr Farquharson's hounds, rough shooting for hare and partridge, coursing and the odd day with the harriers.

Mr Grove goes to Pythouse. Charlotte says, on the 5th, *'I hope his & Mr Benetts plan will answer for the sake of old England.'* This was to do with the Corn Laws. Foreign imports of corn were banned unless home-grown corn had reached a price of 80s a quarter. This was of benefit to farmers and therefore landowners, but it kept the price of bread artificially high. Mr Benett and Mr Grove were pro the Corn Laws. Charlotte's father could not be away for two days without lament: *'We miss My father very much indeed.'*

January 7th *'My Father returned. They had A good Meeting at Warminster though the officious Mr Hunt tried to make it as disagreeable as He could.'* This was Henry Hunt, known as Orator Hunt, drawn to our attention now with the bicentenary of the Peterloo Massacre, which occurred in the August of 1819 in Manchester, where a perfectly peaceful crowd were dispersed by the military with very bloody results. Hunt was a Wiltshire landowner, but unlike most of his peers he was a radical, certainly violently opposed to the Corn Laws and he had a peculiar distaste for Mr Benett. In truth, the memory of the French Revolution was a most disturbing one, not at all easily forgotten by even the lesser gentry of the period: they did not necessarily see reform was a better answer than repression.

January 8th *'Sir Byshe Shelley is dead – My Uncle succeeds to the Baronetcy.'* Charlotte announces this with no other comment and goes on to talk of walking the poodle. Later she refers to the dog as Blucher, so they must have changed its name in honour of the renowned Prussian general, Prince Blucher, unless they had two poodles.

She pays a visit to the Marklands, her friend Helen, at Tollard Royal, escorted there by Hyscock, a groom at Ferne. She seems to have walked there, and five days later Captain Markland walks her back.

With her Jackson cousins, on the 25th, they go to stay at Lyttleton. *'We had A merry Rubber of Whist in the Evening.'* The purpose of the visit was to attend a Blandford ball, which they do the next day.

January 28th *'A thaw. Fanny & Myself walked out though it was excessively dirty.'* Fanny is Fanny Jackson.

On the 30th, the weather must have been worse because *'We read Novels all Day.'*

The following day, *'At Dinner time poor Henrietta had A violent Hysterick Fit.'*

February 1st *'Arabella very impudent to Me, Henrietta kept Her Bed.'* They dine at Langton and play a *'merry Game of Speculation'*.

By the 2nd, Henrietta is recovering. There is *'A Female Party to Tea at Mrs Farquharsons'*, which Charlotte describes as *'Hum Drum enough'*.

On the 3rd they return, calling on the Marklands at Tollard on the way. *'Helen I think looks worse.'*

The month proceeds as usual. *'Mrs Doyle wrote to My Mother about the Blind Boy whom C Benett has got into A School in London.'*

Captain Markland is a frequent visitor. His aunt is Mrs Cooke living at Donhead Lodge, that favoured destination of Charlotte's brothers. She has been away. Charlotte remarks that *'Miss Cooke grown very plain'*.

February 21st *'We have as yet only 4 Lambs.'*

On the 22nd, they go to Whatcombe, the Pleydell's house near Winterbourne Whitchurch. Charlotte manages to win six chess games out of eight against Miss Pleydell.

At home she is not so lucky when her opponent is Captain Markland, who frequently beats her.

On March the 11th and 12th, the shattering news is out that Napoleon has escaped from Elba. Charlotte says, with many underlinings, *'It is true that Buonaparte has invaded France – I hope that He will be soon killed (The Traitor).'* After dinner, they toast the French royal family.

March 16th *'This is the Day appointed for the sale of Ashcombe. I wonder who will buy it.'*

March 17th *'Harriet & her two little Boys called upon Us. Carey in high spirits. The Paper says Buonaparte has An Army of 50,000 Men. The Duchess of Angouleme & Wellington are arrived in England.'*

March 22nd *'Good News from France. I think Buonaparte will be defeated – Tom called upon Us – Ashcombe is not yet sold. I wish A Friend of Mine may have it.'*

On Good Friday, *'Mr Boys gave Us an excellent Sermon on The Crucifixion – The sad News that Buonaparte is again Emperor of the French, & Lewis 18th in England. Tom dined & slept here. We are all anxious in one Topick.'*

The next day, Tom and Mr Farquharson call in on their way back from hunting. Charlotte says they appointed her father as negotiator. This was undoubtedly to do with the purchase of Ashcombe.

March 26th *'The King of France is gone into the Netherlands – where I hope he will be successful.'* This corrects the previous information.

March 28th *'The Allies have declared War against Buonaparte.'*

April 2nd *'My Mother & I went to Evening Service at Berwick. I took A long Walk with Blucher as My attendant. Mr Easton dined with Us – My Father proposed his accepting A Chaplaincy in the Navy to which he agreed.'* This was the clergyman without a living. According to Patrick O'Brian of *Master and Commander* fame, the Navy would have been an unpleasant option as the sailors considered having a parson on board unlucky. They often had the added task of giving the midshipmen their lessons.

April 3rd *'My Mother & I called at Wardour – We saw Both Lady Mary & Mr Arundell – Lady Mary looks more beautiful than ever.'*

On April 8th, *'A shocking circumstance happened at Donhead Hall, A servant had secreted a child She had had ever since Christmas.'*

April 10th *'Tom called in his way from Pythouse, where He was rather heated with The hospitable entertainment He met with.'*

On the 10th, *'Mrs Knellers Maid Servant that secreted the Child is run away.'*

On the 15th, they dine at Wardour where they meet a French émigré just arrived from France. There is the usual walking and visiting. Captain Markland dines often but without his wife, which seems to have been a normal practice. He and Mr Easton sometimes dine two days running.

April 20th *'I took A long Walk with Blucher as My Guard. He carried My Fur Tippet for Me.'*

April 22nd *'My eldest Brother called upon Us & was as usual very entertaining. My Father rode A little way with Him & was caught in A tremendous Hail Storm.'*

April 25th *'We heard the good News, that Tom has purchased Ashcombe.'*

April 26th *'Mr Bond & Mr South came in the Evening to settle the business relative to Ashcombe.'*

On the 27th, *'The Business relative to Ashcombe finally settled & It is My Brothers – (How happy this has made me).'* As the journal unfolds, this turns out to be far from the case. Charlotte goes on to say, *'& This auspicious Day heard that dear Charles has past His Examination'*.

May 4th *'Tom called upon us having looked at his delightful Ashcombe, (The Dining Parlour the same length as ours).'* This surprised me because the picture of Ashcombe shows the house to be far bigger and grander than Ferne.

May 4th *'Tom called upon Us having received A letter from Mr Davies relative to the Sale of Cwm Elan.'* I assume this sale was to assist the purchase of Ashcombe.

May 6th *'I walked to Ashcombe with Susan – My Mother rode the Poney – We met Capt. & Mrs Markland there. My Father also went with Us – I went into every Room in the House.'*

May 12th *'Capt. Markland shot the young Rooks – Mr Easton called. His Son has been in An Engagement & He is in A great fright about Him.'* He had a son in the Navy.

May 14th *'Blucher behaved very ill running after the Sheep & we had Him tied up.'*

Charlotte and her mother then go to stay at Sedgehill. They call at Clouds. *'We saw Mrs Still, Miss Still, Lady Parker & her very plain Children.'*

Charles comes home with his friend Mr Phillips. They are soon off to *'drink Tea'* and spend the evening at Mrs Cooke's.

May 22nd *'Tom called here & Mr South. They will not settle about the Rent of Ashcombe till Michaelmas.'*

May 23rd *'I took A nice Walk. There has been A mad Dog killed that has bit 3 People – in the Evening Charles taught My Father Back Gammon & I played Chess with Mr Philips.'*

May 24th *'My Aunt Shelley & her three eldest Daughters – came to Fern. They arrived about 9 in the Evening.'* They are soon joined by their Jackson cousins. They walk, they dance, they *'find out Riddles'*. They visit, I think, possibly a retired nursemaid or nanny to the Groves. They are entertained by the Berwick band.

June 4th *'We all went to Berwick Church – Something occurred I would much rather had not.'* What ever can have happened?

On the 8th, they go in Tom's carriage to Ashcombe and he takes official possession of the house.

A party of them go to church in Upper Donhead. *'Mr Prowse preached & in A most Theatrical manner.'*

The battle of Waterloo is fought on June 18th. Henry Percy presents the dispatch and two captured French Imperial Eagles to the Prince Regent on the 21st. The news reaches Ferne on 23rd. Charlotte says, *'The glorious News that Wellington and Blucher have beat Buonaparte.'* She then adds, mundanely, that she and Harriet walked to Knoyle to buy a cheese. She is staying at Sedgehill at the time.

June 27th *'We past A most pleasant Day at Stourhead & partook of A cold Dinner at the Tower – Mr J. Still met Us on the Downs & told us Buonaparte has abdicated the French Throne.'*

They often go to Ashcombe, but brother Tom is still living at Lyttleton. Her father has made eight ricks of hay. Mr Easton and his son William, who had caused his father so much anxiety, *'has lost his left hand in an engagement.'* They hear of the taking of Paris. *'I very much fear Buonaparte has escaped.'* By the 28th, they hear he has surrendered to the English.

The year goes on with a visit to Aunt Grove at Netherhampton. As usual, they visit the Penruddockes at Compton on the way home. *'Painting going on in the House. The smell of it does not agree with Mrs Penruddocke.'* There was no doubt lead in the paint.

July 13th *'Lewis 18th is returned to Paris.'*

July 14th *'Mr Wyndham called. He is engaged in A Chase Cause against Ld. Rivers, in which I sincerely hope He will be successful.'* One of the ongoing situations in the diaries was Mr Wyndham's 'Chase Cause' against Lord Rivers. It was to do with Lord River's right to the deer within the bounds of the Cranborne Chase. Those farming the land became increasingly annoyed by the deer damaging their crops and being prohibited from taking any action. Mr King, Mr Wyndham's tenant at Norrington, had an altercation with the Chase keepers. From reading *Hundred of Chalke*, I understand Mr King lived at Samways. Norrington was occupied by labourers and had not been maintained since 1787. Charles Bowles bewails its ruinous state when he published his book in 1830.

July 18th *'We drank Tea in Our new Drawing Room for the first time.'* I find this puzzling. Where have they been drinking tea in the meantime? They have been at Ferne nearly four years.

Charlotte walks to Tollard to stay a few days with the Marklands, escorted by the footman, Daniel.

At the end of July, they go again to Netherhampton for the Salisbury races and the ball.

At home, they have Miss Catherine and Miss Laura Arundell to stay. Miss Julia is to marry Lord Talbot. They are joined by Miss Kneller, Mrs Long and Aunt Grove. *'The Miss Arundells sung to Us. They sung very well.'*

August 3rd *'I walked with The two Miss Wyndhams to Ashcombe. My Mother and Mr Whyndom went there in the Phaeton. We had A scrambling Walk Home by the Summer House on the Hill.'* There is an 18th-century print of Ashcombe that Desmond Hawkins depicts in his *The Grove Diaries* that clearly shows this and another similar building on the high ground above Ashcombe. It also shows the very considerable extent of the house and buildings.

They stay at Lyttleton for the Blandford races and subsequent balls.

Back at home, they dine at Mr Gordon's. This would have been Wincombe. *'A sumptuous Dinner of Turtle & Venison.'*

August 16th *'Sir Richard, Lady Glyn, their three Sons & Miss Plumtree came.'* The Glyns owned Gaunts in Wimborne. The present Sir Richard's charitable foundation runs it as a centre for holistic and spiritual learning. When I was a child, they lived in Gillingham and Sir Richard's parents were friends of my parents, so my brother Peter and I were sent over 'to play', I think without enthusiasm on their part or ours.

August 17th *'The Party went to see Wardour with The exception of My Father & Self…We had A very merry Game of Commerce & danced with 8 Gentlemen.'*

The following day, they invite additional friends for more dancing.

August 20th *'Tom dined and slept here – We talked about the bad times for Land holders.'* I imagine the post-war agricultural depression was setting in.

Charlotte's other brothers are mostly at home at the minute, except for George. William joins one ship or another at various moments. Charles often has friends to stay, Mr Phillips and Mr Wallinger. We don't learn their Christian names, but John Lane says Mr Wallinger, clergyman, was John Arnold. He later married Harriet Devonsher and her brother married Louisa Cooke, with whom Charlotte's brothers spent much time.

They visit *'Bourne'* for a few days, where the Tregonwells are living, and get very wet walking by the sea.

August 25th *'I played Waltzes. Mr Wallinger & Charles danced with Chairs. John & Mr P. played at Chess.'*

The rest of the month and the beginning of the next are taken up with the usual walks and visits. On September 3rd, *'I accompanied My Mother & Charles to L Donhead Church – We called upon Mrs Fletcher & Cooke, & afterwards on Mrs Burlton & They were not at Home. We saw two of Mrs C Benetts children very plain (I think them).'* These would have been Mrs Burlton's grandchildren, her daughter married to Captain Charles Benett. Mr Fletcher was Rector of Donhead St Andrew.

September 7th *'Tom came. He dined & slept here. He thinks He shall get into Ashcombe the 10th of next Month. John & Him laughed at Me but I did not understand their joke.'*

The following day, *'My Brothers Bailiff Mr James & his Family arrived from Wales – They dined here & went to Ashcombe afterwards.'* The sale of the Welsh property must have gone through promptly.

September 11th *'I was waked about 3 in the morning by a summons from Tollard for My Mother Mrs Markland being taken in labour.'*

September 12th *'I heard the joyful News that Mrs Markland is brought to Bed of A Son. I went in the Phaeton to Tollard to fetch My Mother home, & saw Helen & her little Boy – Both quite well.'*

On the next day, *'We dined at Wardour & saw Miss Julia's Lover Sir J Talbot, & A silly Man He appears to be.'*

September 14th *'The Harvest Home. Betty Stretch was assisting as alertly as ever, Betty Pickford looks very ill.'*

They stay at Gaunts. September 17th *'I took an Excursion to Horton Tower with Miss Plum Tree, & drove Her in the Donkey Cart.'* I don't know if Charlotte's spelling of this name is accidental or not.

John is starting to practise as a doctor. September 20th *'John & Wm. called at Wardour – The Former saw his Patient recommended by Lady Mary Who is better for his advice. Charles called on Charles Bowles.'* Charlotte does not say who the patient was, perhaps a servant. A qualified doctor was beyond the means of most. An apothecary, of doubtful, or any, qualifications, was the substitute.

On the 24th, *'John went to Hook to see Mrs Strictland, Who has caught cold since her lying in.'* He makes several visits.

September 30th *'Tom called here, My Father accompanied Him to Ashcombe, where Henrietta was very busy unpacking.'*

October 5th *'Tom came here. They got into Ashcombe yesterday. Emma & Harriet accompanied Me in A Walk there to call upon Henrietta. We were very merry all the way.'* They have the Helyars and the Waddingtons staying. On the way home, they call at Tollard. *'Helen still looks delicate. The Child very well.'*

Despite the innumerable visits of married sisters and their children, the sporting activities of brothers and brothers-in-law and quantities of people to dine, Charlotte is still very happy when left alone with her parents. *'Our comfortable trio sat round the fire.'* They get through lots of novels.

Mr Grove attends the *'Turnpike Meetings'*. These were held at the Glove, presumably to discuss the upkeep of what is now the A30.

October 14th *'My Father heard from Mr Methuen But not anything in favour of Williams promotion.'* William was obviously going to need considerable 'string pulling' to get his career underway.

On the 30th, *'The Gentlemen dined at Ashcombe.'*

October 31st *'Dear Harriet left Us – Our spirits rather low being The last Day of Emma's staying with Us.'* Charlotte immediately goes off to Sedgehill.

November 1st *'The poachers were fined at the Justice Meeting.'* I was interested by this comment because the poaching laws were draconian.

You could be sent to Australia for having a rabbit net, but it is good to see ordinary charity and common sense could prevail.

November 2nd *'I accompanied Caroline & Harriet in A Walk to Knoyle called at J Snooks & left My Gown to be made.'* This typifies the way a length of cloth was referred to as a gown long before it was one.

Charlotte is, as ever, critical of other people's children. Of a Mrs Doyle, *'I never saw such an object as Her little Girl.'*

She and her mother visit Helen Markland at Tollard. She does not look well. *'The little Boy grown – But not pretty.'*

November 14th *'My mother and I walked to Eddys. My father has permitted Robert Lathy to make her Husband A new Wooden Leg.'* Lathy must have been the estate carpenter.

November 20th *'Tom and Henrietta came to Ashcombe for A few Days – The Former sent My Mother & Self A Present of A Cloth Cloak like the Princess Charlotte of Wales's.'* This is the equivalent of wearing the same garment as seen on the Princess of Wales. Cloaks could be purchased ready-made, as could most garments worn by ordinary working people.

Her brother does not seem to be living at Ashcombe full time. They are also living at Weymouth.

November 27th *'William set off about seven Oclock in the Morning for Cattistock in order to hunt with Mr Farquharson's Hounds – There being no Frost.'* This was a distance of about twenty-six miles if William had gone as the crow flies and probably about a third more only using roads. It was customary for a wealthy foxhunter to have a 'covert hack' to ride to the meet and then to change on to his hunter that his groom would have brought on earlier, or even the night before. His groom would have provided him with a second horse to change onto halfway. Hunting as a child, I remember strings of grooms hacking along quietly at the back of the hunt with the second horses. Francis tells me only one person has a second horse with the Blackmore Vale now and the meeting up is of course all organised by telephone. William was one of several younger sons, so I doubt he had such arrangements at his disposal, but

Mr Farquharson may well have provided him with a fresh horse when he got there. He returns nine days later, or more, which suggests being lent lots of horses. Charlotte reports his return twice, on the 6th as well as the 12th, this sort of confusion is out of character. Aunt Grove, the Netherhampton one, gives Charlotte her harpsichord. It is placed in the hall between the pillars, surrounded by pot plants. A Mr Parker comes to tune the instruments.

December 1st *'My Mother and I sung very finely to the Harpsichord.'*
December 2nd *'Helen is much better since She has weaned Her Child.'*

On the 7th, William is off to dine at General Garth's to meet a large party at Weymouth, including Mr Farquharson and Tom. General Garth leased Ilsington House on the edge of Puddletown between 1780 and 1829. He had been equerry to George III. Princess Sophia, the King's fifth daughter, had a child by him. It was said the Princess was so innocent that even in an advanced state of pregnancy she had no idea of her condition. Of course, the matter was kept a great secret, but there was a lot of gossip at the time and the wretched Princess was condemned never to marry. General Garth, a bachelor, brought the child up and always acknowledged the boy was his but would never say who the mother was. Later Tom Garth, as he was called, made an attempt to blackmail the royal family.

December 15th *'Mrs Markland has bought Mrs Burltons donkey. A foolish Purchase as They are very stubborn and never go the right way.'* Mrs Burlton was a widow, sister of Charles Bowles, living in Donhead St Mary. Her monument is in that church and also that of two of her grandsons killed in the Indian Mutiny. A house there still bears her name, Burltons. It is said to have been lived in by her poet/parson brother William Bowles whilst he was curate at East Knoyle.

The rector's wife, Mrs Boys, is not well. Her health, like Henrietta's, is a cause for concern.

On the following day, they are glad to see Tom. *'It did Us good to see Him. He is so Cheerful.'* He has been paid the money for Cwm Elan. A few days later, he calls to discuss *'the Ashcombe Business'* with their father. On the 22nd, a Mr Chitty comes *'on the Cwm Elan Business'*.

The year ends as usual. They are entertained by the Upper and Lower Donhead singers, also the Bulls and Mummers. What are Bulls? Ralph Perry Robinson tells me a mummer wearing a bull's head.

At the end of her journal, she does a tally of chess games won and lost. There is, as usual, a list of clothing items she packed when visiting: petticoats, shifts, night caps, etc. She does not mention stays nor underpants, or drawers as they were called. There is a general idea these were not worn until Victorian times, but this is nonsense. There is an ancient pair on display in Wilton House, made in two parts and tied with ribbon. The officers of the Peninsular War were always writing home for more pairs. Charlotte may have been too delicate to name such intimate garments. I have various books on underclothes, but unlike wedding dresses, the original articles were not preserved, which makes research tricky. 'Sleeves' and 'bodys' are mentioned as separate items, so I suppose one could ring the changes.

1816

The diary starts with a note to say Mr Portman married Sir Edward Halse's eldest daughter. *'A suitable Age for Him & likely to be A good Mother in law to his Children.'* This term was used where we would say stepmother. The correct name was Hulse.

They have a house full of friends and relations, including Charlotte's friend Miss Popham. On January 2nd, the gentlemen dine at Ashcombe. Charlotte's father is coursing his greyhounds. *'Master Farquharson came with His Beagles & went into the Wood to look for Rabbits But could not find any.'* If a lad came from a sporting family, he could be given a pack of beagles for himself.

On the 11th, they go to a ball at the Knellers. *'Mrs Cooke told Harriet A Report about Me. (I wish It was true).'* This I find a rather wistful entry. Is Charlotte regretting her unmarried state? We will never know, and she gives no hint. They do not get to bed until six in the morning.

On the 16th, they walk to Ashcombe and spend an hour with Tom's wife Henrietta. *'A most dirty Walk. Nearly stuck fast in A ploughed Field. I took a bundle of clean Stockings and Shoes with Us.'*

January 22nd *'Miss Popham went to Ashcombe. She rode the Poney & her Maid & Trunk went in the cart.'* Laetitia Popham had her own maid. Charlotte never mentions having one herself. She regularly moves from her bedroom into the *'East Room'* because her fire smokes but is glad to be able to return.

They read *Mansfield Park* and *'Miss Burneys novel of Evelina'*. Tom and William go to Montacute, which catches fire whilst they are there. Helen Markland asks her to Tollard but she cannot bring herself to leave *'Our own comfortable fireside'*. She complains of William sleeping all evening, *'A very bad Plan'*.

Her father has not been well for a few days, but when he is better Charlotte announces it with obvious relief. *'I cannot bear to have anything the matter with Him dear little Man.'*

There is much coming and going between Ashcombe and Ferne. *'Mr Wyndham called, he is very earnest about His Chase Cause against Ld. Rivers.'* The news from the outside world is still of Napoleon. Their friend Lady Bingham is going to join her husband at St Helena where he is brigadier general of the staff of the island. Lady Emma Bingham was a Pleydell from Winterbourne Whitechurch. *'We look at A Print of St Helena in the Ladies Magazine where Buonaparte is now A State Prisoner.'*

Her father and William *'ride to Great Ridge to see the Rides Mr Bennet has cut there'*.

February 21st *'I walked over to Ashcombe, Tom showed Me all his Improvements. My Brother and Sister accompanied Me part of the way Home.'*

On the 22nd, *'Prince Leopold of Saxe Cobourgh is arrived, the destined Husband of the Princess Charlotte.'* The latter was the only child of the Prince Regent, so second in line to the throne.

February 23rd *'My Mother had some Shrubs planted on the Lawn before the House. A Cedar of Libanus opposite My Window & one in Front of the House. I had planted An Acorn Laetitia gave me.'*

Tom and Henrietta visit, Tom leading his wife on a little Welsh pony.

Charlotte visits Sukey Clowter in Berwick, who she fears *'has A Cancer'*.

On the 27th, *'It was not very fine But I walked into the Garden & saw the Cucumber Plants which are looking very well.'* Ferne had arrangements for heating pipes and glasshouses in the smaller walled garden, the remains of which could be seen in our day, but they were probably the Victorian edition. They surely would have been necessary for cucumber plants in February.

On the same day, Charlotte reports on the Princess Charlotte going to Brighton with the Queen to see the Prince of Saxe Coburg.

In March a lot of gardening goes on, William helping the gardener transplant laurels, and he also pulls up the docks in the park. *'We had some firs transplanted on the Green.'* When Charlotte returns from staying with Henrietta at Ashcombe whilst Tom is away, she *'found My Mother busy planting'*.

March 12th *'Sukey Clowter intends going to the Infirmary.'* This was in Salisbury. Her husband George manages to visit her there. I cannot help thinking that hospital is bad enough in the 21st century, let alone for people who had possibly never gone as far as Salisbury in their lives.

Lady Shelley arrives with her four daughters. Charlotte is silent on the subject of the poet, but it must, I suppose, have been a sad subject for Mrs Grove and her sister to rake over. He was nineteen when he eloped with Harriet Westbrook, a schoolgirl friend of his sisters. They had a daughter. His father cut off his allowance and declined to allow them to visit the family home. Shelley then fell in love with Mary Godwin, aged sixteen, and eloped with her, abandoning his wife, pregnant with their son, in 1814.

Charlotte and her brothers take their cousins Mary, Helen and Margaret to afternoon church in Berwick. There is no mention of Elizabeth.

March 26th *'We read Lara Ld. Byrons Poem, the Poetry beautiful But story confused.'* So much for Lord Byron! He and Shelley knew each other well.

The Helyars and Charlotte's brothers are hunting well into April. On the 10th, Mr Bowles calls on them but does not come in on account of *'the Gentlemen gone hunting'*.

April 13th *'Wingreen Hill was covered with Snow. I took a Walk with My Mother But it was an unpleasant task. The weather being so cold.'*

This month they again go to Bath. Charlotte notes her Jackson uncle is looking very ill. I see from a Pilfold family tree the Jacksons had twelve children, but it does not say how many survived childhood.

They dine at Sedgehill on their way home. Her brother-in-law has lumbago. Later she says he has gout in his foot. William Helyar is thirty-eight at this time, so it seems young to be getting such complaints.

April 20th *'I walked over to Ashcombe & staid some time with Henrietta. Tom very busily employed working in his Garden.'*

Two days later, they are hunting in the Chase. *'Charles much fatigued with His Days Sport.'*

Harriet is expecting again. Charlotte goes to Sedgehill on April 24th. Her habit of making announcements without explanations is on the increase. Whilst walking in the plantation, *'We met with an extraordinary occurrence'* or *'I saw something in the Salisbury Paper that pleased Me'*. As in the unfortunate incident in the church, we are none the wiser.

The marriage of Princess Charlotte is noted on May 2nd.

William Helyar's sister Caroline, known as Aunt Mouse to Harriet's children, stays at Sedgehill at the same time as Charlotte. *'Caroline very much annoyed with A fancied speck in one of her Teeth.'* The underlinings indicate Charlotte's irritation, but she is fond of Caroline. William Helyar goes about, shoots rooks and dines out but *'the ladies'* stick to walking and minor excursions.

The male members of the family frequently go to Norfolk or Derbyshire, where they had property.

June 10th *'Mrs Hoare and Miss Fanny Still called upon Us. Caroline and I went down to Them. My sister being too nervous for Company.'*

I note the frequency with which husbands dine out minus their wives, even without pregnancies. It seems to have been a normal practice. Captain Markland is often dining at Ferne without his wife.

June 12th *'Wm. H dined at Clouds – the Party consisted of Mr Mrs & Miss Pryors – Mr & Mrs Hoare Miss Annie Ogle & Mrs J Hellyer. They waltzed in the evening.'* Mrs Helyar was there without her husband,

William's uncle. It seems random. You would have thought William could have taken his sister. The day before he had dined at Mr Ordes, the Rector of Semley. When at home they might all, or only one or two of them, dine at Ashcombe.

Also on the 12th, *'We walked out on the Turnpike & met Edwards who had been to Warminster to reclaim A Silver Spoon that had been stolen from us by a Gypsy last Autumn.'* Edwards was the Ferne butler. The spoon would no doubt have had the 'Talbot' engraved on it and thus be identifiable.

Like missing the train, it was possible to miss the coach! June 19th *'Wm H went to Shaftesbury to meet the Yeovil Coach to go to Coker – He was too late & obliged to return again.'* He made a more successful attempt by leaving before breakfast the following day. A man of William Helyar's standing, heir to a large property, was happy to use public transport.

William Helyar returns on the 25th, having been to a ball at Sydmouth. A pregnant wife was definitely no requirement for these jollifications.

Travelling on the coach was a more intimate business than travelling on a train. The mail coaches were set up in the late 18th century to replace post boys delivering the mail, carrying passengers to offset the cost. They were so successful that stage coaches, with passengers on the roof as well as inside, soon came into being as a rival enterprise. The roads were improved and the inns became clean and efficient. By the 1830s, the railways started to creep across the countryside and eventually the coaches disappeared.

On the 23rd, *'Harriet not quite well in the Evening. She sent for Mr Ames. The pains went off again.'*

Three days later we get the real Charlotte. *'A wet Day. I was in A great Fright, I found out something in the Evening that subsided My Fears.'* I suppose these entries were aide mémoires. She would always remember to what they referred without having to commit indiscretions to paper.

June 28th *'About two in the Morning We were called up & Harriet was brought to Bed of A little Girl A minute before Mr Ames arrived. Mr Hodson named Her Ellen Harriet.'* Mr Ames was her doctor.

Charlotte notes at the end of this month her brother-in-law's disapproval of Mr Benett of Pythouse being made one of the stewards at Salisbury race course. The Benetts of later generations were certainly strange. My mother-in-law dined there as a young woman and was surprised that Jack Stanford Benett threw fruit at his wife down the whole length of the table. The guests, of course, politely ignored the goings-on.

In July, Charlotte is back at home, having seen her sister through the last months of her pregnancy. Her brother Tom sends his *'Carriage for Us & We dined at Ashcombe – Old Mrs Farquharson was there.'* This would have been Henrietta's mother.

Her father gets a new mare all the way from Hertfordshire. *'She is very pretty called The Maid of Kent.'* There is no explanation for this anomaly.

On the 9th, *'Capt. Markland called. John accompanied Him to Mrs Cookes – Both the Capt. & William have offered their services for the expedition against the Algeirenes.'* Charlotte's attempts at spelling this are no better than mine. After the final bottling up of Napoleon, the armed forces were short of work.

July 9th *'Susan & I walked to S Clowters to try to persuade her to go to St Bartholomews as She has A cancer, But we could not succeed.'* This must have been the London hospital, so I can see why she might have demurred.

On the 11th, George returns.

July 14th *'We went to Berwick Church. Tom met Us there & received the Sacrament to initiate Him to be A Justice.'* You could make no progress in the world without being solidly proven C of E.

July 19th *'A Wet Day. Tom was so kind as to put My Fathers Sheep into Ashcombe It being very tempestuous Weather on the Hill.'* I assume the sheep must have been in the vicinity of Win Green. The Grove farming activities abutted Ashcombe, an added incentive to join the two properties.

On the 21st at Berwick church, *'Mr Pike did the Duty A relation of Mrs Pinkneys.'* There is not much mention of the Pinkneys. Philip Pinkney has his memorial in the church on the south side of the aisle. He died in 1807 and his son, also Philip, aged ten, died in 1806. His wife Elizabeth lived until 1844. In Goodchild's copy of the tythes due to be paid within the parish for 1840, Philip Pinkney is listed as owning quite a lot of property in Berwick, farmed by Charles Foot. At this juncture it was probably Henry Foot, Charles' father. If all the Pinkneys follow the family habit of being called Philip, it makes things confusing. Did they live in Berwick and, if so, where? The daughter of Philip Pinkney's sister was married to Samuel Foot, the one-handed lawyer of Salisbury and the much older brother of Charles Foot: there was seventeen years between them.

July 22nd *'Tom & Mr Brown dined with Us – Farmers Grove & Co croaked exceedingly about the Weather.'* Some things never change.

July 27th *'John played 3 Games of Chess with George & beat Him. I looked over Them – A little dispute between Them about A Pawn.'*

July 29th *'I accompanied My Mother to Sedgehill & read Mrs Jervis's Poem of Ines in the Carriage.'* They always took something to read. George has his revenge by beating John four times at chess.

Backed by Mr Wyndham, a legal action was brought between Thomas King and Lord Rivers. It was regarded as a test case. On the 31st, *'Charles went to Salisbury to hear Mr Wyndhams Chase Cause.'*

August 1st *'Charles returned from Salisbury. The Chase Cause not finished. He gave Us A very good account of it.'*

August 2nd *'Mr Wyndham has gained his Chase cause against Ld. Rivers. I am delighted about it.'*

August 4th *'We went to Berwick Church. Mr Boys did not rejoice so much as He ought upon the Chase Cause being gained.'*

I am glad to find Charlotte in support of the rights of the common man as opposed to the powerful Lord Rivers. She also says, obliquely, after George had dined at Ashcombe, *'I am determined now never to believe anything I am told',* much underlined.

On the 6th, *'My Father & Tom dined at Shaftesbury Club as did Capt. Markland & Mr Wm. Helyar.'* I wonder what sort of club this was.

Soon they are off to Netherhampton and the races. Charlotte mentions all sorts of vehicles. As horse-drawn equipages were made to order unless bought second hand, it was like being able to order your motor car to your own design. There was a variety of general types but variations on the themes. She goes with Mr Bromley on the barouche box: *'I got rather wet.'* The following day she goes in the *'landelet'* with her mother, and Mr Bromley was on the box. Some vehicles were owner driven, more fun, and some, like the larger carriages, were driven by the family coachman.

On the 9th, *'I betted every Day with Mr H Hetley & won upon the whole.'* There were dinners, a ball and a concert. On the way home, on the 10th, they visit the Penruddockes of Compton Chamberlayne. *'Their House is newly painted & furnished & looks beautiful.'*

The Miss Frasers are often staying at Ashcombe. These were cousins of Henrietta's, the daughters of Sir William Fraser. He had three sons and eleven daughters, so it is no wonder some of them were offloaded on Tom and his wife.

It is now the turn of the Blandford races. They stay at Langton House, built by the Farquharsons, calling at *'Brianstone'* on their way there. Charlotte danced every dance at the ball.

Life returns to normal apart from the news of the death of *'My Uncle Jackson'*. They do not attend church on the 25th as a consequence, I suppose a form of mourning. It is confusing exactly what mourning entailed, because otherwise they seem to go on much as usual. On the same day, *'George arrived at Our Breakfast time. He is appointed second Mate to the Rose East Indiaman.'*

On September 15th, *'Week's child had A fit during the Service. I accompanied Miss Brown & Mr Boys to S Clowters to try to persuade Her to go to Bartholomews Hospital But We could not succeed.'* A few days later they suggest she goes into the Salisbury Infirmary.

September 17th, *'I accompanied My Mother in visits to Mrs Cooke & at Donhead Hall – The elder Mrs Kneller sillier than ever. We dined at Mr Boys's. Mrs Boys very ill But John did Her A great deal of Good. He is so clever.'* It is apparent John has as yet no regular practice of his own, but he sees the sickly Mrs Boyes quite regularly. What we do not know is whether he was paid, but I assume he was.

There is a charming informality in the visits and counter visits of close friends and relations, some staying to dine, some going home, some staying a night or two. Dining was a late afternoon/early evening affair; the further you get into the 19th century, the later it becomes. Tea was taken after dinner and suppers were served, in which neighbours might share. Charlotte does not talk of suppers, so it was probably not a Grove habit. In the 18th century, dinner was closer to two o'clock, so supper was more of a necessity. Breakfast, not taken very early, was another meal that could be shared. *'John went to Sedgehill to breakfast.' 'Capt. & Mrs Markland breakfasted with Us'* – though on the whole it was a masculine habit.

Charlotte, when at Tollard staying with the Marklands, says, *'I went to Church twice & heard Mr Bliss whom I do not like as A Preacher. A long Sermon & Methodistical.'* As a regular church goer, she was in a position to judge the parson's performance, and she certainly did not approve of nonconformists. Bliss was curate at Tollard Royal. They go to *'Tollard Green & to the Shop'*. They were a great deal better served with shops than we are, though she does not mention one in Berwick.

September 28th *'A Wet Morning All My Fathers Wheat is carried. The Barley cut Today.'*

October 13th *'Poor George snapped the Tendon of his Foot again.'* This sounds very painful, but no information is given as to what could be done about it.

John's courtship of Miss Jane Fraser now becomes more apparent. Charlotte always called her Jane, though she is Jean in the family tree. October 15th *'John brought Us A letter. He is in high Glee with The contents of it.'* The following day, he showed them a letter from Sir William Fraser. We are not told what was in it, but with Sir William having eleven daughters, though I do not know if they all survived to grow up, you would think he would welcome any faintly respectable son-in-law.

They are visited by Mrs Fitzgerald, who was a daughter of the Penruddockes. After a few days, they walk with her to the Glove so she can catch the coach to Compton, so well-to-do women were also using public transport. She probably travelled with a maid. They spend a few days at Gaunts with the Glyns where *'Lady Glyn shewed Us several of her Tricks.'* George Banks dines with them. He *'entertained Us very much. He is A very pleasant young Man.'* I take him to be a Banks of Kingston Lacey. When they get home, they find *'The Cattle have been upon the Green & spoilt some of Our Shrubs.'* The Helyar children are growing up. *'My Niece Agnes is more entertaining than ever. Ellen is very much improved.'* The enthusiasm for chess does not abate, but her brothers and the Miss Frasers play loo. This was a popular card game of which there were two versions. One was played harmlessly at home and the other was a serious gambling game that could rapidly lead to the loss of whole fortunes.

November 5th *'We are very much amused with The Novel of Pride & Prejudice.'*

November 7th *'My father received A letter from Charles to say He is not elected at All Souls & He came here just before Dinner — We consoled Him as well as We could on the occasion.'* This would have been to become a fellow of the college.

November 18th *'Mr Bedford and Charles rode to Summer Lease & hunted with Mr Wm Helyars Hounds.'* William Helyar's father was also William. Mr Bedford was a friend of Charles' with whom Charlotte plays chess most evenings and is merciless in beating him every time. On the same day, she meets Betty Stretch and Sukey King on her walk.

On the 19th, *'not clear enough at 8 in the morning to see The Eclipse of The Sun'.*

There is an alarm on the last day of the month, there being a fire in the chimney of the bailiff's house, but *'It was speedily put out.'*

As December proceeds, there is sometimes too much frost to hunt. Her father and her brothers go out with Mr Walter Long's hounds. Charles' horse falls with him; *'Providently He was not hurt But Harcourt's*

Knees were very much cut.' I wish Charlotte would give us more of the mechanics of getting to hunt at such distances from home. They were back the next day in time to be reading sermons; *'Charles one of Hornes Sermons on Daniels praying in the Den of Lions.'*

December 9th *'Capt Markland has bought Farnham of Mr Mills.'* The way Charlotte says this, one would think there was only one house in Farnham.

December 11th *'Many Snow Storms, But I got An half hours Walk – Tom called here & Charles rode with Him to A sale at Motcombe – Mr Bedford & Charles dined at Ashcombe. George returned with Them at Night.'* The next day, *'Tom called in the Morning & We prevailed on Him to dine with Us. It was A very stormy Night for Him to ride Home.'* Despite their apparently leisured lives, I get the feeling these were tough young men, not put off by darkness, snowstorms or Mr Bowles' *'impassable roads'*. There was plenty of shooting of snipe and pigeon.

Mr Bedford is still being slaughtered at chess. He has only won one game so far, though he has been staying since November 16th.

December 16th *'George & Charles & Mr Bedford rode to Salisbury to see the Indian Jugglers.'*

On the 18th, *'I was beat A Game of Chess by the combined Powers of Mr Bedford & George, & afterwards I won A Game of the latter.'*

The Helyars come for Christmas. December 20th *'Mrs Mansell Miss Mary Pleydell & the three Miss Frasers called upon Us – They were very much pleased with Harriets pretty children.'*

December 21st *'I accompanied Harriet in A Walk to Berwick, we called on Sukey Clowter, Betty Pickford, Sukey King & Betty Stretch.'* How much I should like to know where they all lived. Sukey Clowter is obviously not in hospital. Charlotte goes on to say, *'Mr Bedford & George went out Shooting Mr B. shot 2 Snipes & George 6 Pigeons. I played at Chess with George & He beat Me 3 Games.'*

On the 24th, William Helyar returns from a visit to Coker. *'He was much entertained with His Stage Coach passengers.'* Christmas was as usual.

In the evening, the children were entertained with the mummers and bulls; *'Carey was rather frightened at Old Father Christmas.'*

Captain Donaldson is often mentioned, usually in connection with the Farquharsons. December 31st *'George heard that the Proprietor of the Rose is dead & He wrote to Capt Donaldson to know what He should do, who advised Him to go to Town immediately.'*

There is not much in the back of the 1816 journal except the Bath address of a stay-maker. She had the reassuring name of Mrs Allwright and lived at Number 17, Green Street.

1817

There are some brief entries, mostly to do with money, including the numbers on Bank of England notes. Charlotte informs us that Miss Eyre of New House married Mr Matcham, the nephew of Earl Nelson, on February 14th. This is the same Miss Eyre who John had courted. However, better things were to come, for his engagement to Miss Fraser is now official. On January 8th, Charlotte says, *'I like My intended Sister Jane Fraser better every day.'*

On the 1st, George went to London on *'Business relative to his Ship'* but came back a fortnight later *'not able to succeed in getting out this Voyage'*. We hear no more about the Algerians. Having occupation in the Royal or Merchant Navy was far from guaranteed.

Mr Bedford is still with them, but his chess is improving.

They are visited by their widowed Aunt Jackson who *'felt it very much at first seeing us'*. She leaves them to take the coach to Lyme Regis. Later they hear *'The Sea overflowed My Aunt Jacksons House at Lyme. They were much frightened But got out in safety.'*

Sunday January 12th *'We had Church at Home – Mr Bedford read Prayers & Charles preached.'*

January 14th *'Mr Blackmore does not consider the feelings of A Widow.'* Mr Blackmore was the new incumbent for the parish of Donhead St Mary, or Upper Donhead as it was called. As the widow of the last incumbent, Mrs Jackson would be liable for *'dilapidations'* on the Rectory.

February 2nd, after dining at Ashcombe, *'My Father walked Home at Night'*. Mr Grove is fifty-nine, which would have been considered quite old in this period, but I feel his powers did not diminish, and if a benign spirit hovers over our landscape here, it is his.

February 4th *'Tom paid Us a nice long Morning Visit. He is in excellent spirits talking about his farm at Ashcombe.'*

Though they are still working their way through novels, on the 7th *'my father wishes to make Me A Politician as He makes me read the Speeches every Day after Dinner.'*

February 10th *'A Man picked out of A Sand Stone A very complete Fossil, which I bought of Him. My Birth Day 34 – I copied out A letter of Verses, Charles wrote from Bath to George & A very pretty Composition I think.'*

On the 11th, *'The old Woman of My Aunts Lodge at Zeals was robbed & came before My Father Who committed the Man to Salisbury Gaol.'*

John wishes to get married in May but *'The Baronet answered He could only give his Daughter to Dr Grove.'* I think this must mean John had to have some position, rather than his not being qualified.

Mr Bedford, who went to Bath with Charles, sends Charlotte a present of *'some very nice Chess Men'*. Later that day, the 17th, *'Capt. Markland came. He dined and slept here, I played at Chess with Him & He beat Me two Games I am sorry to say.'* They have a Mr Drummond and a Mr Steward staying. Charlotte played chess with the latter, who she initially defeats. After that, she is trounced for days but she is kind enough to say, after he has left, *'I miss My Antagonist at chess, very much.'*

February 28th *'My Mother received A letter from Wm. He has had A bad Cold, But They have had excellent Sport in Hunting at Cattistock.'* Jokes about sailors and horses were obviously not applicable in William's case.

March 1st *'Buonaparte is ill They say from want of Exercise at St Helena.'*

On the 4th, *'We received A letter from Aunt Chafin to tell Us Charles is taken ill in the Measles at Bath. Dr Parry attends Him. We are very anxious about Him (Poor Fellow).'*

March 5th *'My Father went to the Justice Meeting, there was only Himself & Mr Benett. He returned to a 7 o'clock Dinner, & was overfatigued. But smoking his Pipe in the Evening did Him A great deal of Good.'*

On the 6th, they get a good account of Charles, but George *'set off in the coach for Bath where He is gone to nurse his sick Brother'*. I am surprised it was a brother who went off to do the nursing, not a mother or a sister. *'I got an hours Walk though A very stormy Day. My Father has adopted A new Plan for the Poor at L. Donhead.'*

March 7th *'The Papers say the Princess of Wales is coming Home. I hope not. She is better out of England.'* This was Caroline, the estranged wife of the Prince Regent, who gallivanted about Europe from which much scandal resulted. Despite this, she had considerable support owing to the unpopularity of the Prince of Wales, who had treated her badly. She was Princess Charlotte's mother.

On the 10th, they go to Whatcombe. They stay a few days and are entertained with roe buck hunting for the men, and in the evening music and singing.

March 11th *'I read Sir George Bingham's narrative of Buonaparte & saw a Picture of Boney very ugly & very fat and bloated.'*

March 13th *'On our return Home found Charles here & looking very well after the measles.'*

On the 14th, they have a letter from John; *'Like all the rest of My Brothers He makes but A desponding Lover.'*

On the 16th, they pray for Susan Clowter in church.

They are reading Fanny Burney's *Camilla*, but Charlotte's comments are not flattering. *'The last Volume is very foolishly written & one too many.'*

March 19th *'My Mother heard from Emma. Little Frederick has been inoculated & got very well through it.'* This would have been for the smallpox. Frederick was their sixth child. Charlotte goes on to say, *'Waddington comes to Us the 26th inst. He is going to let his Farm at Woodcots.'* I am reminded that John Lush's son came to see Charlotte's father about Woodcots. Her brother-in-law duly arrives *'at our breakfast time'*. He rides over to Ashcombe with Tom. The next day, Mr South, the agent, accompanies Waddington to Woodcots.

On the same day, *'We went to Sedgehill to call upon Harriet & They are not returned from Coker, George went on the Box & was very useful as Our Footman &c.'*

William and George went off to Langton to dine and sleep in order to hunt at High Hall with Mr Farquharson. High Hall is at Pamphill near Wimborne and was built around 1666. It was a part of the Bankes estate and was linked to Kingston Lacey by an avenue. Francis and I once passed it in the car. It looks charming but I can only tell you it is a venue for weddings.

March 31st *'Tom came in the Morning. The Gentlemen busy transplanting a Walnut Tree upon the Lawn. Waddington left Us. He went by the Coach to London. My Brothers accompanied Him to the Glove.'*

April 1st *'We got up to An 8 Oclock Breakfast as the Gentleman hunted in Knoyle SummerLeaze. My Mother took Me to Sedgehill. Harriet and The Children are quite well. Mr Wm. Helyar dined & slept at Pythouse. Mr Benett has A large party of Foxhunters staying there.'*

On the second day of staying with Harriet, *'The Gentlemen played at Whist. The Ladies talked & It was A rather dull evening.'*

April 8th *'I was very much surprised by the arrival of Our Carriage to fetch Me home & A Note from My Mother to tell Me Charles is very ill in A Fever. George is A very attentive Nurse to Him. Dr Bliss attends Him.'* I wonder how far they had to go to get a real doctor. They are soon on visiting terms with the Blisses, so they must have been reasonably close.

April 9th *'Tom came. All the Gentlemen but Wm whose Horses are lame, went out Hunting with Him. Charles is considerably better. Dr Bliss called, & says His Pulse is much lowered.'*

Sunday 13th *'Tom called at Breakfast time. I walked back with Him to Ashcombe, went to Church at Tollard with Them. Dined at Ashcombe & Tom accompanied Me home in the Evening.'* Family life was undoubtedly pleasant, and Charles is well enough to come down to dinner on the 14th.

On that day they hear of the death of *'poor Sukey Clowter'*. Charlotte sees it as a happy release.

April 15th *'My Mother received two letters from John, He is anxious about getting into the Infirmary at Salisbury…Tom came In the Evening to persuade My Father to write to Dr Fowler.'* One immediately sees the family machine getting into action.

April 19th *'We called on Dr & Mrs Bliss. They are very pleasant People. John & George rode to Salisbury. They met Mr Robert Still & were just in time to put off the Election of the Hospital till September.'* The post of a doctor in a hospital must have been done by election. He had failed to get elected to St Bartholomew's.

On the 20th, *'Mr Easton dined with Us. He talked of the H Opera as He calls it.'*

April 21st *'My Father & Brothers John & George called upon Dr Bliss.'*

April 23rd *'Dr Mr & Mrs Bliss – Mr & Mrs Blackmore, Miss E Blackmore & their Son dined with Us. We had Musick in the Evening, Mr Bliss sung.'* I cannot help thinking Dr Bliss had influence in the infirmary elections.

'George escorted Harriet & Myself & showed He had A great deal of patience to a Shop at Ludwell.' She does not say what they were buying. It is the first mention of a Ludwell shop.

Charlotte goes to stay with the Farquharsons on April 28th. *'I arrived at Langton before Mrs Farquharson had crossed the Stour. A pretty sight the Procession with the Palanquin. Captain Donaldson & My three Brothers of the Party.'* Mrs Farquharson was in poor health, so I suppose she was carried about. In the subsequent days, Charlotte walks beside her, often with Mr Farquharson and Captain Donaldson. The latter lived at Montacute, but he spends a lot of time at Langton. *'Captain Donaldson dined with Us. We on April 28th played at Whist in the Evening. Mrs F & Myself equally bad Players.'* The following day, she teaches Mrs Farquharson and Captain Donaldson chess. The next day she gives them another lesson. Eventually, *'They played together & A fine confused Game They made of it.'*

Mr Farquharson goes off to the New Forest to buy some hounds. He was, of course, a celebrated master of foxhounds. Even here Charlotte's brothers come and go, other visitors arrive, people come to dinner, *'a great deal of Chess & a great deal of Laughing. Capt. Donaldson is very much improved in that Game.'* She teaches everyone chess and they all play each other.

May 11th *'Mr Dansey called. He says Mrs F is to remain still longer on the Sofa.'* We do not learn what is the matter with her but unlike Henrietta, who *'has got the Rheumatick Gout'*, she had children, schoolboys at this juncture.

Charlotte stays at Langton until the end of May. She leaves *'with very great regret'*. The day she leaves, I learn exactly when the Groves had dinner. *'We now dine at four & walk afterwards.'* This sounds a new arrangement, but she does not indicate the previous one. Perhaps it was seasonal, to allow for an evening walk. There is previous mention of their dining at half past three.

June 3rd *'I walked to Edies Cottage. She was at Mrs Cookes. I saw Her Husband to whom I gave the subscription We had made for Him that He may be able to put three Lives for The House he has built.'* This means, I think, he could have the house as tenant for three named lives. I wonder which house it was.

Tom Grove occasionally goes to Derbyshire, which seems a long way off by the available means of transport. They had property there.

Charlotte goes to stay with Harriet. On the 7th, *'Mr & Mrs C Benett Mrs Burlton & Her Daughter dined with Us – Waltzing in the Evening. It made Me very giddy.'* I have decided waltzing was more acceptable than we have been led to believe.

June 16th *'I walked over to Ashcombe & put the Novel of the Antiquary My Brother had lent Me into his Library.'* Charlotte gives such a picture of her brother in full residence at Ashcombe, no thought of its later destruction. *'The Housekeeper heard yesterday from Mrs Thos. Grove. She has not yet recovered the use of her Limbs.'* Henrietta was in Weymouth for her health.

On the following day, *'We walked in the Evening to Bericourt where We saw My Fathers Wheat & home by the Hill. My Father began cutting his artificial Grass.'* This must have been, I suppose, a specially sown crop for hay. I am puzzled as to which hill they went by between Berrycourt and Ferne.

June 21st *'My Brother & Sister Waddington & Their six Children came here. We were delighted to see them all.'*

On the 23rd, Charlotte and Emma walk in the *'South Walk. We met with something which made Us laugh very much.'* Typically, she does not say what. Later she takes the children to the farmhouse to see Mrs Shere and shows them the *'Farmyard and all the Horses'*. I feel the ways of entertaining children in the country have not altered much. A few days later, she walks to Berrycourt with Emma. *'The Shepherds Dog Crack ran after Us & frightened Us very much.'*

On the 30th, they are joined by the Helyars and their children, so ten children visiting altogether.

July 1st *'Little William Helyar put on his Cousins Cloth Dress & I thought looked very well in it.'* William was approaching five. It was around this age small boys were taken out of dresses and put into the masculine wear of trousers, known as being 'breeched'. Perhaps William had been breeched so was reverting when he dressed up in his cousin's clothes.

July 2nd *'The Children busily employed Haymaking & with their little Waggons Rakes &c – The Gentlemen all went to the Justice Meeting dined there & had A good deal of Wine.'* I think a good deal of wine was rather expected of the Georgian gentleman, and Charlotte observes it with amused tolerance rather than disapproval.

Charlotte plays chess with Emma and usually wins. Her father looks on *'though He says the Game of Chess annoys Him very much'*.

There are additional people to dinner. Mr Wallinger has returned. *'Daniel played on the Violin & We had A little Dance. I tried to Waltz with Mr Wallinger But did not make it out well. Little Emma & Caroline danced.'* Daniel was a Ferne footman. It reminds me of our Burns Night efforts in the hall.

Family life goes on, either at Ferne or at Sedgehill. There is a rarely mentioned visit to Shaftesbury where Charlotte buys a flower for her bonnet. Henrietta returns from Weymouth. She *'bore her Journey very well & is much better for her Weymouth Excursion'*. Her lack of a child must have been a cause for concern, as Tom was the heir and as yet none of the younger brothers had married.

July 11th *'Tom called upon Us. My two Nephews & William accompanied Him to Ashcombe to Dinner.'* These were Emma's boys, staying at Ferne whilst the rest of their family were at Sedgehill. John is nine and George is seven. I like to think of them being affectionately cared for and amused by their childless uncles.

July 16th *'We heard that Ld Arundell is dead. My Father & Brothers invited to his Funeral.'* We now are not accustomed to being invited to funerals, we just turn up. They tended to be masculine affairs. Sometimes your empty carriage was sent, I suppose as a mark of respect.

The men play some *'Matches at Battledore & Shuttlecock'*. They also play cricket. *'Mr Waddington & Wallinger have rather hurt Themselves by that Game.'* As bowling was all underarm until the 1820s, you would not think they could be in the dangerous situation of the modern batsman, so it must have been the running about. On the 14th Waddington had *'in his exertions sprained his leg'*.

July 18th *'We arrived at Weymouth in the Evening.'* Their lodgings were *'upon the Crescent close to the Sea'*.

Weymouth was popular with George III and the royal family, so it was a thriving resort. There were Frasers and Farquharsons and Captain Donaldson there already. They walk on the sands, listen to the band and visit *'Harvey's Library'* to choose books.

Charlotte goes on *'A Water Party to Portland with the Farquharsons. The Wind being contrary & going Gunnell to listing Mrs F was so frightened We were obliged to land her again.'* I imagine the water rose rather high. After that, they carry on and enjoy themselves.

Emma's two youngest boys *'went into the warm Bath'*. A few days later *'little Tom was not so well & we sent for Mr Warne who prescribed the warm bath in which he was put 12 minutes & it made Him shriek violently Poor little Fellow.'*

Waddington and George go out in the Princess Charlotte sailing boat.

They go on an excursion to Portland, walk to the highest point on the island and look in the church. The following day they sail to Lulworth: *'The Boys accompanied Us. John very sick'* and visit Lulworth Castle, belonging to Mr Weld. *'It is not so large A Place as I expected.'* There is a ball to attend but Charlotte, her sister and brother-in-law prefer to stay at home. They play a game with the children called Man of France. Charlotte and Emma go in *'the Machine to see My two Nieces & George bathe'*. My own niece had never heard of a bathing machine, a device for preserving modesty. It was a little sort of hut on wheels that was pushed out to sea, and from there you were either dunked in the water by a female attendant or I suppose possibly managed for yourself. There was a horse to drag it back up again. There were plenty of them at seaside resorts. An uncle of mine, who was born in 1901, once described the horror of going in one as a little boy; he was never very robust.

Much time is spent walking on the sands, shopping and visiting. The children are with them. Emma and Caroline buy dolls. *'The two Girls very busily employed making Dolls Clothes.'* There is no mention of nannies or servants, though obviously they had them. There is a notion that women of their background and position only saw their children for an hour or so of an evening, but I have begun to think that was more an Edwardian and Victorian habit. Certainly, my parent's generation spoke of it. They were born in 1911. I suppose there have always been good, bad or indifferent parents.

August 18th *'Emma and Myself went with The Children to see Them bathe. We could not prevail upon John to go in. Little Emma beat Me at Chess with The Queen. I now give Her A Castle.'*

August 19th *'A Foggy Day But We walked about two Hours. Waddinton rode on the Sands & John with Him on A Donkey.'* These were 'hands-on' parents. On the 21st, *'We walked about the Town as usual to amuse The Children.'*

Charlotte says, *'I brought A Brown Silk Gown'* and *'I brought A Gown Emma's Choice & We think A Bargain.'* Some purchases came from an old woman *'with large pockets'*. Pockets were detachable things tied on with tape, hence 'Lucy Locket lost her pocket.'

She remarks on the daughter of Mrs Jordan, Mrs Alsop, coming to Weymouth but not acting because of the ball. Mrs Jordan, the mistress of the Duke of Clarence, had ten children by him, but she also had children from a previous liaison, of which Mrs Alsop was one.

August 27th *'We left Weymouth. I went in the Gig with Waddington, called upon Mrs Farquharson & the Children had their Dinner there. Capt. Donaldson at Her House. We arrived at Ashcombe after 6 – I slept there.'*

The following day, her mother sends the phaeton to fetch her home, but the day after that Tom sends his carriage so that his mother and sister can dine at Ashcombe, where the Waddingtons are staying. *'All the dear Children delighted to see Us.'*

August 30th *'Sir Richard Glyn My Father & Brothers went to Salisbury to vote for John & He was elected Physician of the Hospital & was voted for (with great eclat).'* Who had the vote and why?

August 31st *'We went to Berwick Church. Dr Boys preached his farewell Sermon after having had the living 25 years. He has exchanged Livings with Mr Bingham.'*

September 2nd *'I accompanied My Mother & George to Salisbury. The latter went on to Town. We went to My Brother Dr Groves House & were busily employed buying Furniture &c for Him.'* He was given *'A Present of Tea China'* by their relative, Mrs Long.

On the 3rd, *'John called upon Us at Netherhampton. On our road Home, We called at Compton, & upon Mrs Fitzgerald. Charles rode to Sherbourne with Mr Wallinger who left Fern Today. They saw Ld. Digby & met The*

Farquharsons there.' She spells Sherborne in a way I often want to spell it myself. Society was small but select in more than one direction. Though Lord Pembroke could be called on for patronage and emergencies, Wilton, Longleat, the Somersets at Maiden Bradley and the Hoares at Stourhead seemed to have been beyond bounds. The grandest house in our immediate vicinity must be New Wardour, but the Arundells, as Roman Catholics, would have been in an anomalous position.

September 4th *'I walked over to Ashcombe. Tom asked me many questions about Dr. Grove & His House.'* John, having been elected, is now referred to as doctor.

Emma and her family have been staying at Ashcombe since they returned from Weymouth, so there is much coming and going. Charlotte stays there too, and she and Emma take the Waddington children for an exploratory walk in the wood. They are looking for new walks. *'Emma put her foot in a bog.'* On the 13th, she and Emma walk to Ferne with *'little Emma & George'*. On finding their mother has gone to Sedgehill, Charlotte jokes *'We left Our Cards.'* I suppose they then walked all the way back again. Leaving cards, turning the corners down or not, according to whether or not you called in person or sent your footman, I have never got to grips with.

September 14th *'I accompanied Mr Waddington & Tom to Tollard Church. Mr J. Helyar gave Us an excellent Sermon on Contentment.'*

September 15th *'My Brother & Sister Waddington & Family, accompanied Me Home. My Mother delighted to see Us again. My Father has made all his old Wheat & has quite A Street of Ricks. The Gentlemen played at Whist. Emma & Myself at Chess. I beat Her as usual.'*

When Tom dines with them and John visits from Salisbury, Charlotte remarks on the family all meeting with the exception of George.

A few days later, when various people are dining with them, *'Some of the Gentlemen played at Whist. A stupid Party round the Work Table. The Chinese Puzzle the only resource.'* It was not unusual for women to bring a little sewing or embroidery with them when out to dine on familiar territory, to occupy them over the long evening occasioned by early dining. This obviously bored Charlotte to tears, the word stupid meaning dull. I had no explanation for the Chinese puzzle, but John Lane tells me it is one of those things with lots of interlocking pieces.

The shop at Ludwell is becoming a regular purpose for a walk.

On September 21st, they go to Berwick church, the service taken by Mr Bingham. Charlotte makes no comment on the new rector.

On the 23rd, *'My dear Brother & Sister Waddington & Their Family left Us, to my very great Regret – Harriet walked with Me to Ludwell, & afterwards Mr W. Helyar Herself & Children returned to Sedgehill. The Wheat Harvest got in. My Fathers Labourers worked till near eleven & then had Bread & Cheese & Beer given Them.'*

They go to stay at Netherhampton. Attending the cathedral, they hear *'A most excellent Sermon preached by A Dr Woodcock'*. Her aunt has three beehives stolen in the night. *'My Aunt has had Warrants to search Houses But cannot find out the Culprets who stole Her Bees.'*

Back at Ferne, Mr Grove dines with his tenants. Charlotte and her mother *'had a Tete a Tete by Ourselves'*.

September 30th *'We dined at Mr Blackmores & met Capt. & Mrs Haines Our new Neighbours at Lower Donhead. The Miss Blackmores are sensible young Women.'* She has the satisfaction of beating the eldest at a game of chess. In Donhead St Mary church they have the list of the rectors, and you can see exactly when Mr Blackmore replaced Charlotte's uncle Gilbert Jackson. The Blackmores had ten children, the eldest, Richard, born in 1795. The Miss Blackmores were Jane, born in 1793, so now twenty-four, followed by Ann, Elizabeth, Harriet and Sarah, the last born in 1808, as was the youngest brother, Samuel. They may or may not have been twins, but now they are nine. The sisters are otherwise interspersed with Charles, George and Frederick. Frederick had the second name of Nelson, having been born the year of the battle of Trafalgar.

At the beginning of October, Charlotte goes to Farnham Cottage to stay with Mrs Markland. Their notion of a cottage is different from ours.

In 1947, my family moved to Maiden Bradley into a house belonging to the Duke of Somerset. If you are at all familiar with this village, it is the substantial house on the left if you are facing Frome, opposite the turning to Bradley House. It was called the Cottage, which my mother asked to have changed as she thought it ridiculous, but it is apparent 'cottage' was once applied to any old thing smaller than an actual mansion.

On her way home, she calls in at Tollard. Mr and Mrs John Helyar are there. *'That Place is very much improved The Well being taken away & A Pump erected in the Scullery.'* I am uncertain if she is talking about the house they occupied when building Ferne or the house the Marklands lived in before going to Farnham, which may be the same house, the Old Rectory.

She buys lace in a shop in Donhead and on another occasion took *'A nice Walk to Berwick & back the Carriage way'*. Do we assume that the main route into Berwick is the one we use now?

On the 10th, Charlotte attends the Christening of Harriet's two little girls, being godmother to Agnes. There were Benetts, Knellers, Jervises, Mr T Gordon and a quantity of Burtons. *'We had a little dance. My brothers Tom & Wm were also of the party. The Gentlemen quite merry & pleasant.'*

October 14th *'I walked by Lushes White Cottage to Clay Lane & Home by Berwick.'* Where was Lush's white cottage?

On October 16th, she and her mother set off to visit the Longs at Marwell where there is a fine Romney of *'Lady Hamilton in the character of Circe'*. They go on to visit the Bromleys at Southampton, where Charlotte walks *'up the High Street & into the Market with The Gentlemen.'* My knowledge of Southampton is too limited to know if any of this would be identifiable now.

When they get home, they hear Captain Markland has hurt his hand *'by the Bursting of his gun'*. Guns were loaded with 'black powder', gunpowder in fact, rammed down the barrel.

October 26th *'I accompanied My Mother to the Evening Service at Berwick. Mr & Mrs Bingham are got into their House. The latter is very *stiff & formal.'* Mrs Bingham, like Mrs Burlton, was a sister of Charles Bowles. They were, of course, moving into the Rectory.

Going to Sedgehill, they call on friends in Shaftesbury. Charlotte buys *'A Black Velvet Pelisse'*. This was an outer garment, not quite a coat but worn over a gown, in this case obviously ready-made.

On the 29th, *'The Gentlemen went to Hindon Fair. My Fathers Sheep sold well.'*

On November 3rd, they have the Binghams to dinner. They stay the night though they did not have far to go home. Perhaps even a short journey was to be avoided on a dark evening.

Her walks are still confusing. *'I took A Walk to Berwick went up the Hill by Mr John Lushes, & returned through Berricourt.'* I begin to think Mr Lush lived at Dairy House Farm. I discussed with Francis and Dick Walby what can have been the main farmhouse for Upton Farm, as Upton Lucy House was not originally attached to it. Dairy House seems the likeliest conclusion, in the right place and about the right size. One might ague there is no hill, but Luke Street rises from the Cross. Much later research makes me think my surmises on this are probably wrong.

They are reading 'Lalla Rookh'. This was a long narrative poem by Thomas Moore, who I mentioned previously in relation to Peregrine Bingham. Though he is not well known today, his music does linger on in old fashioned favourites like 'Oft in the Stilly Night', 'The Last Rose of Summer' and 'The Canadian Boat-Song'. 'Lalla Rookh' was much acclaimed at the time, but I found it a bit of a struggle to read. His copious letters and journals I do read and enjoy.

November 7th *'We heard the very disturbing News that The Princess Charlotte of Wales died yesterday Morning having been delivered of A still born Son the Evening before.'* This was only too true. From what I have read, the baby was lying sideways and the physician in charge was nervous and did not intervene with sufficient promptness to turn it round, something a skilled doctor or midwife would have been able to do. Do they still do this now? It was such a catastrophe that the physician in charge later committed suicide. *'The presumptive Heir of this Kingdom & an amiable Princess is now gone & We are much grieved at Her loss.'*

Princess Charlotte had been the golden hope, her father, the Prince Regent, not popular, and his younger brothers mostly unsatisfactory in one way or another. Her death ultimately led to William IV, George III's third son, succeeding, and as he had no legitimate living children, he was succeeded by his niece, Queen Victoria. I have often reflected how the bungling of that unfortunate doctor altered the course of British history. How would things have gone on if we had continued with the Georgians and never had the Victorians?

Charlotte has not finished with the subject. *'The Princess Charlotte when opened was found to have some dropsy in her Heart – But not the cause of Her Death'* and *'The Prince of Cobourgh feels his sad loss most severely indeed.'* This was Prince Leopold, whom the Princess had been very pleased to marry, having dodged William, Prince of Orange. Prince Leopold became surplus to requirements after his wife's death, but later a satisfactory role was found for him when the newly formed Belgium was in need of a King. His descendants are there to this day.

November 16th *'I accompanied My Aunt & Father to Berwick Church. Mr Bingham gave Us an excellent Sermon upon the uncertainty of Human Life, & brought in about the Princess very properly.'*

On Wednesday the 19th, the day of the funeral, they attend church in Lower Donhead. Such had been the Princess's popularity that at the time of her funeral *'there was in all the Churches of London Devine Service performed, & also in most of the Country Churches – in respect of her Memory, She was so universally beloved.'*

Family life continues. Charlotte's youngest brother Charles is ordained by the Bishop of Salisbury and is soon looking for a curacy. He turns one down in Romsey but does *'the duty'* on behalf of the local clergy. Charles' friend Walter Erle, ordained at the same time as him, takes his first service in Berwick in place of Mr Bingham.

Mrs Markland has another son. Charles is amusing himself *'in copying out Parchments trying to make out Our Pedigree'.* They are reading *Clarissa, or, The History of a Young Lady.*

Desmond Hawkins says Charles Bowles lived at Higher Coombe, but Charles rides to Shaftesbury in order to see him. His family were associated with St Rumbold, Cann, now a part of Shaftesbury School. There are memorials to the Bowles family in that church. Apart from writing *Hundred of Chalke*, he was Lord Grosvenor's land agent.

December 7th *'Tom came & went to Berwick Church where We heard Charles preach. My Brothers think the same as I do about his reading.'* My sympathies are with Charles. Think of having to do your first sermons in front of a handful of critical older brothers.

George is likely to get an appointment in *'Capt. Drummond's Ship'*. Charlotte buys muslin in the shop at Ludwell. Lady Shelley writes to say they are going to Bath, their house in the Circus being ready. Charlotte and her mother walk to Lower Donhead and speak to *'the Man at the Work House about the School there'*. There was a workhouse in Ludwell, the tall building on the left after the traffic calming thing, with the pub on the right. Was it this one or was there another? Was the school for the inmates' children or for all children? There were schools of various sorts, but this is long before the Elementary Education Act of 1870, which introduced the concept of compulsory education.

Charles is met with greater approval. They go to Upper Donhead to hear him. *'He preached remarkably well & gave Us an excellent Sermon.'*

George does not get the place he wanted after all.

Christmas is celebrated as usual. Charlotte's father goes out on foot with his own pack of harriers.

December 29th *'My Father called at Wardour, to consult Ld. Arundell about the Ashcombe Business.'*

*

The end papers for this year are extensive. Charlotte takes £3 18s 10d to Weymouth and over twelve pounds to Langton. She lists expenses, a striped silk dress and a green sprig gown, a purple-and-pink satin gown and two of muslin. She pays bills to Mrs Towsey, E. Winters and Miss Domine. Could they have been dress-makers, or mantua-makers, as they were called? But you would have thought she would only use one. They are paid shillings rather than pounds. An earlier list notes what Miss Blagrove charged for making up dresses.

1818

On January 1st, Charlotte says it is the last time she will see her brother John as a bachelor, except, in the strangely formal manner of the age, she now refers to him as Dr Grove.

January 5th *'We had an early Breakfast & My Father & Tom attended by Mr Day set out for London.'*

On the 9th, *'We were surprised in the Evening by the arrival of My Father, Tom, & George. I do not think now they will have Ashcombe.'* She goes on without explanation to describe losing two games of chess.

Her father goes out hunting with four of his sons. On Sunday, Edwards, the Ferne butler, accidentally locks George into the library, where he spends the night. Suddenly there is a new development for George. His failure to get a place on a ship and doubts about the *'India service'*, seemed to have catapulted him into giving up a life at sea. Desmond Hawkins describes him as being in the Merchant Navy. Charlotte says, without preamble, *'George talked in high glee of the Estate He is to have at Sedgehill, & invited me to come & see Him there.'* As this was the last of the Grove sons, apart from the heir, not to be making his way in the world, Charlotte's father must have decided he needed something else done for him.

William has property of his own but stays in the Navy; he is more often at home out hunting with his brothers. The stables at Ferne seemed to have had a large quantity of horses. I remember six looseboxes. Stalls were used, horses tied in rows. If you go to a house open for public viewing, the stables are so often turned into tea rooms, but the bones of the original can sometimes be observed, the stalls with rings on the posts in the passage so the carriage horses could be prepared and then tied to face outwards, ready to be led out.

Charles Bowles arrives for breakfast and offers Charles *'A curacy'*.

January 17th *'We drank The two Brides & Brides grooms Healths in Bedford Square.'* I assume John's bride must have married in conjunction with one of her innumerable sisters. (John Lane says, yes, her sister Anne married Col Edward Keane). The entry makes odd reading to us now, because it is apparent that neither John's father nor any of his brothers attended the ceremony: Tom going to Weymouth that day, William, George and Charles at home, the latter taking the service the following day in Lower Donhead. However, the bride and groom are imminently expected.

January 20th *'William & George went Foxhunting to Dinton. My Brother & Sister Dr & Mrs John Grove came. We spent rather A dull evening. Mourning for the Princess is not out till Feb. 1st.'* They had been to various balls and dances in this period. The 'mourning' probably applied more to what they wore than what they did, but it was universally expected for a member of the royal family. Perhaps Charlotte added this as a little excuse for the dullness of the evening rather than infer it had anything to do with the newlyweds, who may have been self-conscious.

Things settle down. John goes regularly to Salisbury to see his patients and his wife goes out riding with Charles.

On the 23rd, *'John does not like Novels. But his Wife enjoys our reading very much.'* They have gone on to *Persuasion*.

John and his wife, Jane, leave on the 31st.

February 2nd *'My Brothers & Mr Phillips went to Salisbury to attend A Ball there. Edwards Found My Brother Georges Portmanteau after They were gone & He forwarded it by the Mail.'* I sometimes get the feeling things were easier in those days. If you forgot your suitcase now, I don't think it could be put on the bus.

Fanny and Arabella Jackson come to stay. Arabella entertains them by singing. They receive a copy of Rob Roy, *'But my Brothers will not let Us read it aloud'*. On the 8th, *'I accompanied My Cousins to L Donhead Church to hear Charles preach. The Gentleman also went there.'*

February 10th was Charlotte's thirty-fifth birthday. *'Arabella entertained Me with anecdotes of Miss Emily Benett.'* She was John Benett's fourth daughter but, according to R Moody's book, she would have only been ten or eleven. Charlotte reads *Rob Roy* for herself and enjoys it. This novel of Walter Scott's was only just out and was an immediate success. Scott managed to keep his identity as the author of his novels a secret for a considerable time.

The year carries on much as usual, visits from friends and relations, hunting, chess and the reading of *The Expedition of Humphry Clinker*. The shop they go to in Ludwell is called Talbots. On February 17th, they hear of the unexpected death of Sir William Fraser, John's father-in-law. Charlotte's mother hastens off to Salisbury to see Jane, *'who has been ill with repeated fainting Fits since She heard of her Fathers Death.'* She gets back again the same day in time for a late dinner. Mr Farquharson and Tom go to town for the funeral.

February 18th *'A Rumour in the Newspaper, that The Duke of Devonshire is not Heir to that Title.'* This would have been the sixth Duke, whose father kept a ménage á trois with his wife and Lady Elizabeth Foster, having children by both. The sixth Duke was the only legitimate son. The situation naturally caused gossip, the newspapers not differing then from now in this respect.

Charles is offered another curacy, at Bighton, which is near Alresford in Hampshire. Charlotte says, *'I suppose He will be Happy to accept it.'* She obviously thinks he is being far too picky.

She goes off to stay with Harriet, to await the latter's confinement. There was a false alarm. They send for Mr Ames and Betty Stretch, which makes me think the latter was probably a midwife. The baby was not born until March 19th, another boy, baptised Albert on the same day. This time, Mr Ames arrived one minute before the birth.

On the 23rd, *'Mr Ames came. We luckily escaped seeing Him.'*

While she is still at Sedgehill, on the 25th, *'Mr Wm. Helyar went to Ashcombe, to the last Days sale there.'* Tom had been in possession of Ashcombe for two years. What went wrong?

March 26th *'Dr Bliss came to see Ellen whose Ankles & wrists are A little grown out, An indication of Rickets.'* Rickets being a complaint to which the poor were subject, it seems strange. The child is treated by being given warm baths.

Charlotte's great-uncle, William Long, dies. Harriet's husband receives invitations to attend the funeral. Charlotte's father and all her brothers go, Mr Grove returning to Preshaw, being one of executors of the will.

When Charlotte returns home, her father gives her two black gowns. These were probably not made up and intended for mourning for her uncle.

On April 2nd, Charlotte remarks, *'Tom seems quite happy being at Ferne.'* Was he strangely resigned at losing Ashcombe? Certainly the Groves ended up owning the land at Ashcombe, as is evident from the 1840 tythe map.

Charles is reluctant to go to Bighton but *'I hope He will find it better than He expects.'*

April 5th *'Mr Wm. Long has left A handsome Legacy to My Aunt Phillipa & not to any other of the Grove Family.'*

On April 6th, Mr Long Wellesley visits them to canvass them with a letter of support from Mr Penruddocke, but Charlotte remarks it would have done no good even had they been in.

Charles has taken lodgings in Alresford, as he cannot get any in Bighton.

April 10th *'The Ld Chancellor will not permit My Brother to buy Ashcombe & Tollard.'* A legal wrangle of some sort must have taken place, but owing to a later entry, I see the muddle was on the Arundell side, to do with Lady Arundell's jointure. The ownership of Ashcombe must have been in dispute, so the sale to Tom was not legal. It seems astonishing he paid for it and lived there two years before this came to a head, but I am beginning to think he never did buy it, despite the word 'purchase', merely rented it, owing to confusion over Lady Arundell's marriage settlement. The Groves have always been held responsible for pulling it down, but I think the Arundells pulled it down themselves.

Their Jackson cousins come to stay and they enjoy *'nice long walks'*, one *'up White Sheet Hill through Berwick Coombe & Home by Berwick'.* I always enjoy Charlotte walking into the view I have from my desk.

On the 16th, she and Fanny walk to Ashcombe. *'We met with something extraordinary in one of the atticks.'* She does not, of course, say what, but it is easy to imagine the two women poking about the empty house.

The next day, Mrs John Grove, Captain Donaldson and Arabella Jackson go riding. Arabella rides Captain Donaldson's grey mare *'that had never carried A Woman before. It went very well for Her.'* This had to do with a horse being accustomed to a side-saddle. It was probably another hundred years at least before riding astride became acceptable for women. It was considered more dangerous, as a tight grip could be made on the pommel of a side-saddle, making it harder to fall off. On the other hand, if the horse came down, the rider was less likely to be thrown clear. Women rode at this period, but it was unfashionable for them to go out hunting. They hunted in the 18th century and again as Victorians, hence Surtees' Miss Lucy Glitters and Trollope's Lizzie Eustace. We have two early 19th-century prints depicting the Hampshire Hunt and there is not a female to be seen. I am afraid a lady was expected to be elegant and modest with a little delicacy thrown in!

While the Jacksons are with them, *'A dissertation after Tea upon the Gentlemens fashionable long Coats.'*

George buys oxen at Wilton fair. He is building up stock for East Hayes.

It is decided by Mr Grove and Tom that Charlotte should visit Weymouth, where Tom and Henrietta are residing, and she accordingly leaves on April 25th. She does not say how she travelled. Did Tom go with her? Did she take a maid? Tom is certainly at Weymouth. Charlotte says she finds Henrietta quite well but *'I walked on the Esplanade by the side of Henrietta's Wheel Chair'*, which sounds ominous to us.

The Farquharsons are also at Weymouth. They play chess, walk, take carriage rides and visit, and Henrietta *'went into the warm Bath both yesterday and today'*. On the 4th of May, *'Bysshe's Novel of Prometheus came'*. Charlotte is reticent on the subject of this errant cousin. She gives him an extra S.

Some of the Helyars are also at Weymouth. Charlotte visits Caroline, who is not quite well, and a few days later *'I called on Caroline who has used A most desperate remedy for the pain in her Face.'* We are not told what, but Caroline is a little better the following day.

Charlotte leaves Weymouth on the 27th *'with great regret'*. She goes to Sedgehill. There is a note in the end papers for this year recording the cost of hiring horses between Weymouth and Sedgehill, £3 11s 0d. On the 29th, she fleetingly returns to Ferne *'to change My Mourning'*. I imagine this was for her uncle, who had died two months previously. I expect two months was considered about the correct amount of time for wearing black for an uncle, but it must have been pleasant to take it off.

Her walks are no less energetic. *'We walked out in the Evening & over A Hedge Ditch &c.'*

May 31st *'Mr Ames vaccinated little Albert for the third time.'* I wonder why this was. Did it not take in some way?

Her brother John comes to see Ellen. *'He recommends cold Bathing.'* They often walk to East Hayes (now Sedgehill Manor), the property given to George, not so far from the Helyars at Hayes. They walk to Semley Common, her brother-in-law walks to Clouds for dinner, they make a carriage excursion with the children (not Agnes, who had been naughty) to Wind Mill Hill at East Knoyle and see inside the Mill. It must have been pleasant for Charlotte to walk with Harriet who, this time, is not on the brink of having another baby.

On June 15th, she returns home and is soon joined by her mother and several little Waddingtons.

June 16th *'In the Evening I walked up White Sheet Hill with The Children & George.'*

Charlotte walks a lot with the eldest, Emma, who, born in 1807, is eleven. She already has five younger brothers and sisters. They walk to Donhead Lodge, where the Haineses give them strawberries and cream. On the 19th, *'Walked with little Emma & John to Ashcombe the old Gardiner gave Us some Geraniums'.* Somehow, I do not think much talk of tired legs was allowed when walking with Aunt Charlotte. Ashcombe, I feel, is just under caretaker management.

Visits are paid to Suky King, Betty Stretch, Oldy and Mrs Hyscock, Berwick folk.

June 22nd *'In the Evening We walked to Talbots Shop to buy Ribbons for the School at Berwick.'* What school was this? It is long before Mr Downes, who Charlotte marries, built the school house on the corner of Luke Street and Church Street. At the beginning of July, there is an entry that explains it. It is a Sunday school, run by *'Amy'*. The Waddington children listen to the girls say their *'Cathecism'* before church and hand out the ribbons. I think cathecism not the right word; it surely should be catechism. Charlotte's spelling is as bad as mine.

June 24th *'I cannot get any tidings of my near sighted glasses.'* This is the first we know of Charlotte wearing such things.

On the 25th, *'I & My Niece Emma, dried some Grasses & Flowers. I taught her Dancing. She gets on very well indeed. In the evening I walked with My Father, Mother, Wm. George & The little Waddingtons to Berwick to look at Mr J Lushes house that is building. Called upon Mr & Mrs Lush.'*

Upton Lucy House was separate from the farm, so Dick Walby tells me. He says it was the knight's house, very ancient. Mr Lush was tenant at Upton Farm, but he was a landowner in his own right. Initially I thought Mr Lush was building this house for himself but later realised it was all Grove property, Mr Grove building it, probably on the site of an older house. After this initial entry, Mr Lush's house is frequently mentioned as the key attraction on a walk to the village.

Politics are prevalent in Charlotte's journal at this juncture. Elections, often violent, were not for the faint hearted. They went on for days, the different candidates building up their votes. Charlotte records the results, Mr Benett (of Pythouse) v Mr Long Wellesley. There is a good biography of Benett, who the Groves favoured, by Robert Moody. He stood as an independent. Lord Malmesbury described him as 'very unfit for the situation – a democrat, a suppresser of tithes, and a supporter of the Catholic question'. A democrat was considered a very naughty thing in those days. There was a movement to improve the situation of Roman Catholics who could not vote, let alone have a seat in Parliament. They could hold no government office, great or small, nor hold rank in the Army etc. My brother pointed out to me that where a common exists, it is frequently because there were Catholic landlords. At the time of the enclosures, to enclose common land, it was necessary to bring an Act of Parliament, an expensive business and forbidden to Catholics. Semley Common is a case in point, the Catholic Arundells the landlords. I am surprised at the Groves supporting Benett, but he was a friend and a neighbour. Benett retired, according to Charlotte, *'finding by the conduct of his Opponent & Mob, there was no chance of his succeeding.'* Long Wellesley, a nephew of the Duke of Wellington, was certainly a disreputable character. He had married an heiress, Catherine Tylney-Long, and, having no money of his own, fast set about spending hers, though fortunately he only had a life interest in it. He was soon in debt. He was also a rake, so there was nothing about him for the Groves to approve.

June 26th *'My Mother & Mrs Methuen went to Church. Emma & I attempted to go But We had A restive Horse & were obliged to stay at Home.'*

June 27th *'In the Evening I & little Emma walked by Brook Water to Talbots & Home the other way.'*

In June they have a great fright, Harriet being taken ill at Coker Court. John goes there immediately and sends a note to say she is very unwell and he will stay that night. *'My Mother anxious to hear the contents of the Note But We kept it from her.'* There is much relief the next day when John returns, saying Harriet is much better. *'I never in my life was so happy to see My Brother.'*

There are many references to Mr Lush's *'White Cottage',* sometimes in the plural. They still walk to Ashcombe. They also call on Mr and Mrs Foot and Dame Kelly in Berwick.

In Ludwell they buy *'Whips for the two Boys'*. I presume these to be riding whips, as John Waddington goes out riding with his father.

On the last day of July, Charlotte goes with *'Emma P'* in the carriage to Corsham Court, having been invited by the Methuens to stay for a few days. John Lane and I are confused as to who Emma P was, but John concludes it must be her sister, who was Emma Phillipa. *'We arrived at Corsham rather late. A fine house with several beautiful Pictures.'* This house still belongs to the Methuens, is open to the public and has a Capability Brown landscaped park. He died before it was finished so the then Methuen, the one Charlotte would have known, had Humphry Repton finish it.

August 1st *'Emma P. & myself went all over the House. We went out on A fishing Party & caught some Carp & Tench.'* Charlotte does not tell how they caught them.

August 3rd *'We came home by Fonthill, a Man opened A door, & let Us see A rear View of the Abbey.'* William Beckford, who had built Fonthill Abbey, was shunned by society for an alleged homosexual affair. It was never proven, but he was obliged to live abroad. When he returned, he enclosed his Fonthill estate within a six-foot wall, as much to keep out hunting as to keep out his neighbours, and embarked on building the abbey and its enormous tower, which constantly collapsed. He lived there until 1822. A glimpse of this extraordinary place must have been most intriguing to the respectable, and certainly judgemental, gentry round about.

Mr Grove and Captain Markham go *'to the Club at Shaftesbury where They dined'*. I wonder what sort of club this was.

The Waddingtons and Dr John and his wife are staying with them. Charlotte, Emma, Jane (John's wife) and the children walk to Ludwell. *'The Dr & Waddington scolded Us on Our return.'* She does not say why. Was it considered too hot, as it was August? The Waddingtons leave on the 7th *'to my very great regret'*. She has been teaching her nieces to dance. It is obvious she is very fond of the children.

August 7th *'The gentlemen went to Pythouse to dine with Mr Benett & 500 of his Voters in A Tent.'* Electioneering was never cheap for those who embarked on it.

August 9th *'In the Evening I walked with Dr & Mrs Grove & George to look at Mr J Lushes House which is covered in.'*

There are the usual races and balls, but I note Charlotte does not attend them as much as she used to. She stays at Farnham with the Marklands and their little boys. *'Edward Markland A very entertaining Child.'* They go to church. Charlotte is critical of the performance of the various clergy. *'Mr Ridout read very badly indeed.'* Captain Markland drives her home in the gig, taking little Edward for the ride.

On the 17th, *'George has begun digging the Foundation of his House at East Hayes.'* I suppose there must have been a farmhouse there already, probably not considered adequate. The house George built is the present Sedgehill Manor. I have a connection to it because my maternal grandparents rented it from Sir Gerald Grove, Dr John's great-grandson, when they first came to Wiltshire. As Tom had no male heirs, Ferne was inherited by John. John's son Thomas became a baronet but spent too much money, so his son Walter was forced to sell Ferne. George was childless, so Sedgehill Manor would have passed back to John's family. My mother used to mention Sir Gerald, the third Baronet, as a very old gentleman walking up the drive to collect the rent, so definitely a case of 'how are the mighty fallen'. It is possible to look up the Groves on the Internet. Sir Gerald's younger brother went to America where there are claimants to the baronetcy but not proven, so possibly dodgy marriage or birth certificates. Tom Hall, long before he died, told me there was a Wally Grove with him at Shaftesbury Grammar School who was living with his aunt Oenone, who was a sister of Sir Gerald. I think Tom remembered him as coming from California, but I could have that wrong. Walter Philip Grove, presumed fourth Baronet, has dates given as 1927–1974, so he seems a candidate for Wally. Tom was born in 1925, so they could have been at school together. The fifth presumed Baronet is Charles Gerald Grove, born 1929. I wonder if he is still alive.

Charlotte's brothers play cricket and the Waddingtons send her *'A very pretty silk gown'*. This was probably not made up. She does not mention how her clothes were made, no visits recorded of a mantua-maker for herself or her mother. There is a hint in the end papers for this year in as much she paid J Snook six shillings for making a spencer, a sort of short, fitted jacket. Perhaps they had a clever maid, but Charlotte never mentions one nor a maid for her own personal use. In fact, she rarely mentions servants yet there must have been a mass of them. The butler, Edwards, gets passing references, as does the footman who can play the fiddle.

They go to Netherhampton for the Salisbury *'Musick Meeting'*. Charlotte goes with her mother and George to the first evening but they do not stay for the ball. On the second day, Bartleman, Madame Fodor and Mrs Salmon *'sung delightfully'*. On the third day, *'two old Men discomposed Us by chattering during The singing.'* They went on to the ball where Charlotte danced two quadrilles and two country dances with Mr Charles Wyndham. She is thirty-five, which was considered long past youth in those days.

August 21st *'We returned Home. In our way called at Compton. Mrs Penruddocke as usual talked of her Friend Mr Long Wellesley. He has given her A Miniature of Lord Byron.'* Remember, Long Wellesley was the successful opponent of Mr Benett in the recent elections. They also call on Mrs Fitzgerald. We never hear of Mr Fitzgerald. Charlotte makes one of her loaded but unexplained comments. *'My Mother very luckily for Me made A Mistake.'*

The following day she walks to Win Green and meets *'A smart Barouche & four with several Ladies & Gentlemen in it'*. This was a large, heavy contrivance needing four or even six horses to pull it.

There is another shop, Hascals at Lower Donhead, where Charlotte buys lace. George goes off to Woodyates Inn to play in a cricket match *'& his Party won'*. Plenty of cricket goes on and plenty of chess. Tom rides over from Langton, where he was living before he had Ashcombe and is now living again.

As the summer draws to a close, Charlotte's father and brothers go out with the harriers and partridges are shot. I now never see the brown partridge so numerous as when I was growing up and when I came here. The French or red-legged partridge is what we see, a very handsome but imported bird. What has happened to the English sort?

They go to stay at Zeals House, but only for two nights. *'We amused Ourselves with The beautiful musical Clock'* and *'A very nice haunch of Venison for Dinner sent as A Present to my Aunt, from the Marquis of Bath.'*

September 7th *'I walked to Berwick & saw Mr J Lushes House. They have begun covering it with Reed.'* Upton Lucy was originally thatched. Kevin Follet, a Berwick farmer, tells me his grandmother was Winifred Arnold. Her father was then farming Upton Lucy. The thatch caught fire and Kevin's grandfather, Horace Follet, known as Jim, had to bicycle to Shaftesbury to get the fire engine. He reckoned that was a hundred years ago and probably when they slated it.

On the 9th, *'I walked to the bottom of Ashcombe Hill, & Home by Mr J Lushes as also into the Barley Field with My Father.'* They finished the harvest on this day. The following day the men get up early and go hunting at Wardour. Charlotte reports on the Queen being ill. George goes to East Hayes to inspect his building.

September 11th *'I walked to Berwick & called upon Sally Clowter. They live in A miserable old Cottage.'* Charlotte often walks up Whitesheet Hill and back by Berwick Coombe. It is quite a pull up Whitesheet and a steep scramble down into the coombe.

A Mr Boujen (Charlotte also spells it Bowjohn and Bowjen) and his brother and a Mr Rising arrive at Ferne and stay a few days, going out with Mr Grove and his harriers and going to Wilton Fair. On the 14th, Thomas Shere took them to Pythouse, *'& They went over Mr Benett's Farm, which They do not think is at all better conducted than My Fathers'*. I wonder who these men were, some sort of agricultural advisers? Charlotte thinks them *'very sensible pleasant men'*.

September 15th *'I walked through Brook Water to Donhead, called on Mrs Lush at the White Cottage.'* Where was this white cottage? On this year's entry of June 25th, they go with the Waddington children to see the house being built and call on Mr and Mrs Lush, who I take to have been nearby. In the 1841 tythe map of Berwick, there is a house of some sort in the corner of Upton Farm yard, which might have been a farmhouse. There was probably more than one Mrs Lush.

Tom stays with them. He *'was very entertaining & made Us laugh very much'*. Charlotte regrets his departure.

September 22nd *'Our Harvest Home, A sad wet Day for the poor people.'*

The games of chess get more fanatical. On one occasion Charlotte and Mrs John Helyar play seven games, Charlotte winning five of them.

She goes with her parents to Langton and then she goes on with her mother to Weymouth. Harriet is there with little Ellen *'who is rubbed for two hours every Day, to make her legs strait'*. Two hours!

They only stay a few days. On the last day of the month, Charlotte's cousin Charles Jackson dines and spends the night at Ferne. *'He has been visiting Mr Kneller where he had turtle, venison & every Luxury.'*

October 1st *'We went to A Turtle Feast at Mr Benetts'* and *'In the Evening We danced Quadrilles and country dances.'* She and Lucy Bennet played the piano. Her parents sleep there but Charlotte returns with her brothers.

October 2nd *'I saw them making Cyder.'* She does not say where, so I am interested to know if it was at Ferne for home consumption. George spends much time riding off to East Hayes, often before breakfast. They go out with the harriers and the foxhounds. Harriet writes to say the sea bathing does not agree with her. Tom arrives with John *'The former very amusing as usual'*.

October 7th *'H Charles came home.'* I can only think she means her youngest brother, but I do not know to what the H refers. She later says, *'H Charles gave Us an entertaining account of France.'*

Lady Glyn, Mr and Mrs Thomas Glyn and Miss Plumtree come *'rather late, & frightened with the Roads'*. Charlotte was made of sterner stuff, but Charles Bowles must have known what he was talking about when he was describing the roads a decade later.

October 12th *'Mrs Bingham called. My Mother & H Charles had A long Conversation with Her about the Heathens.'*

On the 18th, *'Charles left us for Oxford, George accompanied Him to Salisbury & returned Home to Dinner.'* He presumably caught the coach.

They are reading 'Beppo', a poem of Lord Byron's. Charlotte says, *'But I do not like it much'*. It is hard to imagine Charlotte approving of anything to do with Lord Byron. The straight-laced morality we connect with the Victorians had set in long before, without really diminishing the 'raciness' of the Georgians.

October 26th *'I walked to Lizzy Imbers, I have promised to give her Daughter Marienne A Present if She will learn her Cathechism.'* Later she gives her a prayer book.

On the 30th, *'My Father & Mother went to Netherhampton & George went to Salisbury. I walked to Berwick & afterwards to Vespasians Camp, with Mrs Bingham. I dined and slept there.'* Charlotte, I take it, means she dines and sleeps at the Rectory, which she has never done before, and of course having no idea of it becoming her home for twenty-eight years. Winkelbury seems to have been known as Vespasian's. *'Mr Bingham drove Me home in his Gig.'*

On the last day of the month, Harriet and her husband arrive with a Miss Carter and Harriet's two little girls.

Charlotte's fascination with Ashcombe, which fuels mine, continues.

November 1st *'We went to Berwick Church. I walked to Ashcombe with Miss Carter. The Woman being at Church We got into the House at the Window.'*

They are reading *The Heart of Midlothian*, which Charlotte describes as *'A new Tale by Walter Scott'*. Scott was still writing under a pseudonym, but his identity was generally known by this date.

They receive a letter from Charles saying *'He has not succeeded at All Souls'*. This was his second attempt to get a fellowship.

November 7th *'We went to Rood Ashton. It is new built & very much improved.'* This house was near the village of West Ashton and belonged to the Long family. The architect Wyattville was commissioned to build it in 1808. It passed out of the family in 1930. A later purchaser, in the 1950s, shipped all its lead roofing, fireplaces, panelling etc. to America, leaving it derelict. It was eventually demolished, but a bit was retained and is lived in now (according to Wikipedia).

November 8th *'I accompanied Miss Long in her Tax Cart to Church. An old venerable Clergyman of 80 did the Duty, & gave Us a singular sermon.'* Eighty was very old in those days. I had never heard of a tax cart and am not much the wiser now beyond it being a sprung vehicle upon which a small tax was levied.

Charlotte walks in the shrubbery with Miss Dianatia Long. Some Georgians could be quite adventurous with Christian names, but on the whole they used very few, Charlotte's siblings encompassing most of them.

They soon return home. On the 11th, *'Mrs John Helyar paid Us a long Morning Visit & very politely asked Me to come & see Her at Tollard which I declined.'* Mrs Helyar being one of Charlotte's most ardent chess opponents, let alone her brother-in-law's relative, I wonder the reason for this and what excuse she gave.

On the 17th, Queen Charlotte died. As the wife of George III, she had been Queen for over fifty-seven years. Her poor mad husband outlived her by a year. Charlotte records her death the following day and on the 20th walks to Talbots to buy some mourning. On the 22nd, they *'Went into Mourning for the Queen'*. It seems odd that Queen Charlotte's possessions, clothes and furniture were all sold at Christie's in 1819. The eldest of her thirteen surviving children, the Prince Regent, claimed her jewels, but otherwise even her snuff was sold. Francis has a snuffbox that came to him via an aunt, inside of which is a scrap of paper saying it had belonged to Queen Charlotte. She funded the lying-in hospital that took her name, Queen Charlotte's and Chelsea Hospital. I have read she introduced the Christmas tree from her native Germany, though Prince Albert more often seems to be given the credit for this.

Mr Grove and Tom set off very early on the 20th for London, and on the 30th Mr Grove returns. *'They will purchase Ashcombe & AshGrove if Lady Arundell will give up her Jointure on that Estate.'* So the purchase of Ashcombe starts all over again. A jointure was money or property held for a woman to provide for her in the event of her husband's death. This was a particular necessity in the case of estates where everything was likely to pass to the eldest son.

In December, Charlotte walks up Win Green with Mrs Bingham, who is impressed with the view, *'never having been there before'*. The Binghams had been in Berwick for over a year.

There is now a mention of a shop in Berwick. December 4th *'I walked to Berwick & bought A pr. Of Pattens at Wrights.'* A patten was a wood and metal overshoe designed to keep the wearer above the dirt.

Charlotte goes to stay with Harriet. They walk to East Hayes. *'I like Georges new House But it is A very dirty walk. We called on Mrs Hudson in our way. She was luckily out.'* A lot of this visiting must have been mere duty.

The talk is of Sir Charles Scudamore who wrote a book on the subject of gout, several editions coming out at around this period.

A letter arrives from Mrs Grove, inviting Harriet and her family to Ferne for Christmas. They are delighted. Charlotte accompanies them there on Christmas Eve.

*

In the end papers, Charlotte records taking over twenty-one pounds to Weymouth. She buys, amongst other things, a blue gauze dress, grey gloves, a brown trunk and an ivory *'stilletto'*. Dr Johnson, in his dictionary, spells this with a single L – 'A small dagger which is not edged but round, with a sharp point.' It seems not quite a paper knife, but I guess this was what Charlotte had all the same. She paid over two pounds to E Sturmey, again perhaps a dressmaker, but we cannot tell.

1819

This year continues seamlessly from the last, starting with Mrs Grove's habitual New Year gifts of pocket books and almanacs. Charlotte walks to Talbots, the name of which shop I took to be some sort of complement to the Groves, like our pub, but it turns out to be the name of the proprietor, as *'Mrs Talbot was brought to Bed last Tuesday of A little Girl & She is as well as can be expected.'* They have had a frost for the last fortnight, which would explain Mr Grove and George going to Wyncombe to hunt on foot, which is what the ardent foxhunter does to this day if the ground is too hard to be safe for horses.

January 3rd *'We went out of Mourning for the Queen of England.'* They had gone in to mourning on October 22nd. I was interested to read in a book of letters I have, written in 1796, 'How long are we to Mourn for Sir Henry? It used to be six weeks for a first Cousin; but I believe now not half that time.' What ever happened to the wearing of mourning? Now people only just about get it on for the funeral. In those days, even children wore black when it was considered appropriate.

On the 6th, *'I was going to walk upon the Hill but met My Father who told me there was A Troop of Merry Andrews &c coming down which induced Me to turn back.'* A Merry Andrew was a sort of professional clown or buffoon associated with St Bartholomew's Fair, which was held in August, so we do not know what they were doing here in January. It was obviously expedient to avoid them.

On the following day, John and his wife arrive with Miss Henrietta Fraser, presumably one of Jane's sisters. She was *'too fatigued with Her Journey to dine with Us. Her being nervous made her cough excessively on first coming.'* Though they stay several days, we don't hear of this poor creature again. William and George go off to a ball at Blandford and come back *'much fagged & not much pleased with their Ball'*. John goes off to see *'little Carey whose Leg is still bad'*.

Charlotte reports on Job Dimmer's children having scarlet fever.

January 27th *'I walked up Win Green Hill. I found A sand Stone with White Spar in the Road they are making to Ashcombe.'* I wonder who 'they' are and what road? There is only one road to Ashcombe we know of, and I have assumed it was the road already in use. There is a road from Ashcombe that leads in the direction of Tollard Royal. Everything about Ashcombe is some sort of puzzle. Either way, Tom is *'in very good spirits & looked remarkably well. He made Us laugh very much in the Evening.'* Sickly wife, no heir, no Ashcombe, but Tom seems always cheerful.

January 30th *'A wet Day. My father & George did not return from Hunting till 7 O'clock. William did not return home from Foxhunting till eleven O'clock.'* I have a vision of him hacking along the quiet, rough, muddy country roads through the night, in the rain. He often hunts down in the Cattistock country.

In February, Charlotte *'scolded some poor Woman for picking My Fathers hedges'*. We do not know if she wanted sticks for firewood. People were so poor, especially in places that were not well wooded, like Salisbury Plain, that they could not gather enough wood to cook by, let alone keep warm, and of course, woods and hedges belonged to farmers and landlords.

There are the usual comings and goings, but the health of Mrs Shere is an anxiety. She has a cough. On February 12th, she has her third stillborn son. After seeming a little better, she is worse again. Mr Ames attends her, but on the 16th, *'My Father sent A Chaise for My Brother Dr Grove. He arrived about eleven O'clock at Night.'*

February 19th *'Mrs Shere very ill indeed. John came But He has no hopes of her. About four O'clock She died, having been insensible some hours before. Tho. Shere & Mr & Mrs Futcher came up here in the Evening.'* I believe Mr and Mrs Futcher to be Thomas Shere's parents-in-law, as his wife was Elizabeth Futcher. A few days later, Edwards, the Grove butler, *'Walked out with Tho. Shere which did him good.'* She is buried on 26th, *'Edwards attended and several of the Farmers'.*

They refuse an invitation to dine at Donhead Hall with the Knellers, owing to there being no moon.

On the last day of the month, *'We went to Evening Service at Berwick. Mr Foots eldest Son is dead.'* There is no further explanation. As already said, there was a quantity of Foots in Berwick, Henry Foot farming Manor Farm. It was his fifth son, Charles, who inherited the tenancy.

The Waddington's butler is going to marry the governess. They had snow in February that continues into March, but it is too wet to settle. She uses the expression 'March coming in like a lion', so I wonder how old that phrase is. Charles and his friend Mr Wallinger arrive. Charlotte says she has never seen Charles in such good spirits, thinking the Alresford air must agree with him, so he still has his Bighton curacy. Her bedroom chimney smoked so much she had to move to the nursery attic.

Police officers caught a gang of footpads. This makes me think how crime is scarcely mentioned. Charlotte obviously does not expect to be robbed on her walks or when travelling. She visits, as usual, *'Nurse Marchant, Dame Stretch & King'*. She tells *'Oldy'* of her cousin Mary Shelley's engagement, so surely news suited to a retired servant. Charles Jackson visited them, in order to consult her father about an appointment, but is poorly from coming in the coach without his breakfast.

Thomas Shere has a little niece to stay with him, no doubt to help distract him from his woes.

The shepherd's daughter at Berricourt, Alice Burden, is ill. Charlotte provides her with a blanket but on the 13th, *'My Father sent Alice Burden in A Chaise to The Salisbury Infirmary'*. However, she could not be admitted, though it does not say why. Charlotte visits her on the 15th. *'She is not at all the worse for her journey to Salisbury.'* Mr Grove had his tenants to dine with him.

March 19th *'At Dinner time We were alarmed by the Library Chimney being on fire the 3rd time it has happened. It was swept with A Holly Bush immediately.'*

Charlotte continues to visit Alice Burden most days, whose health is fluctuating.

They get a letter from Henrietta to say Sir William Fraser has *'got A cadetship for William Jackson. I am rejoiced to hear it.'* Friends and relations were essential for getting young men from large families onto or up the rungs of their professions, in this case the military arm of the East India Company. Nobody had heard of nepotism or political correctness. William, who spends his time at Cattistock, *'has bought A new Horse, His little Mare Rosebud is quite done up'*. William was an enthusiastic foxhunter and does not seem to get an appointment on a ship. He probably received 'half-pay' as a Navy officer while not having a ship and as he lived at home, was not put to great expense. He definitely had some property of his own.

Charlotte goes with her mother to Sedgehill. They are obviously worried about Carey. *'He is not better than when We saw Him last.'*

April continues much as March, coming and going of brothers, friends, cousins and Aunt Grove. The men are still hunting, this time at Great Ridge. The arrival of Lady Shelley and her daughters causes *'A great deal of Talking'*. Percy Bysshe Shelley's son Will had died in 1818, and he lost an infant daughter in 1819. They walk to Berwick, where Charlotte's aunt buys things for Oldy at the shop. This must be the shop in Berwick where Charlotte had got the pattens. They hear that Emma has *'another little Boy'*. This would be Emma's last child, Charles. The Binghams join them for dinner and they dance.

Harriet is expecting another child but is not well. Charlotte goes to stay. On the 15th, *'We were called up about one O'clock, Harriet being taken ill. She miscarried of a stillborn female Infant. My Mother called, I shall remain here with My Sister till She gets quite well again.'* Charlotte occupies herself with chess, walking beside Carey on his donkey and playing *'Travelling Man'* with the children. She reports on the children coming downstairs after dinner. William and Carey were denied this when naughty. (There was an element of coming down after dinner, dressed in best clothes, for children of my generation, but certainly not for me. For those of my parent's generation and background, it was the norm. Could it possibly go on now?) Harriet comes down for breakfast on the 22nd, sooner than expected. Little Albert *'was delighted to see his Mama'*.

Charlotte seems to challenge herself when it comes to walking, first four miles, then six miles and then seven miles round the plantation. *'The children had A Maypole with Flowers upon the Green being May Day.'* The family come and go, William Helyar going down to Coker or dining and dancing at Pythouse or *'Mr W. Helyar amused Himself with going to sleep on the Sofa in the Evening.'*

While Charlotte is at Sedgehill, *'The Kitchen Maid at Fern has produced A little One.'*

On the 10th, Charlotte returns home.

May 11th *'I walked to Talbots. I approve very much of the Blue Satin He brought Me from London.'* This rather elevates the Ludwell shop, the proprietor going to London and taking commissions. *'I accompanied My Mother in the Evening to the Orchard, The little Puppies very troublesome.'* There seems to have been quite a turnover of dogs, but Charlotte does not often remark on them. On the 14th, *'The Kitchen Girl & her Baby left Fern.'* Charlotte does not mention this again. Having a baby while in service was not an option.

Mr Lush's new house is still an object for a walk. On the 15th, she walks to Ashcombe and sees *'Farmer Jones children playing round the Pond with a Newfoundland Dog.'*

On the 16th, she visits Oldy and sees her eldest daughter, *'who is returned from service & is ill'*. Charlotte then remarks on Charlotte Wix again having fits.

As usual, they see plenty of Jacksons, Knellers, Mrs Bingham and others. They read, amongst other things, *Castle Rackrent* by Maria Edgeworth, a topical book at the time about Ireland and the absentee landlord. They are amused by Aunt Grove's accounts of dandies, who had reached the height of absurdity.

Lizzie Imbers is not well. Charlotte takes *'Her two doses of Salts'*. A dose of salts, said disdainfully, to perk someone up who appears less than lively, entered our language and I think is now leaving it again.

May 29th alters their lives with terrible abruptness. *'We received A letter from Waddington saying Emma is dangerously ill, My Mother &c I immediately set out for Salisbury: John joined our Party & We went to Stockbridge.'*

May 30th *'Left Stockbridge at 5 o'clock – arrived at Clay Hall in the Evening. Emma has had an inflammation of the Windpipe & is still very unwell.'*

May 31st *'My dear Sister appeared rather better. Miss Hutchins the new Governess is A very nice young Woman. I sat up at Night with dear Emma & she had A good deal of Sleep. (I sincerely pray She may recover dear Love.)'*

So continues this tragedy, hope and despair alternating: *'My Mother & I have completely made up Our minds for the worst'*, *'She looked so clear about Her Eyes & better'*. Charlotte, her mother, Miss Hutchins and Miss Waddington take turns sitting up at night. The see-sawing of Emma's condition goes on until June 9th. *'My dearest Sister felt faint all day. Towards Evening She grew worse & about 12 oclock at Night died without A struggle. Oh what A heart rending Scene to Us all.'*

On the 9th *'My Father is A great comfort to Dear Waddington, dear little Emma & Caroline have felt their loss exceedingly.'* The two boys are sent for from school. They are now nine and eleven.

June 11th *'Dear Waddington bears his severe loss as A good Christian should do.'*

Emma is dressed in *'A White Gown satin shoes &c'*. The boys arrive, not knowing the circumstances. *'A heart rending Scene seeing the afflicted Father & Children together.'*

June 12th *'The dear Children all saw their Mother.'* That day she was put in her coffin and covered with flowers. *'We were obliged to have her soldered up at Night.'*

Tom arrives. *'He is very much affected at meeting Us all.'* The poor governess is worried she will be left at Clay Hall, but she is to go with them. The funeral takes place on the 17th. To my surprise, being clear women never went to funerals, Charlotte and Miss Hutchins attend it, but not Mrs Grove. Emma is *'interred in the Vault with Her dear little Baby Frederick'*. Frederick is last mentioned as being inoculated. I cannot find his death mentioned.

From later readings I know Emma was buried in the church at what is written as Walcheren, but this is the island where Walcheren fever originated, off the Netherlands. John Lane says it is Walkern, about two miles from Stevenage.

They place a hatchment, that is a coat of arms, over the door of Clay Hall.

On the way home, John meets them at The White Hart in Salisbury.

They return to Ferne and life returns to some sort of normality, Charlotte walking Miss Hutchings to Ashcombe. *'I showed her the House & The Garden. We saw Farmer James & His eldest Daughter.'* I remember Tom had brought his bailiff, Mr James, from Wales. If they are not living at Ashcombe and do not own it, are they still farming the land? In the 1840 tythe map, the Groves are farming Ashcombe.

Charlotte remarks on Alice Burden being still unwell. *'I gave her an Order to go in to the Salisbury Infirmary.'* She also says, *'I see Hannah Burden has A Grand-child very soon'* – obviously too soon in Charlotte's eyes. Later she talks of *'Anne Burden, the young shepherd's wife with her baby'*.

Charlotte is teaching music to her niece and walks with Miss Hutchins and the two girls to see Mr Lush's house. I feel any sort of house building must have been a rarity for Mr Lush's activities to excite such interest. She is poorly for a couple of days, an unusual occurrence, she does not say in what way.

June 26th *'Mr W Helyar & my dear Harriet came. Little Tom thought Her so like his dear Mother.'* Tom was the fifth of the Waddington children and the last was Charles, still a baby. The oldest ones were Emma, John, George and Caroline.

They visit Ashcombe. *'Mr Upjohn was there measuring.'* I wonder what and why.

On the last day of the month, Alice Burden is very ill. Charlotte does not think she will live long.

July 1st *'I walked to Talbots paid A Bill & back again in an hour and five minutes.'* I think it would take me more than that to get to the Ludwell shop and back, supposing Talbots to be roughly situated in the same vicinity. I see Talbots like Hine and Parsons when it was all one shop, where you could just about get anything you wanted. Caroline has *'a very cheap bonnet'* bought for her at Talbots.

July 2nd *'I & Miss Hutchins taught My two Nieces dancing. They have learnt rather a wooden style.'* Emma rides the pony, accompanied by her uncle William, to Ashcombe, and a few days later Caroline falls off it *'but luckily is not hurt'*.

Alice Burden is visited at Berricourt. *'I have collected A very good Subscription to pay for the Carriage, to take her to the Salisbury Infirmary.'*

There is to be another election in Salisbury. Charlotte sets about some modest canvassing for Mr Benett.

July 14th *'Mr Parker came in a Velosopied.'* This is how Charlotte spelt it, but the correct spelling is velocipede. The early form of bicycle was invented by a German, Baron Karl Drais. It resembled the balance bikes we now have for little children, thus it had no pedals and was propelled by shoving it along with your feet, no doubt taking advantage of downward slopes. In 1818 the Frenchman, Niépce, the pioneer of photography, an inventive sort of fellow, improved this dandy horse, as it was called, by making an adjustable seat, but an elegant English version, lighter, made of metal rather than wood, was patented in the December of 1818 by Dennis Johnson. As we are now in 1819, I imagine Mr Parker to have one of these, but Charlotte does not mention him again, let alone tell us how far he had come. The craze for this pedal-less, early sort of bicycle was brief.

The first day of the election was July 19th. George attends. Mr Bennet has 302 votes and his opponent, Mr Astley, 199. The voting goes on every day, Mr Benett always ahead. It is not orderly. *A sad Riot at the Election one of Mr Benetts voters much wounded and sent to the Hospital at Salisbury*, and the next day, *'The Free holders voted in A Malt House at Salisbury. The Hustings being pulled down by the Mob.'* The whole business goes on for twenty-two days because it is not until August 4th that Charlotte announces Mr Benett has won.

July 26th *'My Mother drew such A striking likeness of my dear Sister.'* Was she drawing Harriet or the departed Emma? Where is that drawing now?

They still have the Waddingtons with them, the older boys sometimes with the Helyars. One day, Harriet rides over from Sedgehill in time for breakfast with little William and Carey on the donkey. *'They spend A Happy Day with their Cousins.'*

Charlotte continues to teach dancing. When walking she is accompanied by Miss Hutchins and Emma. They visit Betty Stretch in Berwick, which Charlotte is now spelling as we do. Betty Stretch shows them her garden and also *'Chapel Barn'*. Is this now replaced with Chapel Farm? Francis says yes, and we have in our church a 'voussoir', an arched stone, dug up from the site. Those regularly visited in Berwick are Betty Stretch, Mrs Lathy, Ann Herring, Abbot, the Gardiners and Bugden, who has a bad leg, as does Mrs Pinnock. Later, when ill in bed with a *'sick headache'*, Mrs Grove sends her sago and port wine. Betty Stretch walks to Ferne and back in a day and this being remarked on, indicating she was of some age.

'Little Master Benett came to visit John and George Waddington.' Mr Bennet's eldest son was also John. He was a year older than John Waddington. He stays a couple of nights and then rides back to Pythouse with Mr Grove, who drops him off there on his way to the justice meeting.

I mention this because I see it as an example of the close interaction of adults and children, not much cushioned by servants; Mr Grove, a dignified sixty-one, quite old for the period, not too grand to deliver a neighbour's child home on a pony.

August 12th *'William rode to the Blandford Races with His two Nephews.'* Uncle William, that ardent foxhunter, cannot have considered it too far for boys aged nine and eleven. Did they return the same day? Charlotte only tells us they dine at Farnham and spot Lady Bingham on the racecourse, back from St Helena where her husband had been senior officer of the troops in charge of Napoleon. A few days later, their father takes them back to school.

Emma is becoming proficient in chess, delighted to take a game from her aunt and also from her uncle George.

August 19th *'Walter Stretches youngest Boy has met with an accident & I fear his Arm is broken.'*

August 20th *'A sad Fire broke out in one of Mr Blackmores Ricks, burnt 3 others A wheat Rick Barn & Granary.'* Here is Mr Blackmore, now Rector of Donhead St Andrew in place of Charlotte's deceased Uncle Gilbert Jackson, farming an important part of his clerical living. A rick becoming too hot in its centre and catching fire can happen now as it did then. Francis had a special rod for ascertaining the heat of a rick, which he gave to the Halls when they suffered a similar disaster at Lower Bridmore. Charlotte goes on to say, *'In the Evening walked up White Sheet Hill with Miss Hutchins & Emma. Fern looks to great advantage from the Hill.'* This makes me reflect on the varying views of Ferne seen by passing generations, the house preceding Charlotte's of which there is no known image; Charlotte's Ferne; the much-enlarged version of her nephew John Fraser Grove's; then the Duke of Hamilton's further additions, increasingly ugly; then, by the early sixties, no house at all but the stable block much as Charlotte's father built it in 1811; and now something far larger and grander than Charlotte would have known but in a style of architecture she would understand.

August 24th *'My Mother heard from Waddington. He was just going to Clay Hall (poor fellow!) what melancholy ideas must it not recall.'*

Her brother John is now a father. *'Dr Grove came his little Girls Name is Henrietta.'*

On the 27th, *'I walked to Talbots with Miss Hutchins & Emma. The former so frightened at meeting A Man in A Carters Frock.'* This entry really does puzzle me. I had assumed such a thing would have been a common sight.

September 1st *'Waddington & My Brothers Tom & George got up very early & went to Woodcuts to shoot where They killed 9 brace of Partridges, & A Landrail.'* A landrail is a corn crake. In this area a corn crake does predate me, and I have neither seen nor heard one, though they used to be common. There are plenty of them in Russia. Charlotte remarks on William going out by himself and *'was unsuccessful'*.

The shop Talbots caters for everything. *'We walked to Talbots. I settled about A grey cloth Cloak. Mrs T promised to make it in A week.'*

September 4th *'I walked with Miss Hutchins & the Girls to Ashcombe brought some relicks from the House.'* Ashcombe still fascinates, standing empty, I suppose, in some sort of limbo. What relicks can they have stolen, for surely Ashcombe belonged to the Arundells at this juncture?

The normal social round continues. The girls can now dance eight quadrilles. Miss Laura Arundell is to be married to a Col Macdonald. Little Emma Waddington plays chess with Mrs Bingham and wins three games. Harriet arrives with her two girls for a few days. Alice Burden is home from hospital. She is not better.

The time has come for Miss Hutchins to leave them. On September 16th, they are *'all very sorry to part with Miss H'*. She is going to London, staying overnight at Dr Grove's in Salisbury. I assume she is to take another appointment, but Charlotte does not tell us.

September 20th *'I walked with My Nieces to Ashcombe, We saw a Summer House in the Wood, We had not observed before, Caroline took possession of it. The last time I shall walk with the dear Girls before their journey to Weymouth.*' They leave the next day. Charlotte resumes her solitary walking, going up Whitesheet Hill as far as the milestone, but soon she turns her attention to the youngest Waddington, baby Charles, who is still at Ferne. *'I carried little Charles out Walking to Berwick.'* This becomes a frequent occupation and says much for Charlotte's stamina.

On the 23rd, John and his wife Jane arrive with the new baby, *'the finest Baby I ever saw.'* They are accompanied by Keith Fraser, who I assume to be a brother of Jane's. I am struck by his very un-Georgian name.

September 28th *'I walked to Berricourt. Alice Burden gets weaker & weaker.'*

The following day, Betty Stretch comes to see the baby and Mr Grove has his tenants to dine. William and George *'helped to entertain Them. I dined with My Mother Jane & Keith in the Library.'*

On the 30th, Henrietta Grove is Christened in Lower Donhead church, her grandparents and Mrs Thomas Grove her godparents. *'Waddington returned from Weymouth & brought A letter & some Sea Weed from Emma to Me.'*

In October, it seems John is the crack shot of the family. He manages to shoot far more than anyone else. Charlotte visits Langton and the Marklands, who, being at Farnham, can be taken in on the way. Social life continues unabated, as does chess. Charlotte's nieces now seem to be staying with Tom and Henrietta. Alice Burden *'still lives, but that is all'*. On the 11th, *'Mr John Brine eloped with Miss Bastard.'*

There is further curious information about Ashcombe. October 18th *'The Carpenters are taking up the Dining Room floor at Ashcombe for Fern. Two pictures arrived from that House for Me.'* Ferne being newly built, it surely had a perfectly good dining room floor already. Ashcombe is presumably being prepared for demolition. Charlotte then says, two days later, *'My Mother mended my Picture of the Carnival at Venice, which Mr Methuen had shot A hole in when He lived at Ashcombe.'*

I learn Donhead Hall, where lived the Knellers, had *'those slippery stairs'* because the nursemaid fell down them while carrying the baby, but preserved the baby *from any hurt at the eminent hazard of her own life*. Has Donhead Hall the same stairs now? She also says, *'they are very pretty children the little Knellers'*.

George went to Salisbury and *'saw A Gnu at the Fair like A Bull'*. Charlotte buys net *'for my Mothers scarf'* at Hascals, another Ludwell shop, I think. She has Fanny Jackson staying, who visits the Foots while Charlotte visits Mrs Bingham and plays a game of chess. There is a delicate imbalance of social status between the Groves and their Jackson cousins. Charlotte does not think much of Mrs Bingham's stamina when it comes to walking. *'She accompanied Us A Very little way on Our return.'*

Mr Warburton is *'making great Alterations at the Parsonage'* at Lower Donhead.

October 26th *'I walked with Fanny to Talbots bought A very pretty Cap for 3s 6d.'* This is an indicator of Charlotte's age, thirty-six. Caps were for the older woman.

Despite the suppression of Napoleon, there is still plenty of military activity. George *'went out as Cornet in Mr Benetts yeomanry'*.

John comes from Salisbury to attend sick servants. *'The Cook is cured by Dr Groves advice.'*

October 29th *'It snowed very much in the morning. George went with Thos. Shere to the Hindon Fair to buy Sheep But could not get any to suit Him. We are reading the Black Robber the greatest nonsense I ever read.'*

Charlotte does not mention *'baby Charles'*, so he must be reunited with his siblings. On November 1st, John and Charles Jackson are staying, and the latter does an impromptu rendering of Shylock. How necessary it was to be able to entertain and how few of us could pull off a similar act.

November 2nd *'I walked with Fanny to the Lodge at Wardour, through the Wood one Road & back the other passed Horwood, Mr James Lush there, Ld. Arundell is building Him A Gothic Farm House.'* This is of course where Peter Dalton lives now.

Alice Burden dies on November 4th. Charlotte tells us no more than that. She walks with Fanny to Rushmore. *'We saw the House. A beautiful*

Picture of Lady Ligonire Ld. River's Sister.' The Groves did not socialise with Lord Rivers, despite being so close. I understand from John Lane that Lady Ligonire was of a racy disposition, having several affairs, one of which caused her husband to fight a duel. She ended up divorced and later married 'Trooper Smith' of the Blues, which cannot have pleased her family.

George is now frequently out with the Yeomanry. He dines with them at Hindon *'& got very tipsey'*. He has too much of a hangover the following day to accompany Charles Jackson, who goes out with the harriers, but recovers enough to dine with the Knellers.

November 12th *'I walked with Fanny to Talbots. We bargained for some clothes for the poor people for My Mother. Met Hannah Burden, her eldest & youngest Daughter, all in deep Mourning for Alice.'* I note that even those from a fairly modest background observed mourning.

They have various other visitors during November, John and his wife and the baby, Henrietta, who is not very well. The Binghams with their son Edward dine and stay the night. Charlotte wins a game of chess with Edward and his mother but when *'the Miss Benetts of Norton come'*, she has to report *'Miss Anna played two Games of Chess with Me & won them both.'* There is a great deal of chess: Miss Anna does not win all the time. They are also visited by Mr Bromley and Lady Field and her daughter Mary. Charles Jackson tries and fails to get a curacy at Tollard Royal. The Waddingtons have taken a house at Weymouth.

On December 1st, Captain Markland's *'double barrelled Gun went off & shot his left hand very much indeed. It is feared He must lose A thumb & a finger.'* Captain Markland has already had a similar accident. This is just the sort of occurrence I expect to happen when Francis goes off on a 'black powder' shoot, the black powder of course gunpowder. On a 'black powder day', Francis shoots with a gun made in the 1840s. Captain Markland would have shot with a flintlock whereas Francis' is a percussion, an 1820s invention, but Francis says he has watched people shoot really well with a flintlock. He suggests Captain Markland's accident resulted from a barrel bursting, which is what happened the first time, but that is not how Charlotte tells it now. John visits Captain Markland the next day and thinks he won't lose any of his hand.

They are visited by Sir John Pakington after an absence of eleven years. He came from Westwood Park near Droitwich. *'He made Me as Usual play new Music to Him.'* Was this the equivalent of the latest hit?

Mr Grove has gone to London with Tom. They return accompanied by little John Waddington. *'My Nephew very much pleased at coming Home but very silent.'* The following day, his grandfather takes him hunting and the day after that Tom escorts him to Weymouth, presumably to join the rest of his family for the school holiday.

December 15th *'Mr Wm. Helyar walked here and paid Us A Morning Visit. Harriet was so kind as to send Me two most invaluable presents A Ring & Brooch with My dear Sister Emma's Hair, & also sent My Mother A Ring.'* Hair was arranged in an immaculate curl, frequently placed in rings and brooches but also in the backs of miniatures. In the age of selfies we have little concept of losing someone close to us but having no material image of them. Emma was married for fourteen years, during which period she had seven children. I cannot imagine her setting aside time to sit for her portrait. When I look at miniatures, I find them rarely identified and wish people would realise the necessity of writing on the backs of pictures and photographs. We may know who they are, but our grandchildren won't. I had an uncle particularly good at this. A small photograph of my maternal grandmother wearing a boater and tie and looking a little like Perin is labelled with her name and the addition 'dressed for bicycling'. As she died before I was born, how else would I know?

I feel the impending destruction of Ashcombe. December 16th *'I walked to Ashcombe the Road & home though the Wood, They are cutting down the Trees. I saw Mrs James, But could not go into her House, as I was wet with the Snow.'* It is evident Tom's bailiff, Mr James, who came up from the Welsh property, is still living there, presumably farming the land.

December 17th *'Mr Edward Hinxman has written an excellent Paper against the Radicals.'* He lived at Durnford and was a high sheriff of Wiltshire. Charlotte would have favoured him: the Groves were far from radical.

William returns from Weymouth with John Waddington. I like the way these childless uncles step in to ferry about their nephews. There is plenty of hunting. *'Little John very much tired with his days hunting but sat up till after 10 hearing A Play read.'* The next day, Waddington arrives with *'My Nephew George…John most happy to see His Brother, They enjoyed Themselves very much.'* The following day, *'My Father went out Hunting, Waddington his two Sons, Wm. & George attended Him.'* Charlotte then remarks, *'A conversation upon the National Debt'*.

Emma and Caroline arrive but their father returns to Weymouth because baby Charles is ill. They don't go to church on Christmas Day as the roads are too slippery for the horses.

The Jacksons are friendly with the Foots, but it is not until now that Charlotte joins them, overcoming the social divide between the farmers and the gentry. The Jacksons, offspring of a country parson, would not have been considered nearly as grand as their landed first cousins. *'I called at Mr Foots & walked with Miss Foot her brother & Fanny Jackson.'* At this period the Manor was the farmhouse for Manor Farm, owned by the Foots.

There are the usual Christmas amusements for the children, *'the Bulls & The Mummers'*. They play at battledore and in the evening casino and card games with their uncles.

The end papers for this year have short accounts of money spent, including a shilling lent to her mother. There is a note of Miss Susan Still marrying the Rev Henry Worsley. Otherwise, Charlotte has recorded a list of fifteen poems and another fifteen pieces from Shakespeare. Did she learn these by heart?

1820

January 1ˢᵗ *'William heard from The Commissioners of Mr Farquarsons Hunt, & their Ball is fixed for the 10th of February. If I am invited I shall go to it as William has offered both George & Me Tickets.'* This interested me as I see it as an indication of hunts moving away from being private packs towards subscriptions. The ball, with tickets, sounds like the modern fundraiser, but it may have been a means of keeping it exclusive.

The little Waddingtons are still with them. *'The Children in high spirits & very entertaining.'*

On the 3ʳᵈ, Mr Wallinger arrives with Charles: *'The latter has A Wig which does not improve Him.'* Wigs had been out of fashion for some time, but it cannot have been that unusual to wear one. It is probable many of the older generation had not given them up. Mr Bennett of *Pride and Prejudice* was interrupted when in his 'powdering gown', but we do not know if he was having his wig powdered or his hair. Would you powder your wig before putting it on? In 1813, a Peninsular War soldier described General Stewart (later Marquess of Londonderry) taking off his hat at a review and his wig coming off with it. The same soldier, an officer in the 18ᵗʰ Hussars, describes waltzing amongst the English and the Portuguese, so obviously popular before 1814 when the Russian tsar is said to have made it the fashion.

The next day, Charlotte says, *'I like the description of Miss Hopkins, my intended Sister in Law.'* Thus we hear Charles, now twenty-four, is engaged. Elizabeth Harriet Hopkins was nineteen, the daughter of an Alresford family, near where Charles was curate. The Hopkins were related to Francis' mother's family, also from Alresford, and also to the late Sir Sydney Giffard. Francis showed me a family tree of such alarming complexity I could not puzzle it out, but it did have Charles Grove on it and a Giffard. Charles must have kept his courtship very quiet, though Charlotte did say on December 6th, *'A secret disclosed to me relative to Charles.'*

'Mr Wallinger & Charles waltzed with the Girls.' They also dance *'Quadrilles The Spanish Dance Reels & Country Dances'*.

Waddington arrives with Tom. *'Tom quizzed Charles about his Wig.'* You are going to be teased by an older brother if you start wearing a wig. The word quiz has changed its meaning. Now it is to question; then it meant to make fun of something.

The baby now has whooping cough but is recovering, though later it was decided it was not whooping cough, which Charlotte sometimes spells without the W Chess is as prevalent as ever, Emma Waddington defeating the rector's wife in all three games on one visit. Waddington takes his daughters back to Weymouth, leaving the boys, John and George. They join in with reading aloud in the evening. *'The boys enjoyed it & read it very well.'* There is a lot of snow and ice, which prohibits hunting. They have to go on foot. *'The Gentlemen are not so contented with this Weather as the Ladies.'*

January 15th *'The two Boys very entertaining.'*

On the 20th, *'My Father Wm. & the Boys went out Foot hunting. George walked to East Hayes. In the Evening It Snowed hailed & rained.'* We get the picture.

Dr Grove attends *'Farmer Harrison'*, who *'is grown quite old & childish'*. They are visited by Mr Benett and Mr Phipps.

January 23rd *'I walked out escorted by my two Beaux John & George. My Father read the Evening Service & George A Sermon.'*

January 25th *'The Duke of Kent is dead of an inflammation from a Cold.'* This was the father of the future Queen Victoria, George IV's fourth son.

January 30th *'We went to Evening Church at Berwick. Our Seat was quite damp.'*

On the 31st, they hear of the death of the King, who had died two days earlier. *'The Guard of the Coach brought the News.'* Charlotte has not mentioned the Regency, which had existed for the last ten years. She and Fanny Jackson see a newspaper the following day. *'George 4th was proclaimed King yesterday & held his first Court.'*

Charlotte, on meeting a Presbyterian preacher, emphatically announces he is a Whig while she is a Tory. Not having the vote did not mean women had no strong political leanings. The ball she was to go to is put off until November, I suppose in respect for the King's death. She was pleased.

On returning from a visit to Harriet, *'We were fearful our Wheel should be on fire.'* This was another hazard of the road; friction could cause sparks and wheels were mostly wood.

February 4th *'Waddington took his two dear boys to school. They felt The Parting very much, but behaved quite Manly on the occasion.'* I have always thought the stiff upper lip more of a Victorian idea, but it was obviously creeping in.

On Sunday, Charlotte takes a walk with Fanny Jackson. They do not return *'unfortunately until prayers are over and the sermon beginning'*. The strong sense of religious observance at this period contrasts strangely with the image of decadence associated with the late 18th century and the Regency, gambling, drinking and duelling all commonplace.

Poor Mrs Bingham, the rector's wife, not only has to suffer constant defeats at chess but *'She walked part of the way Home with Us and was full of frights.'*

February 9th *'George returned from escorting The Royal Funeral with the Hindon Troop.'*

Charlotte is still visiting *'Betty Stretch, Ann Sturgens, Dane Pinnock & Sally Wicks, & E Stretch.'* She does this all in one go.

On the 10th, *'My father George & Charles Jackson went to see the latters estate at Knoyle.'* I do not know when or how Charles Jackson acquired this or where it was.

February 15th *'I accompanied Fanny Jackson to Sedgehill found Harriet very well but She has caught A little Cold. Agnes's eyes still very bad. Betty Stretch called upon Us before We left Fern. I gave her A piece of Bride Cake of Charles's & took the rest to Sedgehill.'* This is the first we know of the actual marriage.

Charlotte and Fanny walk to East Hayes. *'We waited An hour & 20 minutes for the Owner of that grand Mansion. But he did not make his appearance.'*

The weather is so cold they are in danger of running out of coal and then *'the coal arrives to our joy'.* Did they not burn wood? February 17th *'Fanny & I walked to Knoyle. Mr W Helyar breakfasted at Fern. George returned here with him. Mr & Mrs Twopenny called She is very pleasant but I cannot say the same for Him. He afterwards came again disagreeable Man.'* I cannot find any reference to the Twopennys and wonder how they pronounced it. Charlotte and Fanny walk a great deal, to Knoyle and to Shaftesbury.

On the 22nd, *'A letter from Charles to my Mother full of his dear Eliza'.*

They go to the evening service at Sedgehill. *'Mr Hodson gave Us A Long incoherent Sermon.'*

Tom had come to Ferne *'& amused Mrs Charles Grove very much'.* It does seem strange, as far as I can make out, that none of them met her until after the marriage. Fortunately, they all seem to like her.

Their reading matter is *Ivanhoe*, *'which I think very beautiful indeed'.*

February 24th *'Mr Wm Helyar & his two eldest Boys left Us for Coker, another very wet day. Carey was most anxious about going. William did not care about it. Harriet is so very agreeable that We sat up talking till a qu. To twelve & thought it ten.'* The boys were aged seven and eight. They return on the 28th.

February 25th *'My Brother Charles & his Bride called here in their way from Bath to Fern. She is a very pretty young Woman – Fanny and Harriet agree with Me that Charles is amazingly disguised by his Wig.'* Charlotte then turns her attention to little Agnes, who *'put herself in A passion about having the Leaches applied'*. As she was presumably to have them on her afflicted eyes, one has some sympathy. A few days later, her eyes are worse and she has to have the leaches again *'& behaved like a good girl'*. Her eyes were a constant cause of anxiety. They get advice from a Mr Alexander, which works for a bit.

Charlotte says, somewhat competitively, on the 28th, *'rose myself up from the ground without touching. Mr Wm. Helyar could not do it.'*

Charles and his wife return. Eliza is winning approval. *'I like my new Sister.'* George says, *'his new sister is very good tempered.'* Mr Twopenny cannot be shaken off; *'he stayed two hours & a half.'* On the same day, *'Mr Wm Helyer has A bad Cold & makes not a little fuss about it.'*

There is again to be an election. March 4th *'My Father intends voting for Mr Astley this contest instead of Mr Benett.'* Mr Grove actually nominated Astley. Despite long friendship with Benett, his support for Catholics and Protestant Dissenters must have become too much for the Groves. Charlotte declared herself a Tory and she no doubt got her politics from her father. She certainly disapproved of anything to do with 'Chapel'. Astley was high church. They hear Mr Long Wellesley has resigned the contest for Wiltshire. He was *'hooted'* at the play, I am not sure where, but *'He made A most excellent speech on the occasion, & spoke remarkably well.'* This is the only time I have heard any praise for William Wellesley Long, his reputation very bad. Mr Grove's actions on behalf of the Tory Mr Astley do not seem neighbourly, so it will be interesting to see if there is to be a coolness between the Groves and the Benetts. Benett was basically Whig but not radical. He was in support of the poor but had a reputation of not being good with his own tenants, and Hindon, where he was landlord, was considered one of the poorest parishes.

March 7th *'I breakfasted with Fanny who went outside the coach to Lyme. I hope she will not increase her Cold.'* On the stage coach you could travel on the roof, as depicted in Christmas cards, but not with the mail coaches. Did Fanny travel alone or did she have a maid? There is never a mention of a maid. It makes me think young women had more freedom than we have been led to suppose. Soon William Helyar's sister Caroline arrives *'with her Maid'*, but the Helyars were very grand compared with the Jacksons.

March 10th *'Poor Agnes suffers a good deal with Her eyes. I frightened little Wm about a Plumstone He had swallowed, he pulled A play thing entirely to pieces. Albert was prevented coming down after dinner having thrown A bason of water over his dress.'*

Charlotte walks to church at Knoyle. *'Mr Beauclerc read the Prayers & Mr Majendie the Sermon.'* The latter had *'A hesitation in his speech'*. Clouds, the Windmill Hill and Slades are all part of her walks. Of course they also go to George's house at East Hayes. The Majendies were of Huguenot descent. At this period one became bishop of Chester, who had had the unpromising task of going to sea with Prince William, later William IV, as tutor and supervisor, for which he was given the rank of midshipman!

March 20th *'Mr John Still & his eldest Daughter rode here. He perfectly coincides with me in regard to Mr Benett's conduct in the House of Commons.'* I was amused by a quote from Thomas Moore, the Irish poet, who described Benett as 'a very haranguing-minded gentleman – his wife odious – full of airs, with a hard, grinding Tartar voice, and presuming beyond anything'. Later he revised his opinion and became a real friend of the Benetts, who encouraged him to lodge with them in their house in Albemarle Street when he was in London. He refers, later, to the beauties of Pythouse and Benett's dire financial straits as the result of the expenses of electioneering.

March 22nd *'I walked by myself to Knoyle met Mr Anthony Burbidge A very odd Man who began talking to me. He is going to the Evening Lectures at Sedgehill Church.'* It is interesting to know that so long ago, and when churches were well attended, they sometimes had a secondary use for them.

On the 23rd, it is known that Waddington has taken Wyncombe for two years.

The protracted visit to Sedgehill, since February 15th, was of course due to Harriet's pregnancy. On the 24th she has a girl, Marian Elizabeth – Caroline chooses the names. At first the baby does not seem well but within a few days seems to recover. There is a nurse, Mrs Williams, who shortly becomes ill, but Harriet and the baby seem to go along very well after the initial alarm. Charlotte returns to Ferne on April 1st.

April 4th *'I walked to Ashcombe. It looks very melancholy The trees being cut down and the House pulling down.'* There is no explanation.

April 11th *'Charles has left off His Wig & He looks much better without it.'*

Charles and his bride are staying with them. *'The new married pair both very unwell. They sat up in their dressing Room all Day. I gave dear little Henrietta A coral necklace. My Father very facetious.'* Was he facetious about the new married pair? A coral necklace was often given for a baby to chew on when teething. Henrietta was John's daughter. Charlotte declares her *'A nice Child'*.

On April 18th, Charlotte remarks, *'Miss Laura Arundell was married at Wardoar to Col Macdonald.'* According to Desmond Hawkins she married in 1827, but that is incorrect.

There is much coming and going of brothers and their wives, but then on the 19th, *'Molly & dear little Charles Waddington arrived. We were indeed shocked to see the dear little Baby look so very ill.'* Molly is the nanny. Charlotte goes off to Berricourt *'to fetch the Shepherd's daughter for the Baby & afterwards went for her child.'* I take it this was the need for a wet nurse. On the 21st, *'Dr Grove came to see little Charles. If his Liver is not affected which He much fears there may be A chance for his Life.'*

Ashcombe is still standing, for Charlotte walks there on the 25th. *'Had a Room measured, about which the Gentlemen had A dispute.'* They hear her aunt, Mrs Rudge, has died, aged ninety.

Mr Long from Preshaw visits them. Mr Grove and George make a bargain with him over some heifers. I note they are not at all too grand for this sort of business. The baby is much better. *'He laughed quite heartily at Molly.'* Charlotte is working out the *'nearest way to Wincombe which is I think by Ludwell, & Donhead Hall'*. This is presumably with the idea of the Waddingtons moving there. She often refers to C.H. Grove, which had puzzled me but now she talks of lending *'Charles Henry my 8 vols of Clarissa Harlowe'*, so it is just a new way of mentioning her youngest brother.

May 8th *'I met Mr Dancey & his Father in Law Mr Warburton. They were going to see Ashcombe, which is now completely spoilt as one of the Lions of the country.'* We do not use that word lion to describe someone or something worth seeing, but it lingers in 'to lionise', though my niece, in her thirties, had never heard the expression. The poet Thomas Moore was a friend of the American Washington Irving, he of 'Rip Van Winkle'. He says, 'Took Irving after dinner to show him to the Starkys, but he was sleepy and did not open his mouth; the same at Elywn's dinner. Not strong as a lion, but delightful as a domestic animal.' Mr Dancey was the new Rector of Lower Donhead. In April, Charlotte had gone to church there and approved his sermon, which she described as excellent and underlined it.

There are now references to Susan Highmore being very ill. She was Mrs Grove's maid. John Grove sees her, as does Mr Wills. Betty Stretch sits up with her. More village names occur, Richard Green and Sam Brown.

May 16th *'We hear that Mr Foot of the Farm at Berwick is dead, He dropped suddenly out of his Chair.'* A few days later, *'Miss Foot is much afflicted by her Fathers death.'* This information can be nicely corroborated by Mr Foot's memorial in the south transept of our church: 'Sacred to the Memory of Henry Foot who died suddenly at Torquay aged 69 years'. It goes on to include the death of his wife, Anne, thirty-three years later.

The baby improves in health every day, apart from catching a cold. Charlotte plays with him. The rest of the Waddingtons are still at Weymouth. Charles' wife writes to say, *'they like their new situation at Bighton very much'*. Mrs Markland has a daughter, but both are poorly. William Helyar has taken Agnes to London to try to get treatment for her eyes.

May 24th *'Lady Radcliffe Miss Macdonall & Mrs Macdonall called upon Us. I like our new Neighbours very well.'* Lady Radcliffe was a sister of the Macdonall who married Laura Arundell. Later they go to Wardour *'being Sir Joseph Radcliffes Birthday where he came of age…We had fireworks & danced with the Servants'*. Had they taken a letting of Wardour? The Binghams were also of the party. *'My Father very entertaining with Mrs Bingham.'* I suspect him of teasing the susceptible rector's wife.

May 26th *'Highmores youngest Sister came. She thought little Charles only 6 or 7 months old.'*

Susan Highmore's sisters come to nurse her. At first she is better and then worse. Charlotte says she was made worse by eating cucumbers. On the 30th, Charlotte sits up with her until half past one in the morning, but a little after two she dies. She refers to her as *'dear Highmore'*. Dr Grove and Mr Wills *'ascertain the cause of Highmores death & it was A cancerous Ulcer in the Stomach'* and *'I & My Mother took care dear Highmores Corpse should be dressed properly.'*

On the 1st of June, *'My eldest brother arrived to our great joy'* and on the 2nd *'Tom spent the morning at Ashcombe.'* I include all these little references to Ashcombe in the hope of working out who owned it, who farmed it and who pulled it down and why, though the actual owners must have been the Arundells. That evening, Tom accompanies his mother and sister to Mr Dancey's to drink tea, which is what you did after your late afternoon dinner. It often turned into a social occasion. Mr Dancey shows them his fossil collection.

Now we open a real can of worms. June 4th *'Mr Bingham lent Us Dr. Gardiners Paper the Vindicator, A vile production indeed.'* Curiosity made me turn to the Internet but without much hope for such an obscurity, but there it all was. I could even have bought a copy, currently in America, for two hundred pounds or so. Fortunately the contents were revealed. Mr

Bingham had an aunt, Mrs Sarah Bingham, aged seventy, living in Gay Street in Bath. The 'Mrs' was a courtesy, because she was not married. Her place of worship was the Octagon Chapel in Milsom Street, presided over by the Rev Dr Gardiner D.D. One Sunday in May, on her way out of the Octagon, the old lady (I'm afraid you were very old at seventy), instead of putting money into the poor box, took a pound note out of it. This was seen by a 'servant', whose good character was later verified. He reported she said the note was hers and he corrected her, all of which she afterwards denied. He followed her out of the building. She stopped, looked at the note, which was a Devizes note, returned to the chapel and gave it in at the vestry, saying it must have caught in her sleeve. According to report, she did this on seeing she was observed. Dr Gardiner, in an act that would have been considered far from gentlemanly at the time and even now, especially as he was a clergyman, published two letters under two different pseudonyms – 'Vindicator' and 'Clincher' – in the *Bath and Cheltenham Gazette*, describing the incident. He was actually answering a letter already inserted by Mr Bingham (I am not sure which Mr Bingham, Peregrine or his brother Edward) declaring the absurdity of the accusation against this respectable old lady and how the word of a servant had prevailed. Dr Gardiner stated he wished to uphold the character of the servant, there being several witnesses to the truth of his statement. Mrs Bingham sued Dr Gardiner for libel. She lost the case. Mr Bingham and Mr John Helyar both went as witnesses as to her exemplary character. (Amusingly, her lawyers were 'Dynely and Gatty'. Francis describes this sort of Dineley as a D-winely. They were obviously some sort of connection, and we have a few things that belonged to Dyneleys.) I can't imagine exactly what Miss Bingham thought she was doing on this occasion, but it is hard to suppose she meant to steal the money, though the evidence was decidedly against her. The reference to a Devizes note means the note was printed by a local bank, a practice later stopped, according to Francis, as they were inclined to print more notes than they had money. Dr Gardiner was criticised for writing anonymously, which certainly seemed a mistake, but overall I rather come down on his side, though Charlotte does not agree. Dr Gardiner also pointed out if 'Mr Bingham' had not put his letter in the paper, the whole thing would have been forgotten. Later on 'Mrs S Bingham' stays at the Rectory and Charlotte meets her with some frequency. *'Mrs Sarah Bingham has been sadly traduced.'*

June 6th *'I assisted My Mother in taking out her Pickles &c threw some Pickle sauce over My Purple Gown But luckily did not spoil it'* and on the same day little Charles *'sadly vexed with his Teeth'.*

Highmore is replaced. June 7th *'Mrs Harris came. My Mother's new Servant. She is a tall stout young Woman only eighteen.'* Despite the Mrs, it is unlikely she was married. Charlotte is soon taking her for walks. Charlotte buys from Highmore's sister *'Highmores Collection'*. She hangs it *'over my Chimney Piece'* and says she will always keep it *'for her sake'*, but what was it?

Now that George IV is King, we have the difficulties attached to his estranged wife, Caroline. *'The Queen is arrived in England.'* This is rather what was hoped would not happen. She had been gallivanting about the continent and now wished to join in at her husband's coronation. She was offered a pension if she would stay abroad, but she refused. George IV's anxiety to be divorced from her led to the famous trial of pains and penalties in the House of Lords in an attempt to prove she had committed adultery. Charlotte said, *'The Queen will not accommodate, & She is to have A trial.'* The whole scene was painted by Sir George Hayter and can be seen in the National Portrait Gallery. There was strong support for the Queen, though this was possibly due to the lack of support for the King, neither of them exactly behaving themselves. Charlotte herself was not in favour of the Queen.

Charlotte goes with her mother to visit the Marklands at Farnham Cottage. I wonder which house this actually is and whether it still exists. Mrs Markland is not well, which makes Charlotte break down sufficiently to call her *'my dear Helen'*, the more formal address usually prevailing. She now has two boys and a girl. Otherwise, Betty Stretch has a cold and is sent some *'Doveys Powders'*. Charlotte hears the *'Cathecism'* of Marianne Imbers and Kezia Law, subsequently buying them a present at Talbots. John Waddington arrives from school, as does George with his father. Sir Joseph Radcliffe and various Macdonnells come to dine. *'I like the ladies But cannot say much for the Baronet'*.

On June 26th they spend the day at Sedgehill, *'My Father & Mother, Brothers & Nephews.'* It is Harriet's birthday. *'In the Evening We went to East Hayes to see Georges grand Mansion'*. Thus we know that what is now Sedgehill Manor is progressing.

Waddington and his family have arrived at Wincombe. Charlotte sometimes spells it with a Y. His sons go there for breakfast. Waddington himself dines with them. *'He rode the Mule & returned Home at Night.'* Of course, the Waddingtons being at Wincombe means baby Charles leaves Ferne.

July 1st *'I walked out with little Charles being his last Day here. After Dinner Waddington & all his Family left Us.'*

There are dire reports of Mrs Markland. At one moment when *'sensible'* she takes leave of her husband and children, but fortunately gets better again. Two Waddington children come to visit at Ferne while Harriet is there but go away again, as it is feared the Helyar children and their mother have whooping cough, though John cannot quite decide that is what it is. There is now in general much to-ing and fro-ing between Ferne and Wincombe, Waddington frequently dining with them.

July 3rd *'I walked to Berwick called upon Betty Stretch. She has heard that Her Daughter Fanny who was transported to Botany Bay is dead, & that the Ship in which her property to the amount of £700 was sent to England, was burnt. Edwards wrote to Lyoids, to ascertain the fact.'* This must be Charlotte's spelling of Lloyds. I am surprised it was possible to be transported and then to accumulate a fortune.

On July 11th, Charlotte goes to stay with John and his wife in Salisbury. They have a very social time, much calling and visiting, including a visit to Aunt Grove in Netherhampton who has improved her house with the addition of a French window. Charlotte and Jane go twice to the Cathedral: *'A very bad preacher there'*. They visit the Bromleys at Bishopstone. *'Drank tea at their new House. The Rooms down stairs good, The Bed Rooms very inferior.'* They go to the races, and Charlotte is delighted to meet an old school friend, Miss Weller. Amidst the jollifications, on the 19th, *'My dear Friend Betty Stretch is dead.'* Later Charlotte sees Rachel, her daughter, but there is no explanation for this sudden demise. Was it the shock of hearing the news of her daughter Fanny's death, let alone the loss of a massive seven hundred pounds?

Charlotte attends the races at Salisbury and Blandford and dances at the balls. At home they are visited by the Waddington children, Emma beating her aunt at chess.

August 15th *'Mr Wm. Helyar went to Knoyle in the Morning, to assist Mrs Twopenny in decorating her Ball Room. I accompanied My Brother to A dinner Party, & Dance at Mr Twopenny's, several Gentlemen, & 8 Ladies there. We danced Quadrilles, Reels Spanish dance & Waltzes. Mr Wm. Helyar sprained his Foot from his excessive agility.'* Charlotte does not say Harriet was there. I suspect her of being stuck at home exhausted from the quantity of babies. This establishes the Twopennys at Knoyle, but which house had a ballroom?

There is now a dog called Bango who accompanies them on walks.

August 22nd *'I walked with Emma to Berwick. We were going to call on Mrs Lush But finding Them at Dinner We escaped down the Ha Ha.'* This visiting business was very strange. I suppose they were embarrassed to arrive at dinner time and made their escape unobserved down the sunken ditch that constitutes that garden feature, a ha ha. I imagine the Lush family now to be at Upton Lucy, grand enough to have a ha ha, but if so, where was it? Charlotte goes on to say, *'Bango & A Donkey had A Race'*. Later they dine at the Rectory, perhaps at a more fashionable hour than that kept by the Lushes.

Emma is staying now, plays lots of chess and goes out riding with her uncle William. August 26th is so cold they have a fire. The James family are still at Ashcombe, the eldest daughter gone to be a housemaid at the Marklands. They amuse themselves by singing the Irish Melodies. Charlotte reports on the trial of the Queen. Italians had been imported to act as witnesses against her, but none of the proceedings were very satisfactory and Charlotte says, a bit later, *'I am quite tired of the Queen's trial.'* Little Tom goes out *'with his Grandpapa's hounds'* and on the 30th, when they walk into the garden, *'the Door fell down frame & all'*, which does not say much for the Ferne builders. John's daughter Henrietta now *'runs alone and says Papa'*.

In September, shooting starts. *'Waddington shot 8 brace of Partridges Tom 4 brace, John 1 brace, & George A Rook.'* Of more significance, William Helyar has gone to Coker Court *'as His Father died last Night'*. The following day, Harriet and Charlotte ascend Win Green, Harriet on her donkey: *'We had A particular conversation together'*. As William was his father's heir, they would be moving into Somerset.

Charlotte calls on Elizabeth Stretch. *'Her daughter Catherine Foot very ill. My Mother sent Her some Caudle & I did what I could for Her.'* Glancing through the list of monuments in our church, which is full of Foots, I cannot find a Catherine, but John Lane thinks she married a Foot not immediately attached to the Berwick Foots. Her real name was Christian, but she was called Catherine or Kitty. Some entries later I find her indisposition to be childbirth, and on the 26th, *'Kitty Foot was buried.'* Two days later, Charlotte takes some milk for the baby. As there was no notion of sterilising, bottle feeding was hazardous. Do you remember in *Great Expectations*, Pip's sister was admired for 'bringing him up by hand'? This signifies he survived without a wet nurse, a rarity. Was Elizabeth a daughter-in-law of the late Betty? Later, on October 15th, Charlotte comments on Kitty Foot's baby being very ill. By the 28th, it is better again.

On the 13th, they go to stay with the Farquharsons at Langton. I went to Tarrant Gunville to the horse show in August 2017, which I discovered to be held in the grounds of Eastbury House. According to

Desmond Hawkins, J.J. Farquharson, the foxhunting brother-in-law of Tom Grove, bought this house, or the remains of it, because it was much larger, in 1807. An old gentleman I fell into conversation with while waiting for my granddaughter to do her bit with the pony told me Farquharsons live there now. I cannot remember Charlotte saying she ever goes there. Desmond Hawkins says Tom and Henrietta lived at *'Gunville'* until 1810, so before Charlotte's journals commence.

September 14th *'Mr Knight came to paint Mr & Mrs Farquharsons Pictures, My Mother & I amused in seeing it done…Mr F's picture is very much like.'* So far I can find no mention of this artist.

Tom and Henrietta call on them while they were at Langton, but where were they living now they were not at Ashcombe? Hawkins suggests they were at Littleton until 1815, but we are now in 1820.

On the 19th, they go off to stay with Sir Richard and Lady Glyn at Gaunts. It is so wet they play battledore, presumably indoors. The evening entertainment is the game of loo, but Charlotte and her parents read their books.

At home, Aunt Grove arrives, as does Charles Jackson. Charlotte suspects the latter of siding with the Queen, whose trial still rumbles on. The Waddingtons have a governess called Miss Layard. *'My Aunt thinks the same of Miss Layard that We do.'* She is obviously not popular, though she entertained them with singing. Baby Charles is cutting teeth. George gave a dinner to the *'Hindon troop'*. He is a cornet, the most junior rank of cavalry officer. There were locally raised regiments long after the threat of the French invasion had subsided. They go to stay at Wincombe for a couple of nights, *'The dear Children so happy to see Us.'* On October 1st they return to Ferne, bringing *'The Nurse, & dear little Charles with Us.'*

On the 4th, *'little Tom Waddington rode over to see us'*. He was the Waddingtons' fifth child, so I wondered how old he was. I put his name, Thomas Grove Waddington, into an Internet search and find the 'East Meon Burials'. It is full of Waddingtons, living at Langrish or Langrish

House, including John Horsey Waddington, Charlotte's brother-in-law, and there find little Tom who died on 5th May 1846, age thirty-two. This makes his birth in 1814 and thus six when riding from Wincombe to Ferne: little indeed! Brother George lived to be fifty-seven, so born in 1811, and John, the eldest boy, lived to be seventy-one and was born in 1809. Though I was sad to think of our intrepid mini horseman dying so young, I was delighted to be able to calculate the ages of Charlotte's motherless nephews and nieces, apart from Caroline, but she came between George and Thomas. Thus in 1820, where we are now, Emma is thirteen, John is eleven, George nine, Caroline seven or eight and Thomas six. Frederick died as a baby and we, or rather you, have yet to learn about Charles, but he was born in the April of 1819, so he is now eighteen months. Langrish House is now a hotel.

Charlotte, George and William and their parents go off for a brief sojourn to Zeals, only two nights. One wonders at the trouble of getting there, some in the coach, Mr Grove and George riding.

On the 11th, they go again to Wincombe: *'Miss Layard made poor Emma cry, & again made A strange speech about Me.'* There is definitely something odd about Miss Layard.

Harriet comes for a few days with some of the children. She now has William, Carey, Agnes, Ellen, Albert and Marianne, known as Marian. There are many more to come. Keeping all these children healthy was the major anxiety. Charles Waddington, at Ferne, is constantly teething or not quite well or a great deal better. He was something of a surrogate child for Charlotte. She says, *'He is my Darling'*. Miss Layard takes *'little Tom'* to Salisbury to get advice from his uncle John.

October 23rd *'Harriet rode her Donkey. She made various noises to get it on – I walked by her side.'* Charlotte never thinks much of donkeys.

The business of the Queen is still uppermost. October 26th *'The Queens council is now finished, & it will be extraordinary if She is not found Guilty.'* Charlotte was on the side of morality, but there was not much of that, George IV having but a hazy notion of it; in those days infidelity was considered a much worse crime in women. Does this attitude yet linger or do I imagine it?

On the last day of the month, Mr Grove and William Helyar *'were both sworn in again as Justices'*.

All male members of the family are taken up with hunting or shooting or both, a great preoccupation. Emma Waddington had measles but made a fairly rapid recovery.

November 5th *'My Uncle Pilfold came, who we had not seen for 9 years.'* This was her mother's brother John, who was married to Mary Ann South. The Internet informs me the Pilfolds were of modest descent, yeoman farmers. It also says he married Mary Ann Horner, but in the family tree given by John Lane it sites South, and as Charlotte has him visiting his brother-in-law of that name, living at Charlton, I am more inclined to believe it was South rather than Horner. This was the Mr South who served as land agent to the Groves and was involved in the business of Ashcombe but there was Mr South and Mr G South, so it gets confusing.

John Pilfold had a distinguished career in the Navy. Whilst only a lieutenant, he commanded HMS *Ajax* at the battle of Trafalgar, the ship's captain away as a witness at the court marshal of Sir Robert Calder, but he had seen a vast amount of action previous to that. It is worth looking him up. He was soon out hunting with Charlotte's brothers and her father. On the 9th he leaves Ferne, *'accompanied by the Setter Bango, whom my Brother has given Him'*.

At Talbots, Charlotte *'bought A pretty pink Rosette for My Darling Charles'*.

November 11th *'We heard the Bill of the Queen, is thrown out of the House of Lords.'* The majority was too small and it was abandoned. Passions were high for and against, but the populace were generally in her favour, and on the 13th the church bells were rung in celebration. Charlotte complains of Mr John Helyar coming from Bath and *'talks incessantly about the Queen'*. The Groves were sure she was guilty.

Most of the Waddington children get the measles but recover again. Charlotte worries little Charles, residing at Ferne, *'is not breeding the measles'*.

November 22nd *'I played with dear little Charles. He wanted to have his own way But I will take care & not spoil Him.'* The Bromleys are staying with them. *'Mr Bromley very goodhumordly danced about the room with little Charles.'*

On the 30th, Charlotte calls on Sally Lush. *'She expects to be confined in March when I must have another Washerwomen.'* It is difficult to puzzle out these families. I think of the Lushes building Upton Lucy, not doing other peoples' washing, but there were more than one lot of Lushes. Did they have no laundry at Ferne? She engages Mrs Wilkins of Lower Donhead as her washer woman, definitely making independent arrangements. In the end papers for this year, the paying for washing is recorded for the month of March, but Charlotte is away at Sedgehill for much of that.

Elizabeth Stretch is subject to spasms: I imagine she was epileptic.

December 2nd *'Miss Layard came here intending to go to Town But My Father stopped her wild freak.'* A few days later, *'Miss Layard was very ill after her frisk.'*

George Waddington is home from school, as he has whooping cough. John *'likes Harrow very much'*. The Waddingtons come and go. *'John had a fine game of Romps with his Father.'*

On the 8th, Charlotte visits Dame Pinnock, who is spinning wool she gleaned from *'the bushes the Sheep had scattered'*. She is making a blanket for her brother. There is much village visiting, to the Rawlins' cottage, Mary and Byth Pinnock's and Sarah Blandford. Elizabeth Parsons, Oldy's daughter, is due to be confined.

November 19th *'I accompanied My Mother to Wardoar.'* There are friends and relations. They dance waltzes, quadrilles and country dances. *'I played some of the time.'*

Charlotte then comments further on Elizabeth Parsons. On Tuesday the 19th, she has been in labour since Saturday. On the 20th, she has a son. On the morning of the 24th, both mother and child die. Charlotte says, *'I viewed the corpses.'* This seems to have been obligatory. The funeral took place two days later.

Aunt Grove has given money *'for the poor people'*. Charlotte spends it at Talbots on blankets and petticoats. Arabella Jackson is staying with the Foots, but she goes twice to Salisbury with William and George to attend the balls there. Charlotte does not accompany them. Arabella must have had a chaperone of some sort. I think Charlotte now prefers home entertainment. They have the son and daughters of Mr Blackmore, the Rector of Upper Donhead, to dinner and they dance as they had at Wardour a few days earlier.

December 28th *'I accompanied Harriet to Berwick & We called upon Mrs Foot. Saw Arabella, Miss Foot & some rather vulgar Gentlemen.'* This hints so nicely at the differences between the Jacksons and the Groves, first cousins or not.

The end papers for this year do not reveal much, mostly her expenses when away. There are still references to the stay-maker in Bath, obviously an ongoing need for these instruments of torture. There was a linen draper called Paines in the Market Place in Salisbury. Charlotte lists speeches taken from Shakespeare and some poems, sixteen in all, that she *'repeats by heart'*. The last is *'Monody dear Emma'*. A monody is a poem lamenting a death.

1821

Charlotte notes at the start *'Jeu d'esprit of My Fathers'*.

> They may hang Her or drown Her,
> Divorce her, or Crown Her,
> But talk not of the Queen.
> For it gives Me the Spleen.

Charlotte also made a special note of the death of Napoleon on May 5th. *'He was opened and his disorder was a Cancer in the Stomach.'* No conspiracy theories here, no lead in the paint or poison. She conceded he was *'a great Man'*.

At the beginning of January, Charlotte is still at Sedgehill with her sister. January 1st *'We met little George Waddington with Richard riding upon the Turnpike Road. Settled he should ride here Tomorrow instead of Our fetching Him in the Carriage.'* There is beginning to be mention of Richard, who I take to be a groom employed by Mr Waddington. George is still recovering from whooping cough. The following day they walk to Knoyle. Harriet buys a shawl as a present for the Knoyle schoolmistress.

Snow prevents them from going to dine with the Twopennys, though William Helyar goes. *'We played with the Children & enjoyed Ourselves very much.'*

On the 5th, the Twopennys and Miss and Mr Short dine with them *'notwithstanding the bad weather'*. They get a Mr Turner from Knoyle to play for them, and they dance the usual waltzes and Quadrilles. *'I enjoyed it very much indeed.'*

January 6th *'I whipped Albert as He was very naughty.'*

She and her brother George go home the next day. Charlotte has given baby Charles a knife and fork. *'He feeds himself quite cleverly.'*

Waddingtons and Jacksons of all ages come and go. Mr Grove takes his grandson John out *'foot hunting'*, which means the ground is too frozen for horses. Charlotte visits in the village and plans to ask Mrs Pinnock about the knitting of worsted stockings. William and George go off to balls, Salisbury or Blandford, but Charlotte does not go with them. She has her niece Emma to stay. John Waddington returns to Harrow. A new Berwick name arises, Dorimede. He is ill. An order is got to admit him to Salisbury Infirmary, but he dies there a few days later of *'an Abscess of the lungs'*, leaving a widow and two small children.

Baby Charles is still at Ferne. He is often poorly. His uncle John prescribes for him. They hear that Tom's wife, Henrietta, is *'alarmingly ill'*, so John goes off to Weymouth in order to see her.

January 31st *'Called upon Mrs Pinnock. By Her account I fear that Mary Stretch has been hurt by the Methodists.'* Methodism really was a cause for deep disapproval. Charlotte goes on to say, *'Mrs James Foote was buried at Berwick.'*

In the evening they are enjoying *'Kenilworth'*.

In February, John returns from Weymouth with the information that Henrietta has mumps. Over the next few days, the accounts of her grow worse.

February 6th *'My Father Mother & Waddington went to Weymouth. They called at Langton in their way. I received the sad News that Mrs Tho' Grove died on Monday Morning last. Old Mrs Farquharson is at Langton & bears it with the greatest resignation.'*

Charlotte takes some solitary walks on the forthcoming days. Mrs James, the bailiff's wife from Ashcombe, comes to *'speak to Me about her Mourning'*. Mr and Mrs Grove return on the 10th, Charlotte's thirty-eighth birthday, leaving Waddington to remain with Tom. Charlotte has been left some topaz brooches.

Ally Brockway comes to Charlotte for orders *'about my Mourning'*. She gives her *'My Brown silk Gown'*. This was, I take it, to be dyed. They are reading *Pride and Prejudice*.

February 15th *'My Brothers Dr. Grove William & George went to Langton to attend My dear Sister Mrs. Thomas Groves Funeral. The Pall is to be borne by 6 Gentlemen, Relations of the Deceased, my three Brothers, Capt. Donaldson Mr Waddington & Capt. Fraser. It was to take place at 7 O'clock in the Evening.'* Henrietta had requested her funeral should take place by torchlight.

February 16th *'My Brothers returned from Langton. Mr Farquharson & my Brother went through the Mournful Ceremony with great fortitude.'* This reinforces my general opinion that it was unusual for women to attend funerals. Henrietta's father attends but not her mother.

February 16th *'I walked to Ashcombe, saw Mrs James…She & her Husband feel the loss of their kind Mistress very much.'*

Otherwise, babies are arriving in Berwick, one to Sally Lush and one to Mary Stretch.

March 1st *'I called on Oldy. Her Son in Law is going to be married again, which vexes the old lady much.'*

Tom is visiting them. March 2nd *'My dear Brother Tom seems better in his spirits. We played with little Charles, He is quite diverted with the Songs his Grandmama & I sing to him. His Grandpapa takes A great deal of notice of the Darling child.'* There is still anxiety over his health. His uncle John *'is fearful about Charles's complaint. I hope & trust it is only occasioned by the fever attendant on Teething.'* His grandfather gives him *'A Newfoundland Dog & A Sailor riding it'* and John's wife Jane *'a set of tea things'*. On the 9th, *'I amused Myself with running after Charles in the*

Go Cart.' Earlier she has said, *'Charles walked in the Gocart.'* I tried the Internet for the history of the go-cart, but there was nothing beyond the mechanical racing sort. It must have been a sort of baby walker.

Though it is March, there is still plenty of hunting for Mr Grove, his sons and his sons-in-law. Charlotte has an inflammation of the eye that she treats with Hannah Burden's eye water, which is painful but seems to work.

Ferne is the hub for the family, Tom going to Langton, Waddington to Wincombe, sometimes William Helyar or Dr Grove to Salisbury, but they all return again, including Jacksons and various children. Emma Waddington, now fourteen, occasionally beats her aunt Charlotte at chess. The rector's wife, Mrs Bingham, rarely wins but is constantly required to play.

On March 21st, their friends the Knellers leave Donhead Hall. Later Charlotte says, *'many of Mr Knellers labourers are in great distress for their money.'* It is apparent the Knellers left under a cloud.

There is a hint of courtship. George attended a ball in Salisbury to *'dance with A certain fair lady'*. Laetitia Popham visits them after an absence of nearly four years. The eldest Helyar boy, William, goes to school at Dr Radcliffe's in Salisbury. Charlotte shows her father a *'yarn stocking'* Mrs Pinnock made for her brother and he commissions six pairs to be made from his own wool. In a week or so, Mrs Pinnock starts spinning the yarn.

April 3rd *'My dear little Charles Waddingtons Birth Day. He is two years old.'* It is also the birthday of his brother Tom, who is now seven.

Charlotte meets *'old Mary Pinnock going to Haskels shop. She was much fatigued being 87 & I assisted her up the Hill.'* Mrs Grove sends her some caudle, which was a drink made with warm ale or wine, eggs, sugar and spices. Mary Pinnock dies a month later. *'Old Mary Pinnock is dead which I am happy to hear as She was very old.'* It must be a younger Mrs Pinnock commissioned to make the stockings.

Not much occurs for the next few weeks: the normal visits, the much-regretted departure of Miss Popham and the news of the death of a Pilfold cousin, Elizabeth, the daughter of James Pilfold. When Charlotte has been away, I believe, she makes a beeline for *'dear little Charles'* and *'detained so long by our little Beau in the Nursery it quite offended the other Gentlemen'*.

Donhead Hall now being empty it is an object of curiosity. Charlotte goes to see some portraits left there and talks to the old gardener. *'A very pretty Moss House made by him'*. I find there was one of these at Belvoir Castle made around this time by the fifth Duchess of Rutland.

A short visit with her mother to Harriet ends on 3rd May with the comment *'We left Sedgehill with regret being our last visit to my dear Brother & Sister.'* The Helyars would now be moving to Coker Court in Somerset. On returning to Ferne, they found their expected visitors, Mrs Grove's brother John Pilfold, and his daughter Emma.

May 12th *'I walked with Emma P to Berwick called upon Oldy &c on our return found Miss Layard & Emma here the former in great affliction as the Girls are going to School.'*

The younger Mrs Pinnock has nearly finished a pair of the yarn stockings. A new name appears, Lee Wadly, to whom Charlotte takes some baby clothes. Charlotte thinks Mary Stretch has a tumour in her side that she has kept secret.

May 17th *'A wet day. Amused Ourselves with playing with Charles. My Father & George after Dinner fancied They had found out the perpetual Motion.'* Charlotte, one can tell, is not impressed.

Edward Bingham, the rector's son, who was in the Navy, came to take leave of them before *'He sails in the Il Librador'*.

May 22nd *'I walked to L. Donhead. I called upon Mrs Dansey, Mr Dansey came in whilst I was there & showed me his Farm House & Dairy. We also went into the Church in which they are putting new Pews & A Gallery erected by Mr Warburton.'* Mr Dansey became Rector of Donhead St Andrew in 1820. According to Desmond Hawkins, he married the youngest daughter of Mr Blackmore, Rector of the other Donhead, but not until 1849. This is a previous wife. Farming was an essential part of a rural clergyman's income. Hawkins makes no mention of Mr Warburton.

Emma Pilfold is still with them. She has been lent a donkey which gives the usual trouble: *'The donkey was very obstinate at one place & if We had not met with A Man to assist Us We never could have got it on.'*

Emma has her seventeenth birthday on the 31st. That day, Charlotte walks and Emma rides the donkey to Ashcombe. *'I showed My Cousin the ruins of the House.'* Ashcombe really is no more but the reasons for demolishing it remain a mystery. The Arundells seemed to have let Wardour and have taken up residence in *'the Priests House at Birdsey'* where Mrs Grove, Charlotte and Emma visit them.

The Lower Donhead band coming to play for them on Whit Monday, June 11th. This was a holiday until 1972.

On June 18th, *'heard Mrs Lush of the Farm is very ill & and not expected to live'*. This is the wife of John Lush, who farmed a large part of the parish, including Upton for Mr Grove. On the 20th, *'The Invalid begged to see me. She is very ill But not so swelled with the Dropsy as I had heard.'* She dies *'about 12 o'clock noon'* the following day. Her death is recorded in the list of church inscriptions compiled by Mr Goodchild. Her name was Elizabeth. She was fifty-six.

At this period, Charlotte seems more preoccupied with visits to her poorer neighbours than with her own social life, their existence often an endless battle against ill health. Babies abound. *'I called on Rawkins and found his Wife in labour.'* Charlotte is alarmed for her and sends for Mr Wills, *'But luckily before He could arrive Christian Wilkins brought the little Girl into the World.'* Charlotte adds she was amused by her cousin's *'explanations'*. I cannot help thinking Miss Pilfold will leave Ferne knowing rather more than when she came.

The embarrassment of the Knellers' too hasty departure rumbles on. *'Mr Knellers Wine sold well.'* I am interested in Charlotte's lack of comment on the Knellers' predicament, moral or otherwise, for they had known them very well. Or does she choose not to commit such things to paper?

On July 1st, all the Waddingtons come to spend the day. Charlotte takes her nieces to church but *'My Mother quite unwell & sadly annoyed by Miss L.'* What was it about Miss Layard?

It was probably not strange for the period for the youngest Waddington to be in the care of his grandparents rather than living with his own family. Charlotte's brother-in-law has been away so *'little Charles looked rather shy upon his Papa, not having seen him for 3 months.'* Charlotte records his accomplishments like a proud parent: *'dear little Charles said Pink Cockade & spelt Boy.'* As he is only two, it is interesting he was in a position to spell anything.

July 9th *'Waddington, Emma & George left Us for Bishopstoke. I hope the latter will succeed in his election into the foundation of Winchester School.'* So it seems George is not intended to follow John to Harrow. On the 14th we learn he has not got a place at Winchester.

Charlotte goes to Lower Donhead to engage a Mrs Read to accompany Emma Pilfold back to Sussex at the beginning of August. Charlotte, with her usual blunt assessment of children not of Grove descent, says of Mrs Bingham's grandchildren: *'the little boy looks unhealthy and The Girl delicate.'*

The coronation of George IV takes place on the 19th. *'The Mail came down with A white Flag & Red Ribbons.'* Tom gives Charlotte his newspaper's full of accounts of the event and Mrs Farquharson sent another with pictures in it. Such was life before the invention of the camera, let alone the television.

The Queen really was the preoccupation of the 1820s, but it was soon to end. Charlotte says in her frontispiece for this year *'July 19th The Coronation – The Queen attempted to get into the Abbey. But was refused admittance. Cries from the People of close the Gates.'* The mob had turned against her. *'Go back to Como (the scene of her Iniquity &c).'* She still had a few supporters, who Charlotte tells us broke some windows, but Charlotte herself says, *'Indeed she tried to do all the mischief She possibly could. The King went through the Ceremony very gracefully & with the heartfelt Acclamation of his People.'* This is an interesting take on the coronation of George IV. He spent twenty-four thousand pounds on his coronation robes, which had a train twenty-seven feet long, and ordered a new crown, which was covered in 12,314 hired diamonds, all of which was considered disgracefully extravagant. Though not without charm, he was far from popular. I have been told that the conduct of Edward VIII concerning Mrs Simpson and his subsequent abdication took the country, as a whole, by surprise, the gossip not extending much beyond London. Perhaps it was thus with George IV, though the cartoons of the period make our modern equivalent look very tame: they were outrageous. The Queen's death on August 7th is also mentioned here but without further comment beyond her having an *'Inflammation of the Bowells'*. But Charlotte records it in its correct place in her journal.

On August 6th *'The Queen Consort is very ill & in great danger.'* She still seems to have been given her full title despite the debacle of her trial and her attempts to get into the Abbey. Her body was to be returned to Brunswick. It was decided to have the funeral cortège take a route to avoid the City, but the mob accompanying it was incensed, blockaded half the streets and threw brickbats at the soldiers, so it had to go through the City after all. Two men were killed such was the violence. William and George were disappointed about a ball during the Salisbury races that was cancelled in respect of the Queen's death.

Charles Grove and his wife are to take a cottage at Upper Donhead. His curacy at Bighton must be ending, but it is a bit puzzling.

Charlotte goes with her parents on a visit to their Long relations at Marwell Hall and Preshaw, seeing Aunt Grove at Netherhampton as they go, the latter with her leg up on the sofa having had an accident. They return to find little Charles ill. Dr Grove declared him to have *'The Stone…But A very small one, & I hope & trust though the goodness of Providence He may yet be saved.'* This was, I presume, a kidney stone.

The next day, *'It is my sincere Prayer to Almighty God this darling Child may recover from this sad Disorder.'*

Despite this anxiety, they are off to Netherhampton the following day, the 22nd, and they attend various concerts in the cathedral, including the Messiah. The Waddingtons are there. Tom Waddington is at school in Salisbury and is duly visited as is young William Helyar. They return on the 25th. Charles, though better, is again troubled with his teeth.

There is the usual coming and going of brothers, Waddingtons and Jacksons. Arabella Jackson has a *'Lover Mr Walsh. A very gentlemanlike young Man.'* Do not be tempted to put a modern interpretation on the word 'lover'. Charlotte is asked to be godmother to the Marklands' latest child, Duff Hoste Markland. Caroline Waddington *'set off for school in good spirits'*.

It is decided between Dr Grove and Waddington that little Charles should be sent to London to be under the care of a Mr Abernethy. *'I offered to go up to Town with my Darling But Waddington will not accept of my services.'*

September 13th *'My Mother tried to take A Sketch of dear little Charles.'*

September 17th *'My darling little Charles with his Nurses left Us for Town, to Our very great regret. I fear that I shall never see my dear Boy again.'* Charlotte was obviously upset at the departure of this child, but she is not one to dwell on misfortune.

September 21st *'My Father is planning a new road to the House.'*

September 23rd *'My brother George met with A disappointment. Want of money being the Obstacle to his wishes.'* There is no name mentioned. Though George has his farm at East Hayes it is, on this occasion, obviously not considered sufficient to satisfy the family of whoever it was he was wishing to marry.

The habit of families using the same Christian names is useful in as much it helps in attaching them to the correct set of relatives, but it is confusing when sorting the generations. The rector was Peregrine Bingham, as was his son. The younger Peregrine's wife and children often stay at the Rectory, and Charlotte walks with *'Mrs P Bingham'*. They are visited by Sir Thomas Salisbury. I try to find who this was. It seems the name is sometimes Salusbury, but they are all called Thomas. An early one was executed for his part in the Babington Plot. There was one who is described as a solicitor born in Giggleswick in Yorkshire but married in Salisbury Cathedral in 1795. He died in 1810. This one could be his son.

Over September, Mr Grove is endeavouring to get in the wheat. The poor people glean, walking over the fields of stubble to pick up stray ears of corn. We hardly hear of this except in the Bible, but the word has stayed in our vocabulary with a slightly different use.

September 26th *'I received A Letter from Mrs Cadbury where dear little Charles lodges saying he has Recovered his Journey But has now three teeth coming through the Gums.'*

September 27th *'I walked to Talbots. Dr Foot was found drowned near his own house.'* Charlotte says no more than this. Was Dr Foot living here and drowned in the bit of pond at the top of Water Street or the pond that used to be on the site of Pond Cottages? He is not mentioned as having an inscription on a monument here. If he was deemed to have committed suicide, he would probably have been excluded from the churchyard. John Lane says a Robert Foot was buried in Donhead St Mary on 30th September 1821, aged sixty-four, so surely this one is not a Berwick Foot at all.

October 1st *'My Cousin Arabella Jackson was married today to Mr Walsh, an excellent Match for Her.'* This definitely means she is marrying someone with an established income and no nonsense. *'My sincerest Wishes for their Happiness. They sent Us some Bride Cake & We drank their health.'* Weddings were private affairs, no question of the Groves attending. Charlotte goes the following day to Coombe Priory, a house still in existence in the Coombs, where her aunt had moved after the death of her husband, to congratulate her on Arabella's marriage.

On October 9th, Mr Grove has his tenants to dinner. Charlotte dines with her mother in the library, it apparently not being an occasion for women. Charles and his wife, Eliza, arrive. They have the Binghams, senior and junior, to dinner. Mrs Peregrine *played and sung most delightfully from the Irish Melodies*.

October 12th *'I accompanied Eliza to her Cottage'*. I do wonder more and more about this word cottage. The very substantial house where I grew up in Maiden Bradley was called the Cottage. It belonged to the Duke of Somerset. My mother thought the name so ridiculous they agreed to change it. *'My sister very much delighted with her new Abode. Indeed she seems A happy temper & pleased with every thing. I introduced them to Lizzy Imber to wash for them.'* Later, Charlotte tries out Eliza's *'piano forte'* and *'Eliza much pleased with Her new Parlour & Kitchen.'* This 'cottage' was in Upper Donhead, but I should like to know where. At one point she refers to it as Grove Cottage. Charlotte takes Eliza to Talbots *'to buy some thick Shoes to wear over her Boots'*. I cannot visualise these.

October 16th *'My Father made A mistake in My allowance by which I have lost A Quarter Pay this year.'* She goes on to happily reflect on not owing *'one Farthing in the World'*. This day's entry concludes with an ominous reference to the youngest Waddington. *'Sad news from Town relative to my dear little Charles. He is too weak to undergo the Operation & I hope will soon be relieved from all his sufferings.'* I wonder how an operation of any sort could be performed on a two-year-old child without anaesthetic of any description. Three days later, they get news from Mrs Cadbury: *'dear little Charles is still so very ill that Mr Abernethy dares not perform the operation. My letter pleased the darling child so much that He held it in his Hand all the Day afterwards, & would only be raised out of his dosing state when I or His Grandmama were mentioned.'*

On the 20th they have *'The Harvest Home'*. *'A very wet Day, however the People enjoyed themselves very much in the Coach House.'* Otherwise, E Stretch's daughter has fallen down in a fit and fractured her skull, and two of her sons are *'also ill in a Fever'*.

On the 22nd, *'My Mother has invited Company here, though I think My dearest little Charles is still in A very precarious state.'* This is a rare occasion for Charlotte to be at odds with her mother.

On October 23rd, they get another letter telling them Charles *'gets gradually weaker. This sad news made Me very low all Day. This constant anxiety is worse than to hear the darling child was released from all his sufferings.'*

There is a little hope when Waddington writes on Sunday the 27th, to Charlotte's joy, that the child is to return to Ferne the following Tuesday. *'I am glad I shall have my Darling again.'* By Tuesday he is *'too weak at Present to be moved'*.

Charlotte is watching the post the first few days of November, but they hear nothing until the 4th, saying *'little Charles is gradually declining'* and on the 6th, *'A letter from Waddington. My darling Nephew & Godson, Charles Waddington, expired last Saturday evening, most thankful am I to Almighty God for releasing the little Angel from all his sufferings.'* There was a greater sense of accepting the inevitable than we have now. Charlotte puts on mourning. She relates the child's burial in Walcheren Church *'with His Mother, & Brother Frederick (& has joined in that Heaven most fitted for them all).'* The name of the church is confusing and obviously wrong. I have made a reference to it relative to Emma's death in June of 1819, where Charlotte makes no mention of Emma's actual place of burial.

Waddington arrives. Charles had been *'opened'* after his death and *'A stone taken from him as large as a Bantam's egg. His kidneys were much affected also.'* Charlotte knows he could not have lived and is relieved *'he was so soon released'*. *'Some Play things, I shall keep forever for his sake.'*

November 9th *'Charles & George went to Tarrant Hinton to see the Parsonage of that Place as the former has thoughts of being Curate. Mr Cory the Rector was not there.'* As they were looking at the parsonage, it sounds as if the rector was to reside elsewhere. This would possibly mean it was an advance on Bighton, where Charles had had to live at Alresford.

November 15th *'The New Road is cut from the House & I like it very much.'* Is this the current driveway? If so, where was the original entrance? Francis thinks the lodges at Ferne were built around the 1870s, so long after this period. The following day, Charlotte takes a walk on it and also announces that *'Dear Tom'* has given Harriet his *'Barouchette'*. This was a four-wheeled vehicle with a fold-down hood, a lighter version of the barouche.

November 21st *'I walked part of the way to Donhead Lodge met Capt. Haines who told Me his Wife was gone out, therefore it was useless to proceed any further.'* Desmond Hawkins makes no mention of this family. Donhead Lodge was the original home of the Cookes but was sold by them in 1813.

Charles and Eliza are now established in their 'cottage'. Charlotte says, *'Mr Bingham thinks Mr Phillip Ridout will serve Charles's Curacy.'*

Though Charlotte is devoted to the family, she again comments on being very happy when she is alone with her parents: *'our comfortable little trio'.* She usually records what they read aloud in the evenings.

November 26th *'By the assistance of Dr Leydens beautiful Poetry I have arranged A Monody to my dearest departed Nephew, little Charles Waddington. My Mother has planned A sweet Picture of Emma & her Angel Children.'* The monody has not been recorded in the end papers, but Dr Leyden was the son of a Scottish shepherd who had saved up to send his son to Edinburgh University in the hope of making him a parson. He was, I discover, a prodigy, learning most of the Bible by heart at the age of eight! A donkey was purchased on which he was to ride to school, and a part of the deal with the donkey included an old book, which turned out to be a dictionary of eight languages, all of which Leyden learnt. He went to university, became a friend of Walter Scott, took no interest in becoming a parson, wrote poetry, qualified to become a doctor in six months and died in Java in 1811 from a fever aged thirty-six, able to speak forty languages. I know this is a diversion, but why do we not hear rather more of Dr Leyden?

Charlotte spends some time looking out for servants for Harriet, to the amusement of her Jackson cousin: *'Fanny entertained with My strenuous exertions in the Cause.'* Her father has his sixty-third birthday and John's wife, Jane, has a son, Thomas Fraser, the eventual heir to Ferne.

December 3rd *'A very wet day. My Brother & Sister unable to return to their Cottage. We amused Ourselves with dancing Quadrille steps about the Room. Charles in high spirits not with standing this battle & expense of moving Houses.'* Charles and his father go to Blandford and Tarrant Hinton. They are soon packing up the cottage in preparation for moving to the latter, their goods to be conveyed in *'My Father's wagon'*. They have only been in it a month or two.

Catherine Benett, who Charlotte feared was turning into a Catholic, married Mr Stanton Corry, a widower with two sons. (He was actually Stanford Carroll, according to John Lane.) Mr Grove pays Charlotte her *'St Thomas Day Allowance'*. Waddington has gone to fetch his children from school. Mrs Lush (but which one?) was knocked over by Mr Gold's horse. Charlotte recommended her to see Mr Wills, and it was discovered she had broken a rib. The name Gold is sometimes Gould in the diaries.

'John and little Tom Waddington arrived at our Breakfast time.' John is soon out hunting with his grandfather but Tom has bad chilblains and *'is obliged to keep in the House'*. The children's old nurse Molly is staying. Charlotte visits her in the nursery *'But it gives My Heart A pang whenever I go there thinking of My lost darling Child.'* They are soon joined by Emma, Caroline and George.

December 17th *'Charles rode to Tarrant Hinton. The Upholsterer is very dilatory in getting in the Furniture.'* It is no better by the 21st.

December 23rd *'I accompanied Waddington & My Nephews & Niece to Church. It is fixed that They are to go to Wincombe for A Week at which I am much vexed.'* I like that old fashioned word vexed, which has gone out of use, I suppose. Charlotte longed for the children.

The next day Tom calls on them. *'My Mother & Him did not agree very well as He rhodomontaded A little.'* There is another word that has gone out, meaning exaggerated and rather boastful talk.

At Christmas, the servants have a dance. Mrs Grove *'drew all the little Waddingtons in one Picture'*. I wonder if any of her drawings ever survived.

*

The end papers for this year are brief though they include (sensibly not included by John Lane) the texts of all the sermons, Sunday by Sunday. There are certain other quotes from the Bible. More frivolously, Charlotte *'Laid A Bet of A Shilling with George that He would not have 40 sacks of Beans in his Field'*. She records receiving ten pounds from her father in October, but I take this to be a quarterly payment.

1823

There is no journal for 1822, so we have a sudden gap. What happened to it? Strangely, having been to the archives, I think can tell you, unlike for the diaries for 1827 and 1830. Charlotte had the complete, unused diary for 1822 but she did not fill it in. We have no idea why not. Why stop abruptly on 31st December 1821 and start again, with equal precision on 1st January 1823? What happened in that absent year? However, I did not at the time actually look at this empty diary, so does it actually exist? I cannot tell without going there again.

Presumably, Charles and Eliza moved to Tarrant Hinton. The year 1823 opens with Waddington and Tom getting an invitation from Wadham Wyndham, an MP for Salisbury, to dine at his house with the actor, Edmund Kean, and to see him perform King Lear at the Salisbury Theatre. Kean (1787–1833) first went on the stage as Cupid when he was four, but he had a mixed career. Sarah Siddons said, 'he played very, very well' but 'there was too little of him to make a great actor'. Despite his short stature he was famed for his Shakespearean roles.

Emma Waddington is staying and much chess is played. Charlotte is seeing E Stretch: *'I shall be glad when that poor Sufferer is released.'* Our forebears were more open than we are on the necessity of dying. She also sees *'Widow Kelly who was brought to Bed Sunday of A fine little Boy.'*

We do not know what happened to Mr Kelly. There is concern over the health of Mrs Walsh, her cousin Arabella.

January 5th *'I accompanied My Nephews & Nieces to Church. It is reported in the Papers that Our King is to be married to Lady Elizabeth Cunningham.'* This seems an odd rumour because though Lady Elizabeth Conyngham was his mistress, her husband did not die until 1832. Charlotte goes on to say, *'My Nephews & Nieces sat up late recounting their notable exploits at School.'*

There are various new names, Miss Auber and Master Onslow. Gordons are returned. *'Mr Gordon called upon Us. He is grown very fat.'* William *'is returned home from Hunting in Dorsetshire'*. He is soon off to Langton for the same purpose, but *'I think the Frost will prevent him.'* She was quite right. There is no mention of the Navy now, William devoted to hunting.

January 10th *'I walked with Emma to Mrs Davys. She has twenty Scholars in her School.'* This is frustrating information, as we do not know where this school was or even in which village. Sarah Pinnock had a Sunday school; Charlotte had provided her with a *'Bible & Prayer Book'*. I believe this to have been in Berwick.

Emma Waddington is as keen on chess as her aunt. We get glimpses of the others. *'My Nephew George Grove Waddington is an entertaining little Fellow.'* He is now twelve. They dance quadrilles and Charlotte entertains them on the piano. *'We keep rather late hours now the Waddington Family are here.'* As the Gordons are back, the Waddingtons must have had to give up Wincombe.

As the month progresses, Charlotte is regularly visiting E Stretch. She is light-headed and does not recognise her. The husband has sent for Mr Heard but Charlotte says, *'he is not very skilful'*. On another day, *'she is not at all the better for Mr Heard's prescription'*. She dies on the 27th.

January 17th *'I walked to Upper Donhead, called upon Brockway, & gave him another 5s of My Aunts kind donation. The old Man seemed pleased to talk of the Kneller Family with whom he lived so many years.'* Charlotte never breathes a word in her journal any condemnation of the Knellers.

John Waddington is prevented for leaving for Harrow because the coach was full. He leaves the next day, delivering his brother Tom to *'Miss Noyes School'* en route, in Salisbury. John is now fourteen and Tom nine. It makes me reflect on the responsibilities and independence, or lack of them, we allow the current generation of children. The school was in the Close.

Emma had become a formidable player of chess. January 24th *'I played 4 games of chess with Emma & she won them all. I have made A resolution if I continue to play this Game, not to mind being beat.'*

January 28th *'Waddington & his two Daughters left Us. They went to Netherhampton on their way to Town. We were very sorry to part with them. It continues to rain & I am unable to take my walk. George sent to Tarrant Hinton for our Nephew George's poney, & He is not hurt by his late fall.'* The following day, young George goes out hunting and is laughed at for *'His poney running away with Him from the Hounds.'* On February 1st, he leaves them for Winchester. *'We missed Him very much in the Evening.'* So now he has a place at Winchester. I wonder why he is not sent to Harrow with John.

Both Charlotte's brothers George and William are living at Ferne. George has suffered from some illness as Charlotte remarks, *'I am in hopes he is recovering his Health again.'* This may account for his not being at East Hayes. The missing 1822 diary would have informed us. He buys himself a magnet and *'is going to try to find the Longitude'.*

Charlotte visits Oldy and Christian Chowne. I believe this to be the first mention of Chownes, though I may have missed one. I think of the 1840 map of Berwick, which shows that row of cottages in Water Street, on the right as you walk from the Cross, belonging to Chownes, hedge cottages, each put up in a day on waste-ground next to the highway, which enabled you to claim it your own. They characteristically abut straight onto the road. According to the map, there were five dwellings, which I think belonged to Christian Chown, Philip Chown, Samuel Chown, John Merchant and Robert Chown, but it is very difficult to see it properly. I imagine them getting together to build each one in a day, or at least an outer wall and roof. To bring us up to date, Holly View, where Chris and Melissa Wills live, was rebuilt by old Mrs Dineley, Francis' grandmother; he does not know to what extent. It seems most likely the Boyds' cottage was part of the whole. The Willses changed the name of theirs when the holly tree went.

They have a short visit from the Netherhampton aunt and Mrs Long from Marwell. February 6th *'A Woman named Cheveril had Twins, & her Husband being in Prison excited the kindness of Mrs Long & My Aunt Grove.'* Charlotte goes to Milkwell to deliver 16s and sees the twins, Sarah and Eliza. A few days later, she goes to *'Marshes shop'* to spend the money on their behalf, hoping she does it to *'the best advantage'*.

Charlotte now refers to having pupils, Emma Wicks and Harriet Hyscock. What is she teaching them? I think mostly sewing. She also mentions her *'club'*. This is certainly some arrangement for women in the village.

February 9th *'I walked to Mrs Whites, She is very unwell & has not so many Scholars in her school as she had.'* Another little school we do not know the location of. John Lane says a Mrs Sarah White had a school at Brookwater, so this seems very likely. It is apparent there were lots of 'dame schools' for rudimentary education. There were various schools run by religious bodies, but it was not until 1870 that an Act of Parliament was passed to give all children an education, regardless of denomination. In 1880, it became compulsory from ages five and ten, so fifty-seven years on.

On the 10th, Charlotte is forty. She gives thanks for her health and that of her parents.

We now move back to politics. Mr Portman of Bryanston has died, leaving a worthy son *'to inherit his vast property'*, though Mr Grove says, *'We shall now see what He is, when He acts for Himself.'* It seems Mr Banks of Kingston Lacy *'is canvassing for the County'*. As ever, it seems confusing. Young Mr Portman does not wish to stand in place of his father but that seems to be exactly what happens. Mr Banks withdraws and Mr Portman *'is now the Member for Dorsetshire'*.

In the meantime, Mrs Grove is sending *'Doveys Powders'* for Sarah Pinnock's cold and a *'little Kitchen physic'* to Edith Chowne, who has had the fever. This turns out to be *'Gentian'*. Charlotte speaks to her, cautiously, from *'the other side of the street'*. Her pupils are going to work *'A sampler in Silks for Me'*. Mrs Bingham has promised to employ them in Mrs Lush's school, so this must have been under the patronage of the rector's wife.

George continues to improve in health. His general condition does not prevent him going out with his father and *'the Hounds up White Sheet Hill, & got completely wet through'*.

On the 24th, *'A French Travelling Woman came to the Door, I had a little Conversation with her in her own Language. She was the Widow of a Soldier.'* French would have been a part of Charlotte's education, but I doubt she had much opportunity to practise it.

February 26th *'I went to C Chownes Cottage. The youngest Dorimede very much swelled all over, I desired them to send immediately for Mr Wills.'* He turns out to be William Dorymede. *'He has got the Dropsy.'*

Charlotte, at the beginning of March, declares George to have *'found out Perpetual Motion. I hope He will attain the Longitude.'* I think there must have been some sisterly latitude.

The various Lushes are definitely in different walks of life. There are some at Rowberry, in a neat cottage, the husband getting lots of work as a shoemaker. There is something called *'Hunts Powder'*. Charlotte says it is a good substitute for tea for poor people; is more nourishing and tastes of coffee. What was in it?

Charlotte had given George a book on chess. *'His study of Phillidor, makes Him more than a Match for Me.'* François-André Danican Philidor was a French composer. His book on chess was the standard manual for at least a century, and various chess moves are named after him.

March 9th *'A great deal of snow on the ground. I walked an hour in front of the House. My Father read Prayers to the Family, & I preached A Sermon, at first felt a little nervous being unused to it. George having so bad a cold he could not read.'* There were books of sermons from which to choose, but Charlotte does not tell us if she invented her own.

Miss Bowles sent Charlotte her *'Book of the Childrens Penny Club to look at, with patterns of their Frocks &c in it.'* The missing year of 1822 would probably have enlightened us on Charlotte's club. The general idea was women would give a penny on a regular basis. The accumulated money would then be used for buying blankets or other necessities. We hear more about this in later years. Charlotte, at forty, is moving away from society, the balls and the races. Her interest, after her family, increasingly moves towards the cottages and their occupants. New names appear, Joseph Hascal, a basket-maker, Jesse Abbots and Love Dibbin. They are often ill, attended on by Dr Foot. We know a Dr Foot drowned on 27th September 1821, but this is his son. Charlotte is put out by meeting *'Byth Pinnock who had been as far as Berwick begging'*. Charlotte's activities spread beyond the village, but where did the Pinnocks live? She tells her pupils to save the money they earn so she can buy them a *'frock'*, which they will make up themselves. Thomas Shere married again after losing his wife, so a new Mrs Shere is visited.

March 12th *'Mrs John Grove has another Son.'* This was John, their third child. Charlotte takes a greater interest in her sisters' children than in her brother's. Tom is often *'My dearest brother Tom'* but John is *'Dr Grove'*. She respects him as a doctor. She is certainly very fond of George. William is so busy foxhunting we only hear of his comings and goings, but he regularly attends church.

Most of the family, including Charlotte, have bad colds. Rich and poor have bad colds well into March. Mr Grove was sufficiently poorly for *'Dr Grove'* to be summoned. He hunts when he is well enough, so we see where William gets it from.

March 17th *'I walked to Berwick visited Sarah Pinnock, & afterwards went to Oldy's & C Chownes, I talked to little Grace as She has been undutiful to her Grandmother.'* Grace Chown's name crops up later for regular naughtiness, never quite specified.

The rest of March is taken up with coping with the colds and the normal visiting of the poor.

April 1st *'Philip Chowne was taken up for stealing Hay. But he came off victorious from the charge. My dearest Brother Tom arrived. He is looking uncommonly well & has been very well pleased with the Sport he had at Cattistock.'*

April 3rd *'I walked before breakfast to C Chownes. Dr Foot has attended Love Dibbin & She is better.'*

April 6th *'I went to Church by Myself the rest of the Party having Colds – Mrs Bingham has heard from her Niece Mrs Fenwick, the letter written from the Cape of Good Hope, She has lost her little Boy. He had the Whooping Cough & also some Disorder of the Brain.'* I cannot help admiring these intrepid, genteel women who went so far afield so long ago, no doubt accompanying husbands on desperate missions to earn their livings.

April 7th *'My dear Brother & Sister Helyar arrived here with Their youngest little Girl. She is a pretty little Creature.'* They invite Charlotte to return to Coker Court with them.

On the 14th, they set off. The house has been repainted and *'some other improvements'*. Charlotte describes it as quite neat. She remarks, inevitably, that the children *'are very much grown'*. The next day she is out walking in the plantation before breakfast.

There then follows a round of visiting alms houses, invalids and cottages. It is evident Harriet's interests have gone the way of Charlotte's. She reads the Bible to *'some poor people in her Village'*. There are some social visits as well. A Miss Harbin *'was thrown out of a Gig & very much hurt'*. At Hardington they meet two Miss Perryns and Miss Emily Barnard.

April 18th *'I accompanied My Sister in a Walk to Sutton, where we saw Mrs Windsor & her School for poor children, she has 6d A Week & Mrs Lush at Berwick, only has 2d & teaches more for the Money.'* I take it this is per child, but it seems a huge difference in price. Out of a small wage, two pence was still a lot. Charlotte is soon walking to Sutton to teach some of the pupils herself.

April 19th *'I walked two miles before Breakfast & afterwards walked with Mr Helyar seven Miles to Pen Wood, The Warren &c – Pendoma is A very pretty Village. Mr H Helyar is the Rector of it.'*

William Helyar's duties are much the same as his father-in-law's at Ferne, visiting the gaol as a magistrate, going to turnpike meetings and giving his tenants dinner. Harriet is president of a book society in Yeovil, which involves the sale of books. I can't quite puzzle what it is about, but Harriet is *'quite the Life of the Party'*. Charlotte is introduced to a Mrs Harbin, a resident of Yeovil, who has *'a fine old House. Mr Harbin We saw at A distance dressed exactly like A Labourer.'* I wish she had been more specific, as it is rare to get a description of what a labourer wore.

On the 22nd, they walk to some cottages *'where the Inhabitants are very dirty working at the Loom'*. Charlotte orders a dozen pairs of gloves from a girl working in the gardener's house. Though we are now in 1823, it seems there is still quite a lot of cottage industry.

The impression given is that of tireless visiting of the poor, advising, giving medicine and teaching, with a huge emphasis on religion. It seems patronising and overbearing to us, but the poor were very poor and doubtless appreciated anything they could get. Harriet and Charlotte would have been carrying out what they clearly saw as a duty. They are indefatigable in the task. Joan Day, who I think is pregnant, and certainly has a daughter, has been a penitent, according to Charlotte, for some years and has the Bible read to her sometimes twice a day. Charlotte also says, with significant underlinings, that she is not a widow. Harriet is giving a prize for the neatest cottage, which reminds me of the 'Best-Kept Village', which I fought to resist entering Berwick in while I was chairman of the Parish council.

Pregnancy and childbirth were always referred to as illness, and they were indeed just as dangerous. Charlotte and her sister were sometimes present when a baby was born, I suppose to comfort the mother, but I do not know if they stayed in the room for the actual event.

Harriet's children are under the care of their governess, Miss Lake. Though Charlotte teaches the girls dancing, they do not take the prominent place the Waddington children do. William and Carey are at school, but they come home later in June. I am glad to note *'Mr George Helyar was out all the Day with his two nephews ferreting for Rabbits.'* They take the children and Miss Lake to the play, I suppose in Yeovil. It is *'John Bull & Lillipo, which Entertainment made Us laugh extremely'*.

Charity work predominates over all but there is some social life, occasionally evaded. *'We fancied Morning Visitors & escaped into the Garden.'* There is not much chess recorded and no reading aloud in the evening. On June 6th, they dine at Montacute, *'silver plate but an ill dressed Dinner'*. This Elizabethan house was the seat of the Phelips family until 1911, when it was rented out. The National Trust acquired it in 1931. It has been used in filming various productions, including 'Wolf Hall'.

On June 21st, Mrs Grove and William arrive. *'My Father being rather bilious was unable to take the Journey. George remained with Him at Fern.'*

Charlotte goes about bidding all and sundry goodbye. She has been at Coker Court since April 14th and leaves on June 25th. *'I was very happy to find My dear Father quite well & George is grown quite fat and wears A Wig.'* It does seem strange, this old-fashioned habit of a wig. Do you remember Charles had one they all disliked? They immediately start a new novel, and Charlotte spends the last days of June striding about in order to catch up with all her habitual old women, young women and nursing mothers. *'I heard of the ill behaviour of Widow Bradley (no more Visits to Her).'* She is teaching some women and girls *'to mark'*. What was this? I ask a friend in Milkwell who is an expert on embroidery and we can only think of marking as you do the children's school clothes, perhaps articles that were going to be laundered. Mrs White, to whom Charlotte had been teaching the marking, *'has found out the way to do the letters of the Sampler'*, so one gets a hint. Perhaps more likely it was the means of transferring a design onto a piece of cloth later to be worked. Mrs White must have had a school of sorts because Charlotte teaches *'two of her scholars'* to mark. That September, Mrs White marks a sampler for her. Later Charlotte is taught *'the Spanish marking stitch'* and is soon teaching it to others, but what was it?

In July, she accompanies her mother, her sister-in-law Mrs John Grove and her niece Henrietta to visit her mother's sister, Mrs Jackson, at Coombe Priory. There she sees Mrs Walsh (Arabella Jackson) and her little girl, no doubt the cause of anxiety over her mother's health. Charlotte then says, *'We walked to the cold Bath.'* Where was this? She remarks of her other cousin: *'Fanny is unfortunately grown fatter than ever.'*

John Grove and his wife now have three children, Henrietta, Thomas and John. There is also a Miss Fraser staying, Jane's sister, who is something of an invalid. According to Charlotte, she could not walk for six years, but with the advice of her doctor brother-in-law, she now can. Charlotte thinks her better *'for change of air'*, that old fashioned remedy still occasionally suggested. She also thinks George has taken a fancy to her and says he has become very civil. He must be better from whatever he had suffered because he rides regularly to East Hayes. *'I begin to be more reconciled to My brother George's Wig now He does not wear it so much over his Face.'* The John Groves, Miss Fraser and the children all stay at Ferne, as do as Charles and Eliza and Mrs Walsh and her baby, Anna.

July 10th *'We went to see the Abbey, all the Party but my Father and Wm. Some new Rooms fitted up…'* I was puzzled as to what Abbey Charlotte is referring to, but a later entry enlightens me, because Mrs Grove *'composed some ludicrous lines on our Party to Fonthill Abbey. My father & Brothers said they would give me 6d each if it made Them laugh. I have won My Bet & have got it for My Penny Club.'*

July 12th *'A Sailor was screaming Ballads in the Village which will not do good to the Poor People.'* I have a sense of Charlotte becoming more of a moral watchdog. Some days later she gets caught in the rain, having walked as far as the *'Withy bank'*, and takes shelter in *'Rawkins cottage…*

read Him A Chapter in the Bible'. Were they really pleased to have the Bible read to them, or did they take it as a quirk of the gentry that had to be suffered? We have Charlotte's voice alone, and it could equally well have been either.

Mr Grove must have been quite poorly, because he is still recovering by July 16th. *'My dear Father improves daily in his Health & that gives him good spirits. He observed his Grandson Tom Grove was very clever in purloining Strawberries.'* One of the things I enjoy about these diaries is that while everything was different, everything is the same. John's eldest boy was born in 1822, so was one or one and a half.

They have news of the Waddingtons: *'A very affectionate letter from My Dear Niece Emma.'* She is sixteen and has left school. They are at Caversham, now but not then a part of Reading, visiting a Waddington uncle. They are to go on to *'Glemham'*. There is a Glemham Hall at Little Glemham near Woodbridge in Suffolk.

Charlotte is worried about Mrs White, who has the whooping cough. She visits her often with fruit and medicine. They have a visit from *'Mrs Armstrong'* who lived at Donhead Lodge *'many years ago'*. They also have a visit from Aunt Chafin.

July 24th *'went down to Marshes Shop. I bought My Pupils A Gown each.'* I imagine this was for them to make up. *'I was surprised by Mr Marshes little Girl Eliza proposing to be A free Member of My Penny Club.'* I wish the setting up of the penny club had not taken place in the previous year, for which we have no journal, as I then might have understood the system better. Charlotte punishes her pupil Emma Wicks but she does not tell us for what or how.

Apart from teaching others, Charlotte does not much mention sewing as a personal occupation or project, but she shows her aunt *'the Silk Net Dress that I have worked in Velvet'*. This sounds an elaborate undertaking; I can only think an appliqué of velvet onto the net.

July 28th *'many Showers fell & Our Hay still remains out and cannot be made.'*

July 30th *'I went to Marshes, bought a sampler for two Girls at Mrs Whites…a poor Man quite exhausted with want, fell down by our Gate. My dear Father had him taken in, gave him something to eat & sent him to the Work House for the Night.'* The workhouse was in Ludwell.

July 31st *'I called at the Parsonage & then attended Mrs Lushes School. I selected a Class & was very strict with Them.'* It seems the school was quite large.

Getting someone to go to the infirmary at Salisbury is sometimes a matter of bribery. Charlotte promises *'Elizabeth Longman'* a new gown if she will go. She sends her to *'Mr Wills to have the Leeches applied'*. Mrs White *'I think much worse. I intend to have two of her Pupils on Saturdays.'* On Saturday, *'My Pupils came & Eliza Tanswell A new one. Mrs Wright did not chuse to send her Daughter to me.'*

Miss Catherine Arundell is going to consult Dr Grove. She looks very ill and Charlotte hopes it is not too late. John is soon driving over to Wardour. William, Tom and George go to the races. On August 9th, *'Waddington & his two eldest sons came here.'* The Danseys come to dine. *'We had quite A Feast of Turtle & Venison.'* Turtle has quite gone off our modern menu, and I wonder how you got hold of a turtle.

Suddenly, Charlotte is more social. On the 12th she goes in Waddington's coach, picking up Charles' wife at Tarrant Hinton on the way, to stay with the Farquharsons at Blandford for the races. *'I tried on A beautiful Dress my dear Brother Tom bought Me for the Races & it fitted me very well indeed, made exactly by Mrs Farquharsons junr. Size.'* There are not only the races but the balls. *'I danced every Dance, Country Dances & Quadrilles alternately.'* Tom is a steward at the races and also has a horse running. *'Toms Colt given him by My Father lost.'* They return on the 16th, but Waddington takes his boys to Weymouth. Tom also goes, being a steward at the races there.

On the 19th, Charlotte goes to Zeals with her parents. The following day she walks to *'Castle Hill where the Duke of Cornwall formerly lived'*. I have not heard mention of this before. They come home the next day, passing through Gillingham, which Charlotte describes as having *'many pretty Cottages'*. This is of course Gillingham before the railway.

At Ferne, they still cannot get the hay in: the weather is so nasty they have a fire. Mrs White, who definitely lives at Brookwater, still has the whooping cough. Charlotte is working a baby's cap for Mrs J Grove. On the 23rd, Thomas Shere *'came in the Evening & desired My Father & Mother to accept A Present of A Turbot.'*

They dine at Wardour. *'Miss C Arundell is better for My Brothers advice.'* John's medical practice is definitely expanding.

August 26th *'Mrs Wright is very humble & wants Me to teach her little Girl now.'* It rains so much Charlotte has to borrow a cloak from *'Dinah Grey'* in order to get home.

Here is another school. *'I went to Marches shop, called on Mrs John Dewy. She has 15 Pupils in the free School & 12 of her own.'* Who qualified for the 'free' school and who paid? There was much education going on, one way or another. There is also a Sunday school where Charlotte *'heard My class their Catechism'*. I am glad to note she took the trouble to explain it to them.

John Waddington turns up unexpectedly. His grandfather gives him *'the little filly named Phillis'*.

The Rector of Upper Donhead, Mr Blackmore, and his wife and two daughters have been on a trip to Russia. This seems astonishing if you consider the means of transport at the time, horses all the way once you crossed the Channel if you were to go overland and see other places, or going by sea, courtesy of the Merchant Navy, not necessarily safe or comfortable. Charlotte calls the daughters *'the two Russian Miss Blackmores'*. I think she was as impressed as I am. *'They have each A handsome set of Chess Men from Russia. Ships instead of Bishops &c I won a Game of Miss Blackmore with Them.'* Further research into this revealed the Blackmore's eldest son Richard was a clergyman. There was a large community of British merchants living and trading in Russia who were part of something called the Russian Company or Factory. They employed clergy to administer to the British community there. Richard had married Harriet Hembry in the Russian Company Chaplaincy, Kronstadt. It is all quite hard to follow, but this is the obvious connection between the Blackmores and Russia. I expect even further enquiry would discover if Richard Blackmore was employed as a chaplain there. It seems quite possible.

By the 2nd of September, George has carried half his wheat at East Hayes. He is obviously farming it but enjoying the comfort of living at home. Mrs White is still ill, but her health is variable. The shooting season starts, as does buck hunting in the Chase. Mrs Bingham and a friend, Miss Gattie, *'walked nearly up the Park & were frightened by some cows quietly grazing'*. Poor timid Mrs Bingham! The men take a day's shooting at Waddington's property, *'Woodcots'*.

They have a Miss Mary Grove staying at Ferne, but I do not know what relation she was. John Lane gives me four possible candidates, but we cannot be sure.

At this period there was a lot of interest in Fonthill Abbey because it was on the market, complete with its contents. Apparently the auctioneers (Christie's) added lots of things that had not come from Fonthill at all. Fonthill obviously fascinated the neighbourhood, shut behind a wall by reclusive, scandalous, immensely wealthy William Beckford. Beckford's fortune was based on sugar plantations in Jamaica. The loss of two of these at this period compelled him to sell the abbey and move to Bath. It was bought by John Farquhar, an arms dealer. When it was first on the market, it was said six to seven hundred people a day visited it. The tower was 145 feet high. It had fallen down, but Beckford had it rebuilt.

September 11th *'I accompanied My Mother Miss Mary Grove & my Nephew John Waddington to the Abbey. We went into the Sale Room But the Books do not sell very well. My Father has A free ticket for Himself & Family. Our little Beau very polite.'* Waddington goes with George on the 13th when *'The books sold higher Today'*.

September 13th *'The Villagers were gone out Gleaning, some of them encroached in My Fathers Field.'* What were the rules on gleaning? It seems unlikely Mr Grove would have forbidden it.

September 14th *'Waddington called on Mr Weld. He intends little Tom shall be under his care.'* This is the first mention of Mr Weld. John Lane and I puzzled over Mr Weld, he convinced he was a Weld of Lulworth and I saying the Welds are Catholic and always have been, not Church of England clergy. Eventually John got to the bottom of it, finding two Joseph Welds, one from Lulworth, one ours, a completely separate family, initially from Cheshire. He was born in 1796, so he is now twenty-seven. His wife was Elizabeth Weekes and they ultimately had fourteen children, all boys but one. Their second son, Joseph Corbin Weld, was born this year and baptised in Alvediston. This made me think Mr Weld was possibly the curate at Alvediston, as why else Christen your child there? Alvediston was managed by Ebbesbourne Wake, the advowsons belonging to Kings, Cambridge; Alvediston was just supplied with a curate. On Wikitree, which our niece had a look at, it says, 'Weld was the curate at Broad Chalke, Wiltshire, from May 29th 1820 till sometime in 1823. From 1823 to 1826 he was curate at Annseley, in the Parish of Berwick St Johns.' Well, here is some sense and some nonsense! John even managed to find photographs of Mr and Mrs Weld, albeit at a more advanced age, he lean and handsome, on the craggy side, and she round-faced.

Charlotte then goes off to Netherhampton for a few days, going with her aunt into Salisbury, visiting. She sees her sister-in-law Jane Grove. *'Baby is quite well & looks very pretty in My worked Cap.'* She walks about with Jane: *'her little dog killed A chicken & wounded another'*. Just the sort of thing one prefers to avoid. She also sees Miss Popham and the Eyre party. I think back to the disaster when John thought he was nearly engaged to one of the Miss Eyres. I presume this to be the same family. John goes off to Blandford by the mail to see Miss Fraser, I take it Jane's sister, and then Tom drives him to Ferne in his gig. *'I accompanied Jane to the Cathedral & directly afterwards set off in the Gig driven by My Brothers Servant to Fern. A very wet ride indeed.'* Charlotte was tough. Think of going from Salisbury to Ferne in an open vehicle drawn by a horse, on a wet day, prior to the invention of the mackintosh.

New names start to appear. We have Miss Gattie and Miss Erle and now Col and Mrs Pine Coffin and Col and Mrs Farrer. The Farrers must have lived in the combes or Milkwell direction, because Charlotte visits them going via Brookwater. Desmond Hawkins does not mention any of these people, but Miss Erle was Mrs Bingham's niece.

Charlotte refers to the parsonage rather than the Rectory when visiting the Binghams. She sees *'Mrs Sarah Bingham'* and *'I am very happy to see her looking so well.'* Despite the lost libel against Dr Gardiner, the old lady's reputation is apparently unscathed. Whilst Charlotte was there, *'Miss Foot came in, her hand which she cut is much better.'*

Charlotte does not approve one of her class missing Sunday school. September 29th *'I visited Mrs Foot. Mrs Hodgekinson her Family & Mrs Greenway are staying there. Miss Foots hand is better & She is in excellent spirits. Mr Pinkney of Salisbury, & Miss Pinkney came in whilst I was there.'* I think of Charlotte only visiting the Foots, at what is now the Manor, when with her Jackson cousins. She definitely gravitates more towards the village, what with her penny club, pupils and Sunday school. Ferne itself is in Donhead, which no doubt encouraged her to extend charitable activities in the direction of Milkwell etc. I still wonder about the Pinkneys. They must have, at one time, lived in Berwick, but when and where? Certainly, there was a *'Mr Pinkney of Salisbury'*. They had property here according to the 1840 map, and there is a Pinkney memorial in the church. At some stage they had married into the Foot family.

On the same day, Mr Grove has his tenants to dine, but having a slight bilious attack, *'my Brothers did the honors'*.

The day after that, Charlotte reports on George: *'I am sorry to say not quite so well again.'* John Grove and his family come to stay. *'Henrietta* danced when I played the Piano-Forte to Her.' She has Jane and *'her little girl'* as company for ensuing walks and visits. They are soon joined by the Charles Groves.

At the beginning of October, she is visiting the school *'& gave A Boy named Burt some instruction in writing. I intend also to teach some of the Boys to Cypher.'* I think this Mrs Lush's school, which I believe to be in Berwick, but where was it? I looked up ciphering in the dictionary and cannot quite work out what she was going to teach these boys if it was different to writing. At Mrs White's she *'whipped A little Boy that was naughty'*. A few days later she says, *'I find the little Boy I punished was not in fault, must not be so hasty again.'*

On the 10th, there is a little bit of Ferne building history. They visit Mrs Shere. *'I then showed my Sisters (in-law) the Riding House that is now creating.'* Francis always reckoned this to be the long building in the Ferne stable block next to the dairy building. In the Hamilton days, it housed the electric batteries that powered the house.

On the 11th, both married brothers and families leave. Jane and Eliza were not quite as hardy as Charlotte when it came to walking in inclement weather.

October 12th *'Not any Service at Berwick. Mr & Mrs Bingham have received the sad News of their Son Edwards death. We therefore went to L Donhead Church.'* He died 15th June 1823. I tried to find more information on the Internet and found out lots about his father and his brother, but nothing about him. We have his plaque in the vestry upon which we are told he was killed by 'banditti' in Peru. The inscription includes the later death of his father. The following Sunday, *'Mr Bingham gave Us A most excellent Sermon on his late Affliction. I am glad We have so good A Clergyman near Us.'* Charlotte sends a message to the parsonage to ask if Mrs Bingham would like to see her, *'But She refused'*. Eventually she sees her in church on the 26th. It is not until November 2nd *'Mrs Bingham We were happy to find in a much more composed state of mind.'*

In the meantime, Laetitia Popham has come to stay, and normal life carries on. A mad dog was *'killed at the London Elm'* but not before it had bitten a puppy belonging to Mr Grove and *'We sent down to Mr Lush to hang his Dog as it was bit by the Mad Dog.'* Before kindly needles, this was the method of disposing of dogs. Rabies was common here. The London Elm was the coaching inn at Swallowcliffe. It was on the main road but was demolished sometime in the last century. There is a photograph of it hanging in the Swallowcliffe village hall.

We often think the weather suspiciously odd, but in my opinion it was ever thus. October 31st *'A deep Snow fell. An extraordinary circumstance in October.'*

Charlotte has taken a shine to *'that nice little boy Thomas Gould'*. He was at Mrs White's school, *'a very clever engaging child'*. On the same day, *'I met the Wife of John Butcher who has just been sent to Gaol, his old Mother & Family are in great distress, I shall give the wife some materials for buttoning.'* How much money could be made making buttons? I cannot think much.

November 9th *'Mr Foot has had a fall from his horse and is very ill.'* I imagine this to be Charles Foot, who would now be farming Manor Farm in place of his father, Henry. They hear of the death of John Helyar, William Helyar's uncle.

November 10th *'I visited Mrs Whites & paid her My Mothers six weeks schooling.'* So that is how some of it was funded. *'She receives something for cooking the dinner of A Labourer that works at the Glove Inn. I went to Jesse Abbots & found his Wife eating some Bread of Their own Wheat.'* Charlotte is obviously surprised by this, so it is apparent it was not the normal practice. The grinding of it up must have been the problem. She visits Haskal's House at *'five Ways'*, so it was called that then as now. She is busy choosing blankets and *'stuff'* gowns at Marshals and Talbots for her clubs. Stuff was any manufactured cloth, here probably wool or linen. A mixture was made of the two called 'woolsey-linsey', which entered the language as meaning neither one thing nor another but has now, I take it, departed again.

Charlotte says she has four pupils on Saturdays, but she mentions Emma Wicks, Hannah Gould, Eliza Weeks, Susan Wright, H Hyscock and Eliza Tanswell. She does not always get all of them, and I do not know which ones have dropped out.

The Coffins and Farrers are now regulars when Charlotte pays visits with her mother. Mrs Farrer has a new baby as has Mrs Dansey, the wife of the Rector of Lower Donhead. The Coffins are at Donhead Lodge, so they must have replaced the Haines.

November 17th *'My Father went out Hunting & They mounted Daniel on the Mule.'* I am rather surprised they had one.

November 23rd *'I walked to Berwick with Eliza. We visited S Pinnock, The School, Oldy, & Mary Kelly. I am in hopes the Widow Kelly will now recover.'* The school is elusive. In the 1840 map, a Mary Kelly is living in her own house just up from the Chown cottages, but it is all too tiny to make it out clearly.

November 26th *'A sad Accident James the Clerk & A Glazier met with. They were upon A ladder doing something to the Church. It slipped & They both fell. James had his Leg most dreadfully broken.'* Charlotte visits on the 27th and the 30th. He *'is very patient under his sufferings'*. On December 2nd, he sends word that *'Mr Wills had set his Leg'*. Nowadays we would like to have our leg set a bit sooner. Charlotte then visits him regularly. He is in great pain. By the 8th, *'visited the poor Clerk who appeared lightheaded & very drowsy. I hope the symptoms do not indicate A Mortification.'* Mrs Bingham writes off to Mr Wills *'to come immediately to poor James'*. She records his steady decline. On December 12th, *'Fanny & I visited the poor Clerk Who was dying. Mr Coates had been sent for in the Morning But it was too late. Tho's James expired about seven o'clock in the Evening. He has left A Wife & 5 Children.'* At the Sunday evening service, *'Mr Bingham gave Us an excellent Sermon applicable to the Clerks death. He is so kind to the Poor.'* When you read all this there seems a terrible inevitability about it, the ignorance and the delay. He was buried on the 17th. Charlotte sometimes refers to him as J James but settles for T.

Charlotte is also visiting *'Anne Roberts'* who has *'a cancer in her breast'* and *'She is in great danger The Cancer has bled so much.'*

December 3rd *'Fanny called upon Mrs Foot. Mr C Foot suffers very great pain in his head, & is in low spirits.'* On November 9th he had had a fall from his horse. Fanny and Charlotte visit him on the 8th and he is declared to be much better.

December 4th *'We walked to Ludwell, visited Mrs White, little Tho's Gould repeated some Verses to Us. Called at some Cottages & Mary Woodfords School, to whom I took some Spelling Lessons. It was extremely dirty as We walked without Pattens.'* Yet another school! Charlotte's own spelling was quite odd.

December 5th *'I bought A pr. Of Pattens for Fanny & Myself & We sallied forth to Marshes Shop to look at the Club Blankets. I bought one of them for Mrs White. We then went to Mrs Dewys & I never saw A greater Trollop than She is become.'* Charlotte talks of wearing pattens earlier in her journals but must have left off the practice, now to start again. When you see a picture of them, they do not look very comfortable but they obviously would have helped keep a long dress out of the mud.

December 11th *'I gave Mrs Lushes eldest Daughter A Black Willow Bonnett.'*

George's health still seems a cause for concern. *'My Mother assisted me in Reading As Georges Eyes were much inflamed.'* That was on the 16th, and they are no better on the 27th.

December 17th *'My Nephew Tom Waddington came by the Coach. He is looking very well. My Aunt Grove came. Daniel obliged to break open her Chaise Seat the lock being hampered.'* We do not use the word hampered for locks now, only for people or events that hold us up.

On the 21st *'I visited the Sunday School, obliged to discard one of My Pupils & take another, made an example of Grace Chowne which I hope will shame her.'*

December 22nd *'I visited My treasurer of the Club, paid her pension for the Year. We measured the new Blankets, They are larger & weigh A Lb heavier than last Year. The purple stuff Gowns are also highly approved of.'* I suppose there was no apparent anxiety on the part of the women if their gowns were all purple, they just must have been pleased to have an article of clothing provided.

They had a quiet Christmas that year, though the following day they have the bands of both Donheads, Berwick and Ansty to play. *'Tom Waddington went out Hunting & rode as well as any of the Party.'* He is nine now. Charlotte makes further resolutions about not minding chess defeats.

December 27th *'I walked to Sarah Pinnocks, the 2 pieces of Stuff she had for a Gown do not suit. I must rectify it in some way. I played a game of Chess with George & He won it. It is some little relaxation to Him as his eyes are so inflamed He cannot see to read.'*

There is little in the end papers for this year. Charlotte again lists the texts for sermons and makes a note of a few shops, e.g. that of a pastry cook called Garrett, Cross Keys, Shaftesbury. Perhaps I should not omit the slightly intriguing mentions of *'Morrells Portable Pens'* and *'Atkinsons Curling Fluid'*.

1824

The notes Charlotte makes here are rather obscure, possibly easier to make sense of when the text is studied. She records the death of Louis XVIII and the succession of his brother, Charles X. Her cousin Charles Jackson marries Arabella Knightley, whose latter name has an Austen-like ring to it. More significantly, Charlotte writes down her mother's 'impromptu' verse on Tom Grove's engagement to a Miss Hill. There are other jottings and addresses that do not mean much to me.

There had been some dissatisfaction over the stuff gowns. Charlotte walks to Talbots. *'I paid my Club Bill there. He behaved very well relative to the Stuff gowns.'* It sounds as if she got him to take them back or maybe took a reduction. The following day *'I visited S Pinnock, & carried her gown.'*

There is a fever in the vicinity. *'Ann Dimmer is dead of the Fever & two others taken ill'* and two days later, *'I desired the Children not to attend the Funeral of Ann Dimmer As She died in A most putrid State.'*

Charles has duties at Tarrant Hinton because he *'went home to attend his Church'*. George wins a game of chess but *'though I lost the Game did not lose my Temper at the same time'*. George is winning rather a lot at the minute. The book by Philidor Charlotte had given him made him almost invincible. Tom Waddington has been with them since before Christmas, the only child in residence. His old pony has died, but *'Mr*

Hascal has lent Little Tom A Grey Poney.' (Pony usually appears with an extra E.)

January 8th *'We walked to Mrs Maidments Cottage, Ann Roberts remains much the same. We met old Farmer Maidment in the Lane & I thought I should never get Eliza away. She was civily listening to his long stories.'*

The news, noted by Charlotte, is of the trial of a man called Thurtell who murdered a William We are over a gambling debt. Two others were implicated, Hunt and Probert, but Probert 'Turned King's Evidence' and was let off. Thurtell was hanged, but Hunt was sent to Botany Bay where he lived for years. The case was celebrated for the judge complaining that the press had condemned Thurtell before the trial, and indeed they built the gallows before he had been condemned. It was importantly the last trial under 16th-century principles where the accused had to defend himself, without counsel, after the prosecution had made their case. Madam Tussaud's made a wax work of Thurtell, which demonstrates the public interest.

Wills is attending the fever invalids in Berwick but says they are getting better. Charlotte has been walking to Berwick but not visiting.

Poor Mrs Bingham has now heard her niece died last August in the East Indies. She died of an *'Anurism in the Head, the same her Baby died of. A disorder that had nothing to do with the Climate of India.'* One hardly needed the help of the climate to finish one off in those days.

January 12th *'I walked to Talbots, to execute some commissions for my Mother & Self. Mrs Talbots very ill & I went up to see Her as She was in Bed. Mr Wills came whilst I was there. I received my Quarters Allowance due St. Thomas Day. A new Shaftesbury Bank set up by Mr Storey.'*

On the following day, Mrs Long *'made me a Present of a very pretty Net Half worked in Worsteds for the Head'*. I try, with difficulty, to visualise such an article.

Charlotte's pupils still attend her class on Saturdays. Her brother Tom sends five pounds to aid the sick in Berwick, which was plenty of money then.

January 19th *'I played a game of chess with George. I did not keep my resolution but I will try to next time. Mr Weld called Upon Us. Tom Waddington is to go to school on Saturday.'* Tom we know to have been at school in Salisbury, but this is the new arrangement. On the 24th, *'Tom hunted with his Grandpapa the last time before he goes to School.'* The next day, actually Sunday, *'I accompanied my Mother to Church. We first called on Mr Weld & left My little Nephew Tom Waddington there. He felt Our Leaving Him, But will I dare say soon be reconciled to his School.'* When I first read the diaries I could not understand where Tom went to school, but much later readings have informed me. The house was what is now the Priory. I cannot say when it got to be called the Priory, but Charlotte only calls it thus at the end of her life. How much of a school was it and how many pupils did it have? On February 4th, *'I visited little T. Waddington. He is very happy & says He feels quite at home at Mr Welds.'*

January 22nd *'I visited Mrs White & found Her rather better I gave her A qutr. LB Senna & arranged that She shall have two portions once A Month.'* They were very bold in administering medicine to the hapless poor.

Charlotte says, *'Time passes delightfully at Home these Winter Evenings.'* She remarks, *'My dear Father continues so well & enjoys his Hunting (Blessed be God for it).'* Mr Grove is now sixty-six. Mr Wyndham sends him an invitation to go to Dinton to *'hunt with Mr Codrington & He seems inclined to do it.'* Charlotte loses many games of chess this January. She never should have given that chess manual to George. Some of her penny club want to pay two pence a week so they can have a cloak at the end of the year. On the last day of the month, William *'hunted at Gaunts & had no sport'*. A keen foxhunter travelled any distance, Gaunts being about twenty miles from Berwick. If his father hunts at Dinton, he will have a hack of eleven miles or so.

February 1st *'I accompanied My Mother to Church. We did not see little Tom though I believe he was in Mr Welds pew.'* Tom may have been extra small, but I think this hints at the box pews they were likely to have had in the church at that time, with tall sides easily able to swallow up a little boy. I also think Mr Weld's school was for only a few boys.

February 6th *'Mr Weld came up here to tell Us poor little Tom Waddington is very unwell. I went to see Him & never saw A poor Child so reduced in a short time. We heard unpleasant news of John Waddington. I hope it will be his first & last Fault. Two Members of my Club have behaved ill in Buying & Selling Blankets & I have excused it, being the first time.'*

February 7th *'Mr Weld sent up word little Tom has so much Fever that we sent off immediately for Dr. Grove. My Mother spent the morning with her little Grandson. On the Doctors arrival He found Him better & not at that time feverish. Mr Welds treatment of the Invalid had been perfectly right.'*

The next day, Mrs Grove sits with him while Charlotte attends church. The child continues ill for about a week.

February 10th *'This Fever has prevented My visiting the Cottages in Water St.'*

February 13th *'I visited My Nephew. He is very weak from the effects of the Fever. I called upon Mrs Bingham. I played A Game of Chess with Her & won it. I returned Home in A very heavy rain. They pressed Me much to stay: at about four Oclock A most heavy Snow came. I congratulated Myself at being in My own dear Home & not snowed in at another Persons House.'*

February 14th *'A heavy snow & very deep…My Father has put his Ewes & Lambs into the Riding House this inclement Weather. We are exactly the number four which is agreeable round the social Fire-side.'* George, having built his house at East Hayes, or what is now Sedgehill Manor, does not seem to live in it, but he definitely was not in very good health. William has gone to stay at Coker. Her father frequently rides in his riding house.

February 15th *'We received very good accounts from Mr Weld of little Tom Waddington. His brother John is gone to School to A Clergyman in Essex.'* I suspect John, now fourteen, was expelled from Harrow for the unexplained misdemeanour. There is plenty of snow.

On the 16th, *'large Branches have been blown off the Trees this Weather. I met some poor women picking up the Sticks & accompanied them as far* as Berwick.' Having sufficient firewood for warmth and cooking was a terrible difficulty. *'A man nearly frozen to death in the Chace as when A Boy found Him he was just going to Sleep.'*

In the meantime, John Waddington senior has gone to attend the wedding of *'his brother Spencer Kilderbees'*. I was entranced by the name but could not see in what way he might be a brother to Waddington. John Lane informs me Waddington's mother married Samuel Kilderbee after the death of Waddington's father. There were five known children, of whom Spencer was the eldest.

By the 21st, little Tom is able to ride to Ferne, Mr Weld lending him a pony. He stays a few days.

On the 24th, they receive the news of Tom Grove's engagement to Miss Hill. They are all delighted. *'She bears a most excellent character.'* A few days later they get a letter from Mrs Farquharson, the mother of Tom's late wife, saying she *'is quite pleased at My Brothers intended Match'*.

Charlotte now has five pupils on Saturdays. They have more snow and many people are still a bit poorly. The Groves have colds so Mr Grove reads prayers on Sunday and a sermon of *'Allisons'*. On the last day of February, it is colder than it has been all winter. The start of March is not much better. *'James Kelly is sent to prison for deer stealing.'* It is apparent from what one reads of the period that the laws on poaching etc. were strict and the punishment dire, talk of people sent to Australia for possessing a rabbit net, but I am coming to the conclusion that magistrates were much more lenient. The previous month, *'My Father has convicted some poachers about here & I hope they will be well punished as it is the ruin of a poor family.'* Charlotte does not make the observation they might not poach if they were less poor, but there is no talk of Hanging them.

March 2nd *'I walked to Bericourt Farm. Mr Herridge is planning out a very neat Garden…A very cold day & March is certainly begun with the roaring of the Lion, may it end with the gentleness of the Lamb. A letter from Tom. He is deeply in Love, & they all come here next Monday.'*

March 3rd *'A very stormy Day with Sleet Rain & Snow. It broke A piece out of the Best Bed Chamber Window. George joined Me in my Boudoir & We had 2 Games of Chess which He won, & I bore the defeat with magnanimity.'*

March 5th *'I visited Mrs White. She was taken very ill with Spasms in her Stomach whilst I was there. I sent her after my return Home A Medicine which I hope will be of service to Her.'* Was she still taking the senna last prescribed?

The Jackson cousins are still regular visitors. *'Charles hopes to procure an Appointment in the West Indies.'* In the meantime, he goes out hunting with his uncle. They are visited by the Miss Nortons of Bavant. Miss Anna immediately beats Charlotte in a game of chess.

March 6th *'George rode to East Hayes the first time he has been able to inspect his Farm this Winter. I visited S Pinnock. I met Richard Green. He promised me he would never again pawn his things. My 5 pupils came. My Mother has given me permission to keep E Wicks & H Hyscock on at school until the Haymaking commences.'* This makes me think Mrs Grove subsidised or paid entirely for these girls to be educated. John Lane found their baptisms in the church records. They were around fifteen or sixteen, so late to be not out at work.

Ill health still prevails, colds and fevers. The housemaid has *'spasms'* in her stomach. If they occur again she is to be replaced with *'My young protégée'*. It is best not to judge our predecessors by our standards of today, but what then happens to the one with spasms? There is another alarm on the 9th. *'A poor man named Crowter has caught the Small Pox, though he was a few Years ago vaccinated, & there are many instances the same at Shaftesbury.'*

There is suspense in waiting to meet Miss Hill. She is to come with Mr and Mrs Taswell. Illness and other things mean the visit is twice postponed. Tom pays a flying visit from Weymouth. Charlotte says, *'The Lady is A famous Rider, & very elegant Figure. Dark Blue Eyes, & about 5 Feet 5 & half. She is just Thirty. My Brother appears deeply in Love.'*

There is still quite a lot of snow. *'Tom Waddington came. He is very impatient to return Tomorrow as it is little Henry Welds Birth-Day.'* Henry, the Welds' eldest son, was born in 1821. He became a surgeon in the Navy and died at twenty-three. The next day being Sunday, Charlotte takes her nephew, before he returns to Mr Weld's, to church, accompanied by Charles Jackson, who takes the service in the absence of Mr Bingham. I had not realised he was ordained. So many young men were.

March 15th *'Mr Gordon arrived here with his Niece Miss Hill to introduce her to Us. Tom accompanied Them. I am so very much pleased with my intended Sister. She is so unaffected. A very elegant Figure an expressive Countenance on which the goodness of the Mind beams forth, & I think that my dearest Brother has every chance of Happiness.'* Miss Hill must have been very special to meet with so much approval, as Tom, born in the same year as Charlotte, I think the absolute favourite brother.

March 16th *'Our Party left Us & I was nearly mad with Joy at the prospect of having such A delightful Sister. To show the Vicissitudes of Life A letter arrived to my Father announcing the death of Mrs E Long last Evening at 6 Oclock. But I am happy to hear that She did not suffer But went off in her Sleep quite worn out being 90.'*

March 20th *'On my return from my Walk before Breakfast, I found A strange Man had got into our Library & locked the Door. My Father, Tho. Shere & George questioned him & He said Lord Eldon had sent Him.'* They had some trouble getting rid of him. They *'walked him out of the park But he returned & kept pacing up & down our Road for 2 hours'.* Eventually *'a constable'* removed him to Shaftesbury *'where there was A Man in search of Him. He proved to be A Madman & possessed of great property. Mrs Shere & I protected each other in a walk to Berwick.'* We probably never will know who this poor chap was, but Lord Eldon was Lord Chancellor and had his seat at Encombe, which must be one of the most desirable estates in Dorset. His heirs sold it in 2002.

On the 22nd, *'I played two Games of Chess with George & was defeated in both. The last I was angry. How can I be such A Fool: I will try to behave better next time.'*

March 23rd *'My dear Father left Us for Netherhampton as He is to attend Mrs Eleanor Longs funeral, Tomorrow, & open her Will afterwards.'*

They go into mourning. Though he was only gone two nights, Charlotte says, *'We do miss my dearest Father so very much. Fern loses half its attractions without Him.'*

In the meantime, Mrs Grove is administering to *'Our Kitchen Girl very ill of A Fever'* and William returns from Cattistock, presumably at the close of the hunting season. I do wonder about William. He is only thirty-four, but the Navy is never mentioned. He obviously had sufficient property elsewhere to support himself and he may well have been getting half-pay.

The death of their cousin Mrs Long was profitable to the Groves. Charlotte's father is left five thousand four hundred pounds but the main beneficiary was the spinster Aunt Grove. *'She will come into a great Property & is most truly deserving of it'.* She has already promised to purchase *'a Living'* for Charles and renew the lease on John's house in Salisbury. John has *'all her Houses in Salisbury & £500'.* Charlotte, William, George and Charles have one hundred pounds each. Charlotte, a little later, makes a will on the strength of her newfound wealth.

March 26th *'I visited old Wm. Maidment & his Wife, the latter is very ill with the Worms, We gave her the oil of Turpentine which I hope will cure her. They have been industrious People & deserve relief. They showed me An affectionate letter They received two Years ago from their Son Wm. Sergeant in the 67th Regiment East Indies.'* You would cling on to such a letter. Old Mrs Maidment is now visited regularly.

Charlotte, as well as having her Saturday pupils, usually takes a class in the Sunday school, which I assume to have been held in the church.

Little Tom Waddington arrives before breakfast and he and Charlotte walk out in the direction of the Glove to meet Waddington from the coach. Tom will be ten on April 3rd. On the same day, the 29th, Charlotte calls on Mrs Herridge at Berry Court, the Herridges the new tenants there. I had thought Mr Grove was farming this himself, but maybe he is retiring. *'Dr Grove came & my Brother Tom arrived just after We had* dined. George returned from Tarrant Hinton.' The next day, *'The Punch opened My dear Brother Tom's honest Heart.'*

March 31st *'I walked to Berwick…visited Oldy, C Chown & Mary Kelly in Water street, where I have not been for some time the Fever having been so prevalent there. Dr Grove returned to Salisbury. William travelled to Weymouth to fetch A Paper which was of consequence to Tom. He also offered his Mare for the Lady's Riding / there's Civility.'*

April 1st *'My Mother gave her Diamonds for Bessy.'* This was Miss Hill. Tom Grove and Waddington go off to inspect John's new property in Salisbury.

April 5th *'The Cottages my Father has built nearly finished. Ann Herring preparing as well as Cull & her Family to get in tomorrow.'* Which cottages are these? Charlotte visits there on the 9th. She is delighted to hear Tom has taken Wincombe.

Otherwise, April continues much as usual. Ann Roberts is the ongoing invalid. Charlotte's uncle Pilfold is very ill. William Jackson has *'gained A good Appointment in India & has made his Brother John a present of £100'*. It really was a problem how to get all the young men in these respectable families suitably employed, so few options open to them, so little considered 'suitable'. Charlotte's club was sometimes troublesome. *'I am determined Widow Bradley shall be expelled My Club next Year, from bad conduct.'* Her elder pupils have worked a sampler for her *'with some of the Verses on Charles Waddington'*. Poor little baby Charles is obviously not forgotten, though Charlotte does not mention him. She visits Mrs Dewy's school. *'I heard the Children their Catechism many Dunces among Them.'* Charlotte has grasped how to spell catechism, I note. *'Little Emily Dimmer read very well She is not quite 5 years old.'* Another promising scholar, often mentioned, is *'little Martha James'*.

April 16th *'I finished Capt Franklins journey in the northern parts of America very interesting & they were nearly starved to death poor Creatures.'*

Tom sends *'A droll letter to my Mother some Bride Cake & Bunches of Ribbon &c sent: it is to be quite A Public Wedding on Easter Monday,*

& They are to breakfast at their Aunt Peaches.' There was no question of any of them attending it.

April 19th *'My very dear Brother Thomas was married to Elizabeth Daughter of Jere Hill Esq., Almondsbury Glocestershire. I wish them every Happiness this Life can possibly afford. The Servants had A Bowl of Punch & A Dance on this joyful Occasion. A large Wedding Cake arrived & the best I ever tasted.'*

George has been staying at Netherhampton and has obviously seen John. *'The Doctor proposes pulling down some of the Wall of the Dining Room at Close Gate. I Hope he will be persuaded against it as it may bring down the old House upon His Head.'* I was interested in this because it gives us a better idea of where John lived. It shows a Close Gate on a map of Salisbury you can view on the Internet, once you get past the Mothercare safety gates etc. It might be 75, New Street, listed Grade II, or 47, but someone cleverer than me must have a go.

They had a great scare over Uncle Pilfold but he is now going to Cheltenham for his health. They found Brighton *'very expensive'*. Aunt Grove has also been ill but is getting better. Whilst staying at Ferne, Charles takes her out in his gig.

April 24th *'I rewarded my two eldest Pupils for the Sampler They worked for me in Silks.'*

On the 29th, *'Tom arrives with his bride.'* The following day, *'My Brother & Sister Tho. Grove walked to Ashcombe. It was so stormy A Day I was fearful lest her Sylph like Form might be blown away. My Father & Brothers went to see the living of Compton Abbas But it will not suit Charles.'* Livings varied in income enormously from one church to the next, a bone of contention at the period, some clergy wealthy, others really poor, but we do not know what criteria Charles had. Maybe he did not like the parsonage. Berwick was considered a good living and had, as we know, an excellent rectory. It is strange to us how these livings were bought and sold. My father told me he could perfectly well remember advertisements for such, giving details of the age of the incumbent, as, if the livings were rectories as opposed to vicarages, you could not take possession until the position was vacant.

Charlotte goes on to say, '*My Mother & Aunt drove to Berwick in the Carriage to see Our Monument erected in the Church. Eliza, Myself, George & Charles walked there.*' You can see this in the north transept in our church, with later additions. As the church was 'done up' in the 1860s, what did they actually do to it? Most of the monuments in the church predate 1860. They must have taken them down and put them back, surely a delicate job. Looking at Neil Burton's article in the March 2016 *Berwick Bulletin*, they were to take the walls down to a few feet. Lady Giffard's book *Biography of a Country Church* needs to be reread. The floor must be the same because it is full of old inscriptions. To see box pews with high sides, such as might hide little Tom Waddington, visit the church at Croscombe in Somerset, which is truly astonishing, or that of Puddletown in Dorset.

There is a general gathering of the family with the addition of John, his wife and children, now two of them, Henrietta and Thomas. Little Tom Waddington usually takes his Sunday dinner at Ferne. He does not seem to see much of his father or his siblings.

May 1st '*My love for My new Sister increases daily. I walked with Eliza to L Donhead, we called upon Mrs Dansey & saw the Children dancing & the May pole finely dressed up with Garlands.*' So where was the maypole in Donhead St Andrew?

Ann Roberts has been very poorly for a long while. May 3rd '*We visited the poor Invalid at the Mill. She is speechless But she knew Me.*' She dies on the 5th. There are two of the most obvious mills to choose from in Donhead. This was probably the closer one. If you cross at Whitsans Cross and then take the left turning as if you were going to Donhead St Mary, there is what was a mill at the bottom of the hill on the left. Charlotte and her sister-in-law go on to see Sarah Maidment, who has a swelling in her neck. '*I desired Her to go to Dr Foot.*' On the 10th, Charlotte visits her again. '*She is very ill. Mrs Candy & her Niece two*

Methodists came to see her But I would not let them have any conversation with her.' Charlotte's disapproval of the Methodists is always obvious, but this seems extra draconian.

The family party is increased with Jacksons, Mrs Walsh and Charles Jackson's fiancé. *'Mrs Walsh sung to Us some of the Irish Melodies in the Evening.'*

I now begin to work out what happened at Sedgehill after William Helyar inherited Coker Court. I believe he swapped houses with his widowed mother. *'My Brother & Sister Helyar dined here & returned to Sedgehill in the Evening. After their departure Mrs T Grove though very frightened sung to Us & delighted Us extremely. She plays and sings so well.'* Tom's wife, affectionately known as Bessy, is a great success with her new family. They leave the next day to visit old Mrs Farquharson. Introducing your new bride to the mother of your late wife must be a painful moment.

The Helyars come to stay, bringing Ellen and Albert. The three elder children, William, now twelve, Carey, eleven, and Agnes, ten, were possibly at school. Ellen is now eight and Albert six. *'The baby is left at Sedgehill.'* There was also Marian, now four, and Emma, the baby, who was born in 1822. They only stay a few days, but Charlotte is to go to Coker in September when Harriet is again *'to be confined'*.

May 20th *'George rode to East Hayes. He dined with Mrs Helyars Sedgehill.'* Charlotte worries when George dines at Coombe Priory and does not get home till late. *'I hope He will not catch Cold.'*

There has been a scheme for Charlotte and her parents to go to London with Aunt Grove. Waddington writes to say he has taken a house for her, 70, Wimpole Street. They set off on May 26th and arrive at Netherhampton. *'My Aunt rather in A Bustle about her journey to London.'*

May 27th *'We set out upon Our Journey. I sometimes was the Companion of one Carriage then of the other.'* I start to think of the logistics of the journey. They must have taken the Ferne carriage as well as Aunt Grove's. Did they take four horses each or two? They would have to have changed horses along the route. They dine at Overton and stop the night at Hartford Bridge. *'A comfortable Inn. Mrs Perkins the Landlady A Widow with 7 children.'* The following day they dine at Staines and reach Wimpole Street at seven o'clock: *'every thing very comfortable under the direction of Waddington.'* What an excellent addition he was to the family. It is apparent he is at the minute living in London, because he visits with Emma, who is now sixteen and *'very much improved in her figure'*. They are in Burlington Street. Charlotte is grieved to see *'Molly looking so ill'*. Molly was of course the children's nanny, who had looked after poor little Charles. Charlotte talks to her of Tom Waddington.

Charlotte is delighted to find a library near their house. They receive visitors and walk *'to The Regents Park'*, admiring the *'elegant new buildings'*. They *'see Punch dancing and go with Mr and Mrs T. Grove to the theatre at Covent Garden'*. She walks to Leicester Square with her father to see *'the Panorama of Ruins of Pompeia'*. Soon they are joined by George, William and Charles Jackson.

June 4th *'we went Shopping & afterwards to see Mr Wests Pictures which We found difficult to leave, They are so well worth seeing. Christ rejected & Death on the pale Horse beyond anything I ever saw.'* Benjamin West, an American, was the second president of the Royal Academy. He died in 1820, so it is interesting his paintings are still on show in 1824. Joseph Farington, an artist who kept extensive journals, describes the astonishment at West's painting enormous canvases at such an advanced age and working in his studio for long hours without a break. *Death on the Pale Horse* was exhibited in 1817 when West was seventy-eight. It is 1' 11" x 4' 2" (59.5 cm x 128.5 cm) and is impossible to describe, like some massive close-up battle scene. It is now in Detroit, but I think there was more than one version.

On the same day, they have an invitation to go to the opera. *'George was our Beau in the Evening. My Mother & I agree We never wish to go to an Opera again so disagreeable it is.'* I am sorry to say this is just what Francis thinks.

Mr Grove *'had a fall but luckily he did not materially hurt Himself'*. The next day he is *'very bilious & now our Plans are altered'*. Charlotte goes to *'the Bazar with My Aunt & We were very expeditious in Our Purchases. She has kindly given Me A pretty Morning Gown.'*

Tom and Bessy have lodgings. Charlotte goes there and *'helps dress the latter & saw them set off for Mrs Miles Ball before I came Home. Bessy most elegantly dressed.'* The following day, Bessy tells Charlotte *'that most delightful news that they are going to live at Wincombe'*.

They busy themselves with the theatre, shopping, having Charles Jackson and the brothers round to dine, dining out and taking tea, getting entertained with singing and going to the diorama. This appears different to a panorama, which was two dimensional, whereas a diorama is three dimensional, but I think there is a bit of crossover: *'the inside of Canterbury Cathedral looks like nature itself, a valley in Switzerland all beautifully lighted up.'* A few days later, they go to the Cosmorana, which seems to be views turned three dimensional with the use of lenses and optical devices. How was this done, long before photography? There was a permanent display at 207–209 Regent Street where it was possible to peer at Versailles etc. There seems as much easy entertainment to be had in London as there is now. And of course they go to church, the *'Marybone Church'*. Charlotte also goes, on the same Sunday, to listen to *'Dr. Andrews the Dean of Canterbury'* preach in St James. She goes to these churches every Sunday.

On the 11th, her parents set off for Norfolk and William transfers to Wimpole Street.

June 14th *'I walked with Wm. To Burlington St. to invite my Nieces to go to the Play But Waddington does not approve of it.'* Caroline is twelve or thirteen. Certainly, the theatre was not peculiarly decorous in those days. He must have relented or a more suitable play chosen, for they all go a few days later.

Two days later, Charlotte goes again to Burlington Street with her aunt and finds the girls at home *'with them Mrs Waddington & Miss C*

Mills. The former has flippant manners.' Who was she? John Lane says Waddington had a brother, Harry, who married in 1810, Mary Ann Milnes, so this seems a likely choice.

They visit the British Museum. *'In the Evening I accompanied My Brother Wm. To Vauxhall. The dazzling brilliancy of the Place far exceeded my expectations. A concert. Fantoccini. Chinese Festival. The Dancing delightful with the finest Fireworks I ever saw concluded the Evening. It was the anniversary of the Battle of Waterloo.'* Vauxhall Gardens was the place to go for entertainment and remained open until the middle of the century. Fantoccini are puppets operated by wires or strings.

On June 22nd, they prepare to return home. Caroline is to go with them. Charlotte is glad it has rained because it will have damped down the dust before travelling. They dine in London and sleep at Staines. I had forgotten that Aunt Grove would have brought her servants with her, *'the fat cook & Mr Barret riding in the Barouche'.*

June 23rd *'We left Staines at ½ past ten dined at Andover where they are repairing the Inn. The cook wanted to mount My Aunts Box and They had an altercation on the Subject. At Winterslow the Wheel of My Aunts Chariot was broken. William Kindly proposed that all the Females should proceed in my Brothers carriage to Netherhampton & conveyed the other safely ½ an hour afterwards.'* Travelling in those days was not always a straightforward business.

At Netherhampton the Dr John Groves hasten to dine. *'We hear the surprising News that Daniel is married to Jane. He is to continue in My Father's service & they will have A Cottage at Berwick.'* Daniel Lampard has I think been working for the Groves for many years. It seems odd no one noticed this courtship, assuming Jane worked at Ferne as well.

Charlotte is happy to get home, though her mother has a bad cold. There is still a question mark over George's health. He is always *'getting better'*, but we do not know what from.

June 25th *'I walked with Caroline to Mr Welds. Her & little Tom equally delighted to meet.'* Thereafter, Caroline spends lots of time with Tom.

'*My Nephew & Niece enjoyed playing together very much*' and '*I began reading Shakespeare with My Niece Caroline. I walked with her to Mr Weld where She spent the Day & played with her Brother Tom.*' Tom had arrived at Ferne on December 17th, and it is now the end of June, so he had not seen Caroline for six months. I am sure nobody thought this arrangement in the least strange.

Charlotte is soon back to visiting the schools, teaching her pupils and minding the invalids, but Caroline is a nice distraction. '*My Nieces Microscope is very amusing to Me as well as Herself.*'

July 2nd '*A thorough wet day. Caroline amused Herself with doing sums out of Square Root with her Uncle George, & in sorting some Shells Miss Benett of Norton gave Me, also making Trays to hold Them which I shall place in my little Cabinets.*'

July 4th '*I accompanied My Brother Wm. & Nephew & Niece to Church, afterwards I went to the Sunday School. Tom & Caroline Waddington came there before I had finished & the latter heard Them their Catechism & Spelling.*' So you could learn other things in Sunday school beyond religion.

There are many visits to S Maidment. She is expecting her son to return from the East Indies. '*Eliza Wyatt is very ill. I desired Her Mother to send immediately for Dr Foot.*'

July 6th '*John Waddington came in the Evening. He dined at Dr Groves He is now nearly as tall as His Father. His Tutor gives an excellent account of Him.*' John is now fifteen and it seems redeeming himself from whatever went wrong at Harrow. Charlotte certainly approves of him. '*A very pleasing young Man & very diffident.*'

On the 7th, little Tom comes home and Waddington and Emma arrive. Life then proceeds much as normal, with plenty of chess. On one day, Emma wins five games from Charlotte, but it is not always as bad as that. On the 12th, the weather is good enough to cut hay. '*My Fathers Mowers came into the Park. Old H Gurd cut his leg.*' Charlotte is trying to set up another penny club with Miss Blackmore. She also gets a letter from Bessy with *'News which gave Me the greatest of Pleasure.'* There must have been hope that Tom Grove would get an heir with his new wife. I imagine pregnancy to be the news.

July 14th *'Mr J Snook came to put down the Carpet in the Library. We adjoined therefore to the Drawing Room where We seldom sit.'* The habit of keeping the best room in the house unused seems curious but undying.

George Waddington comes home on the 17th, which gets all that family together at last.

Charlotte's anxiety to set up penny clubs is dominating. Miss Ann Blackmore *'proposed Patrons in their Penny Club'* and *'I walked to L Donhead to talk to Mrs Dansey about A Club there. On my return called upon Mrs Fricker & Mrs Gold & Dewy Farmers Wives tried all I could to interest Them in the Cause. In the evening walked to Milkwell & took A list of several of the poor Women who are much pleased with it.'* And so it goes on.

July 18th *'In the Evening I visited Oldy. I read the Bible to Her & Her Son the latter has minded what I said & not attended the Methodist Chapel.'* Francis says the chapel opposite the Priory was built in the 1870s by her nephew Thomas Fraser Grove, who inherited Ferne. He was an MP and, according to Francis, who will have had the information from his father, it was built to curry favour with the non-conformist voters. I feel it just as well Charlotte did not live to witness this. The chapel in Luke Street is a Baptist one, built in 1828. I do not know what chapel Oldy's son was disencouraged to attend. It may have been a room in someone's house dressed for the occasion, or somewhere in Ludwell or the Donheads.

July 22nd *'My Father so kind as to issue A Guinea Reward to find out the Culprits that have robbed the Garden of old Rebecca Pickford. I wrote out the Paper & put it over the Blacksmiths Shop.'* Now, in the 1840 map, that piece of ground where the bus shelter, cottages, forge etc. are was owned by George Burt and is described as house and gardens. Francis tells me the earlier forge was on the site of the bus shelter, which was built by Francis' grandmother and dedicated to the Queen's coronation in 1953. It obviously is, and probably was, the best place for putting up notices in Berwick St John. Francis and Peter bought the present forge, round the back so to speak, in the early 1960s from 'old Harry Burt'. How many generations later?

That evening Charlotte *'walked to Milkwell & was engaged from 6 oclock till 9 writing the names of the Penny Club, & completely tired with my walk'.* I have never known her to confess to tiredness before. Personally, I think visiting could have been wearing. The next day, *'I accompanied my Mother in Morning Visits, We went to Mrs Coffins Mrs Danseys Mrs Burlton & Mrs Blackmoores, Miss Blackmore & her Sister Elizabeth at Home & all the other Ladies – also to Berwick where We saw the two Mrs Binghams.'* How much time did they spend with each?

Charlotte's pupil Emma Weeks is going to stay with a cousin at Dinton who is a mantua-maker, in other words a dress-maker. *'I hope She will succeed well in Life as I am very interested about Her.'* John Lane has calculated her age at around sixteen.

The Waddingtons return from Coker. *'The Gentlemen were quite wet with their Ride. Poor little Tom Waddington had A Fall Romping with his Cousin Agnes, & hurt his nose very much.'* At the same time, they are visited by Mr & Mrs W.C. Grove; *'the former is very pleasant & lively'.* These were the Grove connections of Aunt Chafin.

July 28th *'I walked to Ludwell visited Mrs John Tatchel the Miss Blackmores had talked so fast when they told her of the Penny Club, that she did not understand Them. She has promised me to be A Patron.'*

July 29th *'…called upon Sarah Roberts. Her daughter this morning was taken speechless. I went upstairs to see Her & She appeared in a dozing State. Mr Parker the Priest from Wardoar came whilst I was there.'*

July 31st *'Mr Waddington & his daughters left Us, dear little Carolines Holidays are over. She left her Microscope in my care. I took Rawkins A Present from My Father of a Coat Waistcoat & Hat. Harriet Pinnock & Hannah Gold came. The former has A head for Accounts.'* Charlotte was teaching them more than sewing, which I had wondered about.

They are visited by *'Mrs Henry Auber her two sons & Miss Mary Grove… It was rather A silent Party.'*

August 3rd *'William & his two Nephews went to the Salisbury Races. George Waddington's Poney was ill. He rode his Uncle George's Mare. They were to dine & sleep at Netherhampton.'* We cannot fault the Groves for proper family life.

On the 5th they dine out, but *'George was too much of an Invalid to accompany Us'*.

The children's holidays are finishing. John goes on August 7th. His brothers walk with him to the Glove *'& saw him in to the Coach'*. Tom goes to Mr Weld on the 9th, but George does not go to Winchester until the 28th. In the meantime he amuses his relatives. August 11th *'George Waddington is very entertaining, He desires his Uncle George to assist Him in composing A Novel, the Heroine to be named Deborah.'*

Mrs John Grove has a daughter on the 7th, Jean Helen. This is her fourth child in four years.

They were told back in July by Mrs Burlton that her daughter was to marry Mr Jones, Lord Grosvenor's steward. His income was two thousand pounds a year, so this was considered a very good match. Now, on August 12th, Charlotte says, *'by Mrs Foots account Mr Jones is 29 years older than Miss Burlton. I hope that is A mistake.'* Money was not everything, even to the Georgians.

August 12th *'I visited poor Love Pinnock. I hear that her Son uses Her very ill.'* There were lots of Pinnocks.

Later we hear *'Mrs Bingham…was just returned from the Wedding of her Niece Miss Burlton to Mr Jones… The Bride was dressed in Lace over satin White Hat & Feathers.'* There is no more talk of age discrepancy, but I think weddings were getting smarter.

On Saturday the 14th, Charlotte's pupils come for the last time before the harvest starts. They would be needed to work in the fields.

There is a music meeting in Salisbury to which Charlotte goes with her parents. They visit Close Gate. *'Lady Fraser & 5 Daughters were there.'*

Remember, John's wife was one of eleven Fraser daughters. At the ball, Charlotte takes pleasure in watching her niece dance: remember, it was she that taught her. Aunt Grove gives Charlotte a watch *'(an old friend of hers 40 years)'*. I imagine it still went. The Waddingtons could not leave Salisbury because they could not get horses…like missing the last bus.

Charlotte has now arranged Sunday school into two classes. They are to alternate with catechism and reading. The Welds are called on, *'poor Tom had been in disgrace'*.

August 25th *'I accompanied My Mother & Niece to Farnham where Capt. & Mrs Markland are again settled. They have four very fine Children. The eldest Girl handsome, & the youngest perfectly beautiful. Miss King is there & is to stay with Mrs Markland till after her Confinement.'* The Marklands have obviously been elsewhere, which would explain their not being mentioned for a while. Remember Charlotte's friend Helen Tregonwell, but this relentless production of children is almost tiring to read about.

On the 31st, Charlotte sets off for Coker Court and arrives at three o'clock. She regrets leaving Ferne, but is immediately taken up with visiting the alms houses and all the old, sick and poor of her previous visit, usually before breakfast. September 3rd *'The blind girl has nearly recovered her sight & A Woman who was bedridden when I was here last is now able to walk.'* Despite all, it was possible to recover. The next day, *'Harriet shewed me her Dispensary of Medicine for the Poor people.'* William Helyar, despite lumbago, and his brothers are taken up with hunting and shooting.

September 10th *'Mr Helyar went out to the Cub Hunting in Coker Wood. They caught two mangy Foxes which appeared as if They had been poisoned.'*

September 11th *'Mr George Helyar went to Mr Goodens of Compton & for A fee Rent seized A calf. Mrs G Helyar walked with My sister & Me therefore We did not have so comfortable A Chat.'* Just helping yourself to something for unpaid rent was permissible, it seems. Two days later, the George Helyars return to Sedgehill. Charlotte makes it plain she prefers *'the comfortable trio'* of herself, her sister and brother-in-law.

September 12th *'Church in the Morning & A good Sermon on being prepared whilst in health of Body & Mind, for Death.'*

On the 14th, *'Abbots child had the croup. I remembered how Mrs Herridges Child was treated & took some Antimonial Wine to Him. Mr Shawland when He came put on A Blister & He was much relieved.'* This did, literally, raise a blister. It was a popular treatment for insanity in the 18th century. Even in my recollection, horses' legs were blistered to strengthen them after tendon injuries. Goodness knows if it worked or not, but it surely was painful for a little boy with croup. How was it applied? Antimonial wine was wine left to stand in a small tin cup for twenty-four hours, during which time it became impregnated with tartrate of antimony. It was generally a purge, so I do not know what it did for croup.

September 15th *'About ten oclock Harriet felt A little ill But was not seriously so till from 5 till 6 in the Evening when She gave birth to A very fine little Girl.'* This was Lucy Elizabeth.

Harriet seems to have given birth to her eighth child without too much trouble. Charlotte is in charge, sending *'Mrs Sellwood out of My Sisters Room as She talked so much. Mr Helyar went out Shooting & had A cold Dinner sent out to Him.'*

Though Charlotte spends much time with Harriet, she still has plenty for visiting and advising people never to go to the Methodist Meeting. She writes to Agnes, Harriet's third child, now ten, presumably to tell her of the baby. I am assuming the older children were away at school. Emma and Albert were certainly at home, under the management of Miss Lake, but Charlotte does not mention them much. They come down to the parlour if they have been good. Her mother writes to tell her of the death of Dr John Grove's last baby, born earlier in the year. Charlotte's brother-in-law calls her evangelical *'because I do not approve of some of his Sayings'*. I feel a little sympathy for him. She writes Evangelical in a carefully abbreviated script. Nevertheless, he dutifully reads prayers and a sermon on Sunday evening. Harriet comes downstairs for the first time twelve days after her confinement.

October 1st *'I had A conversation with S Hillier as She has A religious melancholy upon her, & gave her my Advice to go to the Church only & not to any Meetings. We now sit in the Library one of the pleasantest Rooms in the House. The Floods are out all round Coker.'*

On the 5th, they have a music meeting in Coker Church. I was interested to hear even then the church could be used for other things, but we are not told by Charlotte if it was to raise money.

There is a new anxiety with a further letter from Mrs Grove to say John's eldest boy, Thomas Fraser Grove, is very ill. They watch the post: *'a letter from my Mother. They are in hopes little Tho Fraser Grove is out of danger. He was in an insensible state for some time.'* Eventually he gets better. They also hear little Tom has been ill again with *'spasms in the stomack'*. Charlotte is afraid of his not recovering, but he does.

Charlotte now goes for walks with Miss Lake and the children. Emma, who must have been two or three, is unwell. *'I advised sending for Dr Bradley which they did and he dined here.'* The social position of doctors is interesting. Actually to have a qualification rendered you respectable in circles such as the Groves and the Helyars. It is my belief the Victorians were more concerned with class distinction than the Georgians. My great-grandmother is said to have wept when asked to sit down to dinner with a doctor and, apart from money, her credentials were nothing much. It takes me back to that cosy time when Joe Ellis, our doctor at Maiden Bradley, was called in to attend on one or other of us children, and, having listened to a chest with his cold stethoscope, sat down with my parents for a huge gin and tonic. But did he have supper? I fear not. I note a few days later Charlotte says, *'Miss Lake drank Tea with us.'* As tea was drunk after dinner, I surmise poor Miss Lake was kept firmly in the school room and had her dinner there: drinking tea with the family was a treat. I realise from my own reading this varied from one household to the next, probably tutors and governesses more likely to dine with their employers when their charges were considered old enough to do so. Emma gets better and her father buys her *'A Coral*

Necklace with which she is much pleased'. Coral was often given for babies to chew when they were teething.

October 28th *'Harriet unwell, her Milk lessoned all at once.'* A farmer's wife, Mrs Lucas, comes with her own little boy to nurse the baby, but Harriet needs a full-time wet nurse. Charlotte writes to delay her return to Ferne. Eventually Phillis March arrives, whose own mother will care for her three children. Harriet gives Mrs Lucas a present for her baby boy, *'a cloak and beaver hat with feathers'.* Charlotte says, *'My Niece Lucy is so beautiful A Baby I wish A model could be taken of her in Waxwork.'*

Harriet gets better and the sisters are able to go about together. Mary Hulls had a sick child who died. *'We saw the corpse.'* On November 6th, *'the Wet Nurse sent away at the desire of Mrs Helyar senior'.* I wonder what was wrong with her. Mrs Lucas returns.

November 8th *'A wet Day. Mr Helyar & I walked for an hour in the great Hall. We searched for old China to ornament the Drawing Room & Library. My Brother & Sister Grove came. A message from My Mother that I am to return home with Them. Bessy not at all the worse for her Journey. She played & sung to Us in the evening.'* Bessy is definitely pregnant. There follows several days of entertaining, singing etc. Mrs T Grove, despite her condition, is obviously the life and soul of the party. *'She danced A Minuet & Waltz with Mr Helyar.'* Charlotte is always thrilled with Bessy who is *'A great Florist'.* There is hunting and shooting.

On the 12th, having *'breakfasted with the Gentlemen who went out Foxhunting',* Charlotte then does a whole round of visiting and returns. *'The ladies had A comfortable late Breakfast together, I read the conversations of Ld. Byron to Them.'* These were published in this year, 1824, by Thomas Medwin who was in Pisa with Byron in 1821 and 1822. Medwin stated he wished to 'lessen, if not remedy, the evil' of the burning of Byron's memoirs.

On Sunday the 14th, they go to the evening service. *'I wore A Velvet Hat given Me by my Sister. Tom quizzed it extremely.'* It is the Helyars wedding anniversary. They have been married thirteen years.

November 17th *'The Baby has had The Cow Pox very favourably.'* She was born on September 15th, so she had this vaccination at about two months.

November 19th *'We left Coker & I quitted my dear Friends with great regret. My Brothers Horses frisky at Starting. He drove Bessy in his Phaeton.'* Charlotte goes in a chaise with Mallet, who I guess to be Bessy's maid. They arrive at Wincombe. *'I was quite pleased with the comfort of the Rooms &c.'*

The journey, this time, has not agreed with Bessy. *'It has determined My Brother not to let her again venture in A Carriage.'* Charlotte *'saw all the beautiful worked Baby Clothes'*. She also says, *'George called upon Us. He was so rejoiced to see Bessy that he did not observe I was in the Room for some time.'* It says a lot for Bessy she did not make the women jealous.

On the 21st, Charlotte goes home. *'The little Man was glad to see me again.'* Now it is William who is poorly, *'still an Invalid on the Sofa'*.

There ensues a terrible wind on the night of the 22nd. Trees are blown down and windows broken. *'Poor old Kimber of Berwick had his House fall in about 10 minutes after he & his Daughter had quitted it.'* They are taken in by Mrs Blugden. Charlotte remarks, *'old Kimber though his House was blown down looks quite cheerful.'* I feel some of these cottages must have been built without any substance, so that one could actually blow down, like a tent.

On the 24th, Charlotte and Eliza visit Mrs Lampard, the wife of their servant Daniel. *'They have got a very neat Cottage.'* She then adds, *'Oldy very silly about some Garden ground being put into the Road.'* I rather sympathise with Oldy here.

They have the *'Miss Benetts of Norton'* to stay. Miss Anna *'appeared very learned on the subject of organic faculties'*. They were very learned altogether, these sisters.

On the 30th, they visit Wincombe, Charlotte travelling in the carriage with Harris, her mother's maid, and the carriage then going back to fetch everybody else. *'I found Tom & George busily engaged repairing Bessy's*

Harp. She played some pretty tunes & I think it A fine toned Instrument. She also sung several delightful Songs.' At her mother's request, Charlotte is going to learn some duets so she and Bessy can play together.

Fanny Jackson is seriously ill. John attends her, but Mrs Jackson thinks not enough. She sends for Mr Coates, whose medicine *'increased her sickness'*. Several doctors are involved. Mr Buckland *'thinks my Cousins A very obscure case'*. John returns on December 5th. He *'thinks her better & that an Abscess has broken'*.

Charlotte is as ever busy with the club, enrolling new members and expelling the ones that do not behave. *'Only Labourers Family's should be admitted.'* The Miss Blackmores *'conduct their Penny Club very well'*. She says, *'A cloak finished which I like very much.'* I suppose they chose the cloth and were now having them made up.

Old Mr Maidment dies of a stroke. Charlotte was too late to get the 2s 6d he promised for the club, upon which she unfeelingly comments. Mrs Weld has had another little boy. Mary Stretch is very ill and dies. Harriet writes that she is not satisfied with her wet nurse. Charles Jackson gets married. Tom Waddington comes home for *'a few Days Holiday'*. The Penruddockes from Compton Chamberlayne come on a visit.

December 7th *'I walked to L Donhead called at Workhouse & saw Betty Butcher advised her to stay in so good A Place instead of starving at Home. I arranged with Mrs Marsh, Shop that my Club are to have Calico 6d with the Blankets.'*

December 9th *'Mr & Mrs Jackson rode to Combe. Fanny had not been so sick But subject to suffocations which I think alarming.'* Mr and Mrs Jackson refer to Charles and his wife.

On the 12th, they all go to church. *'The sermon was on taking improper Oaths.'* This entry ends with *'Tom thinks Mrs Jackson like Emma.'*

December 14th *'I received A letter from My Aunt P Grove inclosing such kind Donations to the Penny Clubs that quite delighted my Heart.'*

December 15th *'My Father had a large party out hunting with him…little Tom Waddington accoutred in his Grandpapas Gaiters was very much pleased.'*

On the 20th, *'Dr Grove in going down the Park his Horse fell, & broke the Harness of his Gig. But luckily neither Him or His servant were hurt.'* Charlotte then remarks Harris, her mother's maid, *'has no taste for arranging a Pin cushion'.* What odd accomplishments were required! She has six pupils on Saturdays at the moment.

The following day, young John Waddington arrives by breakfast time, having been all night on the mail coach: *'he is grown taller & handsomer than ever'.*

Cloaks arrive and are approved and the prices and quality of calico compared, to be distributed to the penny club. Betty Butcher, who Charlotte had visited in the workhouse in Donhead, *'has very imprudently gone Home without a bed or a Blanket to cover Her. My Mother & I have relieved her necessities.'* Later, Charlotte reports on Betty Butcher being more comfortable now she has a bed.

Christmas Eve is spent with Charlotte assisting her mother in giving out *'Beef to the Labourers & Families about 18 others had some'.* Tom Waddington comes home.

On Christmas Day, the Berwick Band comes early in the morning and sings carols. On the 27th, *'The Singers Bulls &c came. In the Evening They concluded with a Dance. My Nephew Tom W. enjoyed it very much indeed.'* He reads to his aunt once a day and she thinks him improved. I have the feeling he was not an academic child, as he is now ten, probably why he was at Mr Weld's and not at ordinary school. His brother John *'has his own & his Fathers Hunter here & I hope that he will enjoy good Sport. He is quite free & easy with Us & seems to enjoy his Holidays at Fern.'* John is fifteen.

Fanny Jackson is at last recovering but Mr Dansey, Rector of Lower Donhead, has lost his brother to *'A Typhus Fever'.*

On the 31st, *'Amy was so considerate as to caution Me not to go down Jerry Street Berwick. The Family of the Beaches having The Fever.'* Water Street was Water Street. I have heard Luke Street was once Duck Street, which would fit with Pond Field, the pond on the site of Pond Cottages, built by Francis' grandmother. On the other hand, Charlotte never refers to Duck Street. Jerry Street left me guessing for a long while, but the evidence was under my nose. While looking for something else in the 1840 map, I found a piece of land abutting on to the top Berwick Road, on the right if you are leaving the village, called 'Jerry Lane Ground'. This makes me think the top road was Jerry Street or Jerry Lane, though the map shows not a single house. The name could have extended to include the piece of road between Upton Farm and Upton Lucy and down Blind Lane to join the top of Water Street. I get no reference to Luke Street until after 1826, but from that I conclude it always was Luke Street. However, on both the 1841 and 1851 censuses it is referred to as Duck Street, but this is not how Charlotte refers to it.

The end papers for this year contain nothing but the lists of texts and sermons.

1825

Charlotte regularly records what book they are reading and whether they like it or not. They are mostly very obscure and sometimes abandoned as *'so stupid we could not continue it'*, the word stupid mostly meaning boring at this period. The year starts on a Saturday, the day Charlotte has her pupils. *'I set S Wright & H Gould the task of doing me each a Sampler.'*

January 4th *'Dr Grove went yesterday to Coker little Carey Helyar being very ill in A Fever.'*

Life goes on as usual for a few days; George Waddington joins them and also Charles and Eliza. William and his two nephews go off to Blandford for a ball but on the 8th *'I received a letter from Miss Lake with the melancholy News that My dear little Nephew Carey Helyar died last Thursday Evening. I sincerely pity My dear Brother & Sister Helyar.'* Carey, sometimes Cary, was the baby born at seven months, *'the least baby they had ever seen',* according to his relatives. He had often been unwell, having something wrong with his leg, sometimes riding a donkey when others walked. He was twelve when he died. Charlotte has a disconcerting habit of continuing the day's events as if nothing were out of the ordinary, remarking Susan Wright had to be sent home as she had forgotten to bring her work to her Saturday lesson.

January 11th *'Mrs Long came her Horses were completely tired out only travelling 14 miles.'* This surprised me as other research gave me to understand horses were changed about every eight miles.

It is suggested Charlotte should go to Coker, but Harriet *'will not by any means allow Me to come at present to Coker. She is always so considerate & kind. Dr Groves Head Nurse is dangerously ill in the Typhus Fever. They proposed bringing their large Family to Fern But my Father would not allow it.'* There is naturally a fear of the fever.

On the following day, Charlotte walks to Berwick and *'met the Harriers in Jerry Lane'*. So there it is again, but as lane rather than street. She offers to go to Wincombe on the 27th for Bessy's confinement.

January 19th *'Betty Butcher I saw at Her Sisters. She is only allowed 9d a Week which is half the usual Parish Pay.'*

January 20th *'I went to Berwick to receive my Club Money & then called upon Mrs Weld. Tom & little Henry wanted to accompany me to the school. But I was afraid of the Whooping Cough which the latter has never had. The Gentlemen had a delightful Chase with the Harriers. My dear Father in at the death. Caroline Waddington Birth day. We drank her Health. She is thirteen.'*

I had thought it was Charles Jackson and his wife going to the East Indies, but it is Tom Jackson, who later writes from on board ship. Charlotte comments on the day they sail, the 23rd. What terrible partings families underwent, for it was surely doubtful if you would ever see them again.

On the 22nd, John and George Waddington *'went by the Mail to town'*.

Charlotte hears, on the 24th, that Mr Wills has attended all night on Tom's wife. *'I mentioned it to George & We agreed not to tell my Mother & Father of it As it might make them uneasy: however I could not help thinking about it.'*

They hear at breakfast *'the joyful News that Mrs Thos. Grove was brought to Bed of A little Girl at about three o clock in the Morning'*. The child is to be called Mary after Bessy's late sister. Charlotte is *'honoured'* to be a Godmother.

January 28th *'I accompanied My Mother to Wincombe. My little Niece is A very pretty Baby. Tom is so proud of his Child.'* Charlotte stays on. *'My*

Brother is going to build A Root House to surprise His Wife on her recovery. Bessy has so much Milk that She is obliged to have A poor Child brought here once A Day.' That certainly is the reverse of the wet nurse business. One definition of a root house indicates it was an extra building for the storage of food, but I do not find it convincing. Later Charlotte says Bessy was delighted with the grotto Tom built her.

On the last day of the month, Charlotte goes in the pony carriage to Sedgehill, where Mrs Helyar senior and other members of the family now reside. She hears little Ellen Helyar, who was thought to have the typhus fever but in fact did not, is better. Caroline Helyar, with whom Charlotte used to spend so much time when Harriet was waiting to be confined, is too ill to see her.

February 1st *'I read aloud to Bessy & Emma P – Harriette Wilsons life As long as the Turk as We call the old Nurse would permit Us.'* Emma Partridge is a niece of Mr Gordon, who owned Wincombe. Just when you think they are at their most prudish, you are astonished to find them reading Harriette Wilson, who produced a memoir in 1825. She was a notorious courtesan who wrote amusingly, frankly and possibly not always truthfully about her various liaisons. A few days later they are reading Tom Jones. The books come in the mail.

On the 5th, Charlotte goes home. Tom has been to Langton and with manifest self-control, *'the whole time he was there He refrained from speaking of his Babe.'*

February 7th *'My Father reprimanded the Housemaids for throwing The Carpets out of the windows and frightened Them.'* Was this spring cleaning?

February 8th *'I called on Mrs Ailes. Maidment was there. He was just returned from New South Wales where He was transported 8 years ago. He gave me some account of the Country &c.'* So it was possible to get home again!

On the 9th, *'A Garnet Ring arrived from Bennetts Jeweller directed to Me. As I never ordered it I suppose it to be a mistake.'* This Bennett, with two Ns, was based in Salisbury. He was a distant cousin of the Pythouse

Benetts. Later Charlotte says, *'My Brother George is the kind Donor of my pretty Garnet Ring which I shall wear in memory of my dear little Nephew Carey Helyar.'*

Things go on much as usual. They have a visit from Charlotte's uncle Pilfold, recovered in health. Captain Markland has *'nearly recovered the use of his Arm'*. Henry Jackson has left the Navy: *'I hope he will soon get into some good Profession.'*

February 16th *'I walked to Mr Welds. We invited my nephew Tom Waddington to come here Sunday. He looks very well & little Henry Weld is quite familiar with me.'* He comes back in the carriage with them after church on Sunday.

February 18th *'Mr Codringtons Hounds came here and killed A Fox in our Plantation. Dr Pole, The Mr Wyndhams &c took their Luncheon at Fern. Mr Wyndham's Brother Charles has bought Donhead Hall & at A high price. 10,000 without Furniture.'*

Charlotte now has seven pupils on Saturdays. *'We talked about the Catholic Question.'* Dr Grove visits, but his wife has rheumatism.

Mrs Shere is visited as ever, but this is of course the second Mrs Shere who had a baby about the same time Harriet had hers. There is already a little Thomas Shere, an especially beautiful child. This Thomas Shere grew up and, I understand from John Lane, appears in the 1871 census, farming six hundred acres in 'Luke Street'. He was married to Mary Ann Tanner and employed a governess for his seven children. Fanny Jackson is ill again.

February 24th *'George rode to East Hayes & called at Wyncombe, Tom was hard at Work in his Garden. My Uncle Pilfold left us. He accompanied My Aunt Jackson to Combe Priory. They comfortably filled the Poney Chaise.'*

On the 25th, *'George after Hunting with my Father called at Wincombe. Miss Ethel Benett was just arrived.'* This was John Benett's second daughter, now twenty. She was Etheldred, like her learned aunt. I cannot persuade myself it is a nice name. Bessy was a relation of the Gordons, who probably had not had a political rift with the Benetts. This Etheldred married a son of the fifth Duke of Marlborough.

February 26th *'I walked to Rowberry. Harriet Lush is gone to the Infirmary to have an operation performed having A Cancer in the Mouth.'* The following day she is reported to be doing as well as can be expected. It makes Charlotte reflect on *'all the Blessings'* she has of health and kind friends and relations, particularly her parents.

Tom tells them that Mr Gordon is to marry *'Mrs Oliver A Widow of large Fortune'*. They discuss Lower Bridmore in case Mr Gordon wants his house back.

At the beginning of March, Mr and Mrs Grove go to Wincombe. They see Mrs Helyar senior before they go. Charlotte says, *'I am sorry to hear my Brother Helyar has not yet at all recovered his grief for the loss of poor little Carey.'* I think this an interesting comment. They lived in a period of hoping one had Christian fortitude to deal with the frequent and unexpected death of the young, let alone the old. Carey Helyar died on January 6th, and it is only now March 1st.

March 3rd *'Tom Gordon was at Wincombe. Mrs Oliver has sent to pay off the Mortgage on Wincombe for Mr Gordon. The latter has I think sold well at his age.'* Rather a sharp comment by Charlotte. The mortgage would explain why Mr Gordon was always letting his house. Tom Grove goes to look at *'Mr Batsons Place But he cannot get it'*. Tom is *'very anxious to stay in the country'* meaning in the vicinity. Mrs Bingham is to speak to Mr Harvey, Lord Rivers' steward, to see if Rushmore is to be let.

Aunt Grove and Miss Popham come on a short visit. Charlotte says the latter *'seems very languid and unwell'*. William returns home *'looking very well. The foxhunting has agreed with him.'*

Daniel Lampard, their footman, now lives in the village. His wife is in a protracted labour. *'Mr Wills was there poor Daniel is in a state of great anxiety.'* Mr Grove sends her some white wine. George stays at Wincombe, *'which is best as Daniel cannot at the present wait on Him'*. I had always supposed younger sons without their own valets were looked after by a footman. Mrs Lampard has a stillborn son two days later.

March 15th *'My father rode to Wincombe. He found Bessy & My two Brothers busily employed nailing Ivy on the Moss House.'* We have heard mention of a root house. In January, Charlotte had said Bessy was delighted with the grotto Tom had built. Now it is a moss house. They were possibly all one and the same thing but perhaps not a very permanent structure, as they definitely have to leave Wincombe.

March 18th *'I walked to Brookwater & Ludwell – visited Mrs Whites School & heard S Wright read. I met little T Gould upon A very large Horse. Harriet Lush has had A return of the Abscess in her Mouth. I am quite apprehensive about Her.'* I think illness now as frightening as it was then, but at least we have anaesthetics for the operations.

Here is another thing we do not have to teach the young: *'I attended the Sunday School & made the Children quit the Room regularly by Classes making Their Bows & Curtsies properly.'*

A round of visits by Charlotte and her mother are of frequent occurrence. I suppose once the carriage horses were got out, as many people as possible were called on in one go. How long were those visits meant to last to be viewed as polite? On the 23rd of March, they go Sedgehill to see Mrs Helyar. *'Caroline was looking very thin.'* They go on to Slades at East Knoyle where the William Chafin Groves are living. William and his brother Chafin were heirs to Aunt Chafin's property at Zeals. Charlotte says, *'Her Baby is very thin, wanting A good Nurse.'* Their last visit was to the Stills at Clouds. *'Mrs Still has been very ill. Her daughter Fanny is looking in high Beauty.'*

Charles and Eliza come over from Tarrant Hinton very often. On the 24th, they call at Wincombe, accompanied by George. *'Tom has thoughts of purchasing Donhead Lodge. I wish him to have some fixed Residence in the Neighbour hood.'*

March 25th *'The Tenants Dinner. My Father & Tom were comfortably happy with the Punch.'*

The following day, *'I walked to Donhead Lodge. I met my Brother & Sister there. The Offices &c are so very indifferent & Capt. Haines asks such an enormous price that it would not by any means suit Them as A place of Residence.'* The offices in this sense referred to the working parts of the house, kitchens etc. Tom then starts thinking he might build at East Hayes. Bessy draws up a plan for it. Charlotte *'perfectly coincide with My dear Father about Bridmore'*. They see it as suitable. Lower Bridmore remained tenanted until Mark Dineley added to it in 2013. The interior is interesting as it retained its original fittings, doors etc. from when it was built. Mark has done his best to preserve these.

I have not quite followed the Maidments. One we know recently died. There were more than one lot, I think. Charlotte refers to *'Dame Maidment'*. She says, *'The Old Man was beating Stones on the Turnpike Road.'* This was how the roads were kept up. John McAdam had come up with the idea that roads should be raised above the surrounding ground, cambered for water to run off them and systematically layered with rocks and gravel. The first to be constructed thus was near Bristol in 1816. I do not know how long it was for most roads to be improved in this manner, but 'the Turnpike Trusts' were in charge of them. Mr Grove goes to turnpike meetings. Tarmacadam or tarmac did not come in to being until 1902.

March 31st *'It continues fine dry weather with an Easterly Wind. A fine blossom on the Trees in the Garden where I walked before Breakfast. My Apple Trees Amy has transplanted & They are grown nicely. Little Thomas Shere I visited.'* Charlotte had grown the trees from pips.

On April 4th she walks to Ashcombe, where she has not been for some time, and sees Mrs James, who is lame from rheumatism. Her *'daughter Hannah is grown extremely fat'*. William, never at a loss for hunting even in April, is off to Stour Head *'to hunt with Mr Farquharsons Hounds'*. His favourite horse *'Evergreen fell down & broke His Knees.'* This was a term used then and when I was growing up to mean a horse badly cutting its knees, rather than actually breaking them. On the 7th, *'I gave*

Grace Chowne A present as She has been A good Girl lately.' We are never told what the child does to be in trouble so much. Mr Dansey writes to Mr Grove. *'He is always wanting alterations to his Church.'* Mr King of Alvediston is *'dangerously ill. He will be A very great loss to the Poor of that Parish.'*

Mr Gordon's marriage to Mrs Oliver is in the Salisbury Paper. They are going abroad for a year, which must allow Tom a little more time.

April 11th *'My Application for my Penny Club successful both with my dear Father & William.'* Penny clubs were heavily subsidised. Aunt Chafin was generous. *'At Walter Stretches I saw a daughter of old Smiths & niece to our old Nurse Mary Dimmer, She is very like her Aunt. Aaron is now taken in to the House as Footman & wears A Livery.'* So even Ferne, which was not such a very grand house, put footmen into livery.

April 13th *'Mr Hater the organist from Mere came to new Leather my Piano Forte.'*

On the 14th, *'My Brother has given up the idea of building at East Hayes & is quite undecided what He shall do.'* They contemplate Bridmore again, going there with a Captain Hill, probably a brother of Bessy's, *'who thinks there is great capabilities in the place. I wish my dear Brother had the same sentiments.'*

On the 17th, they get a letter from Charles Jackson *'dated nearly from the Line – They have had a long voyage & do not expect to reach Bombay till June'.* They had sailed on January 23rd. *'William left Us for Town hoping to get an appointment for Promotion.'* This surprised me, as William's Naval career seems to have been long in abeyance. This leaves Charlotte alone with her parents: *'We are A very happy Trio.'* Little Tom Waddington comes and goes.

April 19th *'I walked over the Hill to Combe Cottage where Mary Ann Kelly one of My Club lives, Her Husband is Hedger to Mr Foot. She has five Children. It is A pretty situation.'* This is the cottage that used to be down the combe in front of Woodlands, to the left of the folly. We unearthed the foundations not long ago. Snowdrops grow there, as does some monk's hood. In the 1840 map, it is described as 'house and gardens and plantation'. The grandchildren look for pieces of old china. I once found a marble, but made of stone. Did one of the five children lose it there? Later there were eight children. Francis talks of Old Ben Kelly, a veteran of WWI whom his father employed. These Kellys were probably his great-grandparents. Ben Kelly did not like his grandfather and refused to go down the combe, though grandfather and cottage had long since gone. According to the Rev Goodchild, it was pulled down in about 1898, so well within Ben Kelly's lifetime. Further information confuses the whole issue because later (1841) it is Stretches living there, and Charlotte visits them. John Lane tried to trace 'Old Ben Kelly' on my behalf, but there is insufficient information.

The fever has not entirely left the area. *'John Young has died in the Fever & left two Orphans to L Donhead Parish.'* On the 20th, *'I saw old Betty Butcher & She is now staying at Home hard at work instead of Begging.'* Charlotte had supplied her with the materials for buttoning. *'On my return found Dr & Mrs J Grove little Henrietta & Tom here. The latter is such a nice little talkative fellow & looks so very healthy. They both wore their little watches given them by their cousin Tom Waddington.'* Tom must be eleven now, quite a bit older than these cousins.

On the 24th, Charlotte remarks that Bessy and Thomas's new baby, Mary, *'has both arms inflamed with the Cow Pox'.* I take it she has been vaccinated, though it is not actually said. Does it mean she was vaccinated in both arms?

They are visited by *'Mrs Chafin Grove & Miss Fanny Grove'*. I have by no means a clear picture of Groves and Chafin Groves, apart from the fact they were all descended from the Grove who originally purchased Ferne. In 1828, a year for which we have no diary, William marries Frances Grove, known as Fanny, which John Lane assures me is this one, the daughter of Dr Charles Grove.

April 26th *'I walked with Miss Fanny Grove to Ashcombe. We rested Ourselves at the Farm House. Mrs James Mother in her 70th year had just* walked there from Knoyle. Ld Rivers is just considering whether he shall let Rushmore Lodge to Tom.' She describes it as 'that delightful place'. Rushmore Lodge is the present Sandroyd School.

Two days later, she walks in the garden, 'a quantity of slugs. The gardener was destroying Them with Lime.'

Ferne is having a general paint. The library is to be painted, so 'We now dine in my Fathers room.' Soon the dining room is finished, 'A pale Raspberry Cream color'.

Harriet Lush is back in the Salisbury Infirmary, under the care of John. Emma Weeks, Charlotte's erstwhile pupil, comes to see her while she has some time off. Charlotte buys 'two net caps that She made'. She was going off with a party of friends to 'dance round the Maypole'.

William returns from London with their new phaeton. It took him eleven hours. Charlotte approves of it: 'it will hold 4 Persons & My Father intends driving his own Horses in it.'

May 4th 'I visited Mrs J Tatchell. She has quite A Colony of Rabbits. I accompanied her on a very pretty walk to the Bath where old Jenny Read lives.' What was and where was this bath? I think in Donhead.

On the 6th, Charlotte 'desired Mary Butcher to bring up some buttons for my Brother William'. She says William has been 'in the Penseroso mood' since his return from London. I suspect, myself, he does not know what to do with himself with the close of the hunting season. However, two weeks later, she says, 'William has no chance of Promotion or being sent out to Sea.' William is thirty-five now, so he may well feel life slipping by.

May 7th is Mr and Mrs Grove's forty-third wedding anniversary.

Charlotte now has nine pupils on Saturdays. Charles Jay's baby has worms. She is hopeful of curing him. Harriet Lush is 'now an out Patient of the Infirmary'.

Little Tom has a new school friend, 'Master Austin'. His father takes the service in Berwick in the absence of Mr Bingham and invites Tom to Tollard, where they are living. 'My little Nephew dined with Us & dressed himself quite the Beau.' A few days later, Tom introduces his aunt to Master Austin and he is declared *'A very unhealthy looking child'*. John Lane tells me, after massive research, he was the son of the Rev John Austen of Tarrant Keyneston. He had no connection with the Charles Austen rejected by Miss Erle.

On May 11th, Mr and Mrs R Blackmore are off to Russia, going to Scotland and from there embarking, so definitely a sea trip. They called *'to take leave'*.

The political issue of the day was that of Catholic Emancipation. At this period, Catholics could do nothing, hold no rank in the army or navy, be magistrates nor MPs. May 13th *'We have a Debate most days on the Catholic Church & their emancipation. My Mother waits for the Ld. Chancellors Speech & opinion thereupon.'* The following day she records *'Mr W Cobbett has written some tracts against the Protestants that is not the way to conciliate Parties.'* William Cobbett was an arch radical, best known for the 'Rural Rides'. He had a little newspaper that the government endeavoured to suppress by putting a tax on newspapers that sold for more than two pence. He immediately reduced the price of his to exactly that, and it gave us the derogatory term Tuppenny Trash, which I fear has completely gone out of use.

Mrs White has made Charlotte a *'little model of A Shirt to teach my pupils'*.

May 15th *'I received a long letter from Miss Popham with A particular account of the month she spent in London where She went for the first time in her Life.'* London was no necessity, even for the educated classes.

Charles and Eliza have been in London with Aunt Grove and had been entrusted with choosing clothes for Charlotte and her mother. May 17th *'Our Millinery arrived from Town, & We like it very much, the Ladies have shewn their taste in chusing My Dresses.'*

May 18th *'Mrs Lewis made A mistake in My Mother's dresses taking Aunt P Grove's measure instead of hers. Alice Brockway I hope will soon rectify it.'*

May 20th *'I walked to Milkwell on my return found Mr & Mrs Hill, & there little twins here. They are two fine boys of 2 years old. We took them* to the Kennell & let them peep through the door at the Hounds: Mrs Hill is a pretty interesting woman & Mr Hill a handsome Man. Tom drove the party over in his phaeton.'

On May 24th *'My Mother took me to Wincombe my dear Brother Tom was so very happy to see Me, he called me his foreign sister as I had not been there lately. Mr & Mrs Hill with their little Twins there.'* Mr Hill is Bessy's brother. *'In the Evening Bessy played on the Piano Forte & Mr Hill accompanied Her on the Flute. The Harp was in A very perverse state.'* I cannot help wondering about Tom and George's repairs to the same.

Mary Grove's Christening is the following day. They have a large party to dinner *'turtle, venison &c'*. They have a concert in the evening, Mrs Hill playing the harp, Bessy the piano and Captain Benett the flute. *'Little Mary behaved very well at this first Ceremony. The Gentlemen drank her health rather too often.'* Captain Charles Benett was one of the late Donhead Rector's sons. He was married to a Burlton daughter.

Her father and William come to fetch her in the new phaeton. Charlotte worries the former will catch cold as he has been poorly and it rains. George is on and off unwell. Charlotte does not specify his complaint. He was three years younger than William, so now thirty-one.

May 27th *'I walked to Berwick. Our late Cook Mrs Blugden & her Husband are going to be dipped in the Pool of Bethesda at Semley being of the Society of Dippers A sort of Methodist.'*

Charlotte administers punishments to her pupils now and again, but she never says what they have done. At least she has become more cautious. *'I heard of some ill behaviour of G Chowne. I must investigate it well before I correct her.'* The child does not escape and is punished a few days later.

On the last day of the month, William drives Charlotte and her mother to Donhead. *'We called at The Lodge. Col Coffin has just attained the Rank of General.'* He was actually John Pine Coffin. He had had a full and very active military career.

Mr Wills and John see Maria Burts on June 5th, *'whom they think is in A Decline'*. Charlotte *'visited Maria Burts whose spirits seem very good, generally the case with Decline'*. What were the symptoms of a decline? She dies on the 12th, leaving four children.

At the beginning of June, George Wyatt *'has been much hurt by Gun Powder that they used for the Stone Quarry'*. On June 6th, Charlotte visits him. *'Mr Blackmore was applying Leaches to his Temple & I hope He will recover his Eye-sight. His right Arm is also much hurt.'* Is this the quarry in the wood at the bottom of the park at Ferne? She sees him again on the 10th. *'Miss Harriet Blackmore is applying the leaches to his eye but he is better.'*

Mr Grove has a tooth drawn by Wills. On the 8th, Charlotte takes *'Calomus Aromaticus'* to Mary Blanchard's daughter Sally, who has the ague. She refers to her as *'my patient'* and sees her regularly. The ague is, from Charlotte's account, like malaria, coming every few days. Sometimes the patient 'misses' a bout or two but then gets another attack. Mr Talbot shows Charlotte *'some excellent Under Blankets at 2s 2d yd. which he will let me have for my Club at 2s 1d.'* They are haymaking. Mr Grove takes the phaeton out regularly. He drives it to the Cribbage Hut, taking his wife, Eliza and George. On the same day, Charlotte walks to Talbots and *'brought to my Mother Patterns of glazed Holland'*. This was linen.

Charlotte does the usual amount of visiting the poor or/and ailing, sometimes with Eliza. She and Charles are often at Ferne.

On the 20th, Mr Weld *'has improved his Pleasure Garden'*. I wonder if the Priory gardens were the same dimensions then as now.

June 22nd *'We went a Grand Cavalcade to East Hayes. My Aunts Chariot, Our Phaeton & my Brother CH Groves phaeton: It is a most beautiful Spot, & much improved since I last saw it.'*

There is a little more information on the workhouse. June 23rd *'We called at the workhouse'* after seeing Jenny Reed who lives at the *'Bath Cottage…find they have their Compliment filled therefore there is not now any excuse for not paying her monthly Allowance'*. I think this means that if they have no room in the workhouse so cannot accommodate a person, they must give them money instead. A week later, *'we proceeded to the Workhouse to see the Children reeling the silks. I rewarded the three Best. We saw all the Rooms. Mr & Mrs Trowbridge seem to conduct it nicely.'* Were they reeling the silk from the cocoons of the silkworm or at some later stage of the proceedings? This is the first I knew of a silk industry in the area.

The children in the Sunday school are to have a reward for cleanliness by Miss Erle, a niece of Mrs Bingham. There are sixteen pupils in two classes.

George has abandoned his wig. Laetitia Popham is staying. *'My friend Laetitia is A most entertaining companion.'* Miss Popham is not as active as Charlotte and spends a lot of time in her room. She takes her walks with Mrs Grove. Charlotte mends Laetitia's gown and her friend *'worked some leaves on mine. We had also a nice Chat on past times.'* They were, remember, at school together. A few days later, *'Laetitia so kind as to make A trimming for My Bonnet.'*

June 28th *'George told me to leave my Dinner & go to Berwick to assuage the anger of two Virago's there.'*

July 1st *'My Father drove Us in the Phaeton to Combe. Mrs Walsh & her Children there. Her little Boy is very beautiful & very much like herself. Fanny is looking in perfect health.'* She had been ill.

July 2nd *'John Waddington arrived from Town. Tom W is come Home for the Holidays.'*

The following day, they go to Wincombe. *'I am in hopes the offer My Brother intends making Ld. Rivers that They may have Rushmore.'*

I see the phaeton was very useful. It was less of a performance to get it out than the much larger family coach, and any of the men could drive it. It could be driven with one or two horses, but for a longer journey they had to send their luggage separately, hence Charlotte saying on July 5th, *'We packed our clothes to go by the Cart to Coker.'*

July 7th *'We left Fern. My Father drove Me my Mother & Harris in the Phaeton. We baited at Henstridge & arrived at Coker by Dinner time. We found all Our Friends there quite well…My brother Wm. With his Nephews John & Tom Waddington rode on Horseback.'* Coker Court is a little over thirty miles from Berwick. It seems a long way. Charlotte says, 'baited', which usually refers to resting and feeding horses, but she does not say they changed horses. It was certainly a good long ride for little Tom. He is great friends with his cousin William.

Charlotte is immediately bustling about visiting. It is obviously very hot. *'Caroline Helyar remained in the shady part of the Hay Field with the children.'* In fact, unusually, Charlotte was poorly. She says she took milk at breakfast instead of tea; *'it made Me ill all Day'.* It was then so hot in church she felt faint, but this does not stop her attending Sunday school. There is further talk of walking in the shade to avoid fatigue but otherwise the alms houses, the poor and the invalids are all revisited. *'The Children in the Evening drank Tea in the Moss house in the Wood.'*

July 13th *'My Father drove us in the Phaeton to Hinton St George Lord Pawletts Place. A most beautiful Picture of the Lady of the third Earl Pawlett Daughter of Ld. Pembroke & in Vandykes large Picture at Wilton. This was painted by Gibson. An extra ordinary carved Oak Frame to one of the Familly Pictures. A fine large Saloon & curious old Tapestried Bed Chambers.'* This house, still standing but divided up in the 1960s or 1970s, belonged to Earl Paulett. His descendant or collateral parted with the last bit of the property in 1968.

On the 15th, they return. The Helyars have promised to come to Ferne in August, which makes parting easier. On the 16th, Waddington arrives with his other three children.

They visit and are visited all the time by several generations of Binghams. *'Little Miss Bingham has translated Gullivers Travels into Latin & only 8 years old.'* It seems to me girls' education was not always neglected.

Horror of horrors, on the 22nd, *'Emma dreadfully won of me 7 games of Chess. It has quite given Me A disgust.'*

Family life is extra cheerful with all the Waddingtons at Ferne. *'Caroline & John made the Tea for Us & were very merry indeed.'*

The phaeton is in great use. Mr Grove drives them to Compton Chamberlayne to see the Penruddockes. Mr Penruddocke shows them his new stables '*& an Archway that leads to Them*'. At Berrycourt, the Groves are building a cottage for the shepherd.

Charlotte is still visiting and taking medicine to G Wyatt, who had the accident in the quarry.

The weather is still uncomfortably hot. The Waddingtons, apart from Tom, go to Wincombe, but William plays cricket with him and they go to Farnham to see the Marklands and their children. '*I shall adopt their plan of shutting the Windows to keep out the intense heat. We returned through Rushmore. It is A delightful Place I wish Tom may have it.*'

July 29th '*Evening I visited Mrs Lush at Rowberry & Mrs White the later has the finest Pink Holly Hocks, I ever saw.*'

July 30th '*The Waddington Family returned from Wincombe. Mrs Walsh her little Girl, & Henry Jackson spent the Day with Us. Dr Grove came. My Father was much amused with little Annie Walsh – Arabella sung sweet Home to Us & some other Songs – my Nephew John W. makes a famous Nurse.*' There is much charm in the Grove family life.

August 1st '*Wm. Drove Me in the Phaeton to Netherhampton, He dined with Us & returned Home in the Evening.*' They are joined by Charles and Eliza. '*I read aloud some of Sense & Sensibility to the Ladies.*' A few days later she declares '*The Ladies much interested in it*'. We enjoy these novels for the characterisation etc. and they are enhanced, for us, by the period, so I find it amusing how much they were enjoyed by those for whom they were contemporary.

On the 3rd, they go into Salisbury. '*We call at Close Gate. Little John I think the prettiest of all My Brothers children.*' They go to Salisbury races: '*not much sport & it was soon over*'. They go again on the 5th. '*Williams Horse Evergreen ran but was beat by Bulow.*' That evening they go to the ball, but Charlotte is distracted by the fact John's wife Jane is '*taken seriously ill*'. She says, '*I tried to enjoy it as much as I could. Miss Anna Benett*

I admire more than her sister Ethel.' Here were John Benett's daughters from Pythouse. Anna was a year younger than Ethel.

Fortunately, Jane is better again the next day. William dines with them and then drives Charlotte home. '*My Aunt was so kind as to give me A very pretty Leghorn Hat made at the Wilton Manufactory the Plait. Mrs Lewis made it up & trimmed it.*' So you could buy the straw plaited up and then a milliner could turn it all in to a hat.

August 7th '*Tom called here, I fear there is not a chance of them getting Rushmore. Caroline is A dear interesting Girl. I hope She will soon get rid of her troublesome Cough.*'

The following day, Waddington takes John and Caroline off to school, young George going with them. They are left with little Tom and Emma. William and his father are going to Oxfordshire.

The remaining party dine with the Danseys on the 10th. '*The party consisted of only 4 gentlemen & 12 Ladies. A young Lady from Russia put on the Costume of that Country, & danced A Dance in Character. She was a Beautiful Girl of only 12 years old & looked to be fifteen.*'

On the 11th, we have a bit of Jane Austen, right to the name. They go to '*the Parsonage*' to congratulate Mrs Bingham on her niece Miss Erle, who has been staying with them some time, on her engagement to Mr Charles Austin. '*She seemed extremely pleased with it. The Young Lady & Mrs P Bingham had gone to Gillingham to see her old Nurse.*' On the 14th, Charlotte visits the Binghams after church. '*Mr C Austin A Lawyer & friend of Mr P Binghams there. I talked to Miss Earle about her intended Marriage & Tollard where Our Family lived two years whilst the House was building.*' I surmise Charles Austin to be a brother of the father of little Tom's friend at school, but this turns out to be wrong. John Lane did an exhaustive search to puzzle it out and concluded this Mr Austin was not connected to Tom's friend but a friend of the Bingham's son. The Austin/Austen business is further confused by alternative spelling.

August 15th *'My Mother paid morning Visits. She heard strange News that Miss Erle has changed her mind & will not now marry Mr Charles Austin. She is going to leave Berwick as soon as possible.'* On the 18th, Charlotte sees Mrs Bingham. *'Miss Erle is gone & her Aunt very much grieved at her Behaviour.'* She is certainly the subject of much gossip. Several days later, when the Helyars are staying, *'Mr Helyar rode to Sedgehill. He had A great deal of chat with his Sister Emily & Miss Harbin about Miss Earl.'* On the 21st, *'Mrs Bingham talked to me of her nieces extraordinary conduct.'*

In the meantime, Charles and Eliza have come to stay with Eliza's friend Miss Round, which seems an unfortunate surname. The Arundells and Mrs Burlton dine at Ferne; *'her Ladyship is grown fatter than ever.'*

Charlotte endeavours to get her erstwhile pupil H Hyscock placed as nursery maid with the Marklands, but unfortunately it does not work out. *'H Hyscock will not at all suit them & this first essay of my Pupil is A very bad one.'*

On the 16th, the Helyars arrive in their *'barouchette'*. Fanny Jackson is also staying but won't walk with Charlotte *'as it threatened Rain'*. Later she visits the Foots while Charlotte visits the Binghams. On the 17th, William and his nephew George, now fourteen, ride to Blandford races, dining with the Marklands at Farnham on the way. They stay in Blandford in order to go to the ball and ride back the following day.

August 22nd *'Mr Helyar & George called at Wincombe But Mrs T Grove was come here with Her Baby being anxious to show her Darling to Harriet. She is much grown & improved. Her Eyes are now the darkest Hazle.'*

August 23rd *'We breakfasted earlier & the Gentlemen went to West Lodge Buck hunting…I walked to Ludwell & bought A silk Shawl at Talbots. Emma won A Game of Chess of Me. We had A long Conversation about the Planets &c – & left off as wise in our ideas as We began.'* This is just how I feel about them, despite the advance in rockets etc. in the intervening one hundred and ninety-seven years.

At Wincombe, *'A Party proposed to the Dorchester Races which I dislike extremely But We must sometimes do disagreeable things to please Others. Tom showed off his Baby to great advantage.'*

August 27th *'Mr & Mrs Helyar prevented by the weather from leaving Wincombe – They sent over their servant for Tom Waddingtons Poney which their Son Albert is to ride.'*

On the 29th, Sarah Harris, Mrs Grove's maid, is ill from *'A Blow she received in her Head three weeks since. Mr Wills cupped & bled her.'*

Charlotte and her parents go off to Zeals, without Harris I suppose. On the 31st, *'My Father visited his Friend Sir R Hoare. He is A much older Man of his age than my dear Father. We had an excellent haunch of Venison for Dinner.'* This is, of course, Sir R Hoare of Stourhead.

September 1st *'I walked to the Lodge & saw A poor travelling Woman at the Gate who had been badly used by my Aunts Servants. We left Zeals – intensely hot till we reached Shaftesbury. We found Dr Grove Waddington & Tom regaling themselves with a hearty Luncheon. Poor Harris is very much hurt by the blow to her head, Dr Grove & Mr Wills are fearful of the consequences.'*

The next day, Harris has her head shaved and her sister comes to look after her. An abscess forms.

September 5th *'Harris suffers much pain But what Dr Grove has used, has brought the inflammation outside her head…Elizabeth Harris went Home. My Mother will take her in her Sisters situation if her Mother & Self approve of it.'*

On the 6th, Charlotte remarks, *'The little baby has A fine colour & looks better for being weaned.'* This was Mary Grove, now over eight months, so that must have been considered an appropriate time for weaning.

September 8th *'We got up at 5 o'clock & reached Dorchester in time for the Races. A large Party at the Kings Arms Inn, entertained on the Course with the Yeomanry & Hunters Races – A very good Ball, my niece enjoyed it & had plenty of pleasant Partners.'* Charlotte does not seem to talk of dancing herself any more. It is Emma that does the dancing.

They leave the next day. *'Mr Garth rode A few miles with Us in his way to hunt.'* Was this Tom Garth, the supposed child of Princess Sophia and General Garth? He would now be twenty-five.

Instead of returning to Ferne, they go to Coker Court. Charlotte is soon visiting the alms houses, a great haunt of previous stays with Harriet. I do not know what happened to Miss Lake, but it seems she has been replaced with a Mrs Smith, who is not liked. *'I think Mrs Smith has very unpleasant manners'* and *'I never saw Harriet take such A disgust as She has to Mrs S.'* Mr Helyar was given the task of getting rid of her but was not entirely effective. *'Mr Helyar spoke to Mrs Smith about her leaving Them. She did not seem to take the hint & I was obliged to put the finishing stroke to it.'*

In the meantime, they walk to see *'Where the Ice House is to be erected'*. There is an ice house at Ferne, but I do not know when it was constructed or if in use in Charlotte's day. Francis thinks it probably early 19th century.

On the 13th, *'Albert had A fall from his Poney which frightened my Sister very much.'* Albert is now seven and goes out coursing with his father and Emma Waddington.

September 15th *'I accompanied My Sister & Emma to Mrs Lucas's to see Miss Day who wishes to undertake Mrs Ls place. Cleanliness wanted, an insuperable objection.'*

September 16th *'A thorough wet Day. Emma beat me 7 games of Chess out of 9 – I suppose the dullness of the Day had some effect on my stupid Head as I had the advantage of Pawns in 2 of Them. Mrs Smith is to leave Coker Wednesday. A Reprieve for Harriet as the Woman haunts Her.'* Harriet seems less robust than Charlotte in dealing with such matters. Presumably it was Harriet who employed Mrs Smith in the first place.

They return to Ferne on the 17th, in Brookwater spotting *'Tom with his Gun & Pointers – made Him A Bow (en passant)'*.

Mrs Grove's maid, Sarah Harris, is getting better, but her sister Elizabeth has been taken on in her place. Eliza is learning to play chess, which hardly seems wise to me. *'She had A Game in the Evening with her Husband & many instructors looking on.'*

They are starting to sell the furniture at Donhead Hall. September 20th *'Second days Sale at Donhead. Pictures &c sold cheap – & inferior articles dear.'* Donhead Hall, at this juncture, according to Desmond Hawkins, was still in the ownership of the disgraced Knellers. I have not made out if it stood empty since the Knellers left in 1821. It was probably let to one or other of the families Charlotte mentions.

September 21st *'Mr King of Alvediston is dead. An irreparable loss to the Poor.'*

September 25th *'Tom W dined with Us. He dressed in his Sisters Bonnet &c & looked so like his dear Mother.'* This must have been a poignant recollection of Charlotte's sister Emma. She does not mention the girls, Emma and Caroline, as resembling her. Mrs Grove went to Combe Priory. *'My unfortunate Uncle James is there, very ill, We fear A Typhus Fever: all my Aunts Family are from Home.'*

They are paid a visit of a few days by *'Miss Ethel & Miss Anna Benett of Pythouse'*. Charlotte says, *'they are true Benetts in regard to the Gift of the Tongue.'* It seems as if any ill feeling between the Groves and the Benetts is finally buried. Anna was a year younger than Emma Waddington. William walks them, and Emma, to Ashcombe to see his horse, Evergreen, where he must be keeping it.

Charlotte gives the Sunday school prize to Martha Bradley. George Wyatt, who had the accident in the quarry, is sufficiently recovered to work, though later Charlotte says his hand is still bad. Mr Grove's tenants come as it is rent day on the 24th. Waddington's tenant also comes, presumably from Woodcots.

October 4th *'Before Breakfast I went to see the Fish taken out of our Pond which has not been drawn for 16 years.'* There was a sort of a wet bit in the woods when we were at Ferne, which Francis reckoned on being a pond, but it must have been more of a pond in Charlotte's day if there were fish in it.

Waddington is considering buying Upwood, near what Charlotte calls *'Hanley'* but I think more likely this is *'Handley'*. I see there is an Upwood House at Sixpenny Handley, a large part of it looking suitable. He and George ride there to look at it.

Charlotte is as busy as usual with club matters. Between losing games of chess with Emma she is walking and visiting as much as ever, but now Waddington and Emma, after a long stay, return to town. *'My niece is a nice pleasant unaffected Girl.'*

October 12th *'Mr Long gave Us A clever dissertation on Craniology.'* Examining the shape of the skull to ascertain character was a craze at this period, though from what I have read it was rarely accurate.

A sort of inherited patronage still exists. October 16th *'Ld Pembroke has John Waddingtons name inserted in the Enniskillen List.'* It is slightly confusing about the name of this regiment, as the Inniskillings sprung from Enniskillen. Later Charlotte says John is going from the 14th Regiment to this, but I have failed to follow it all.

October 23rd *'I attended the Sunday School. I was obliged to punish Grace Chowne. Mr Bingham has gained in the Lottery a sixteenth share of £20.00. The second time he has had the same good fortune. A Foreigner attended the Church without Shoes &c excited compassion by doing his duty to his God & got some Silver, a pr. Of Shoes & something to eat given Him.'* I try to visualise a similar happening now. As for the lottery, a little over a pound does not seem much, but it was twice what a labourer might be earning.

Aunt Grove arrives. She offers to take Charlotte to Bath to see a dentist, which Charlotte accepts, though it means giving up an invitation to Langton. She also gives money for the club. *'Mr & Mrs Bingham & Mrs Sarah Bingham dine with us.'* I take the latter to be the lady who took the one pound from the poor box.

October 28th *'I walked to Berwick & engaged Mr John Lushes Pew for the Sunday School. I called on Mrs J Lush for the purpose, & she easily granted Me the favour.'* This establishes that the Sunday school was held in the Church and reminds us that people paid for their pews. Those who could not afford it presumably scrambled in somewhere. Charlotte goes on to say of Mrs Lush: *'She appears exactly what A Farmers Wife ought to be.'* Sadly, she does not give us any better idea of this ideal.

The following day, *'Grace Chowne has behaved better this week.'* Charlotte Shepherd gets six pence from Mr Grove for being good. Charlotte engages Jenny James *'to attend the children to Church salary 4d month'*.

'George in the Spring will go to Town on Dr Groves advice.' He definitely does not enjoy good health. William, on the other hand, is to go to their cousin, Mr Long, at Preshaw, for a month. The time will no doubt be taken up entirely with sporting activities.

November 7th *'Miss Walsh & Henry Jackson come over in the Gig to call upon Us. The company of some young Ladies makes my Brother George very polite.'* On the same day, *'I hope when A certain event has taken place my brother George will recover his health & our pleasant Castle Building happen.'* What the event might be I cannot make out, but Charlotte obviously hopes George is to marry. She says, *'George told my Father that his hand is much better which I am very glad to hear.'* This makes me wonder if George has some rheumatoid complaint.

On the 9th, Mrs Grove gets a letter from Charles Jackson, who had arrived in Bombay in June. *'They were most hospitably received by General Wilson.'*

November 10th *'Snow in the night. My Fathers room smoked very much. I managed mine so well as to be able to remain in it.'* They seem to have quite a lot of trouble with chimneys.

On the 13th, there is a letter from Miss Lake, somehow reinstated, to say *'that my dear Sister Helyar was safely brought to Bed the 11th inst, of A very fine little Boy.'* This is Charles, Harriet's ninth child.

November 14th *'My Aunt Grove came. Her new Horses will not do at all. They knocked up only coming from Neverhampton here.'* Horses were definitely meant to go much longer distances than I had previously thought. Aunt Grove sends them back, intending *'to go Post to Bath'*, meaning she would hire horses on the route.

November 15th *'I walked to Susan Barters. She has had Twins & has been very ill indeed. The Boy is living. She was in great pain today. Mr Wills came whilst I was there & I hope will be of service to her.'* Mrs Baker was there, landlady of the Glove and a mother of thirteen. *'A very good tempered woman & very kind to poor Susan.'*

November 16th *'Left Fern with my Aunt. We arrived at Bath in excellent time.'* There is always the unexplained illness, this time Mrs Vashti, Aunt Grove's maid. They send for an apothecary *'who did her a great deal of good'*. *'We are comfortably lodged in the York House.'* I see there is a York House Hotel, listed Grade II, in George Street, so I suppose it is likely to be the same place.

There is no talk of quadrilles and balls. Charlotte is now forty-two, and this is a sedate visit with her elderly aunt, though they do go to the theatre, dine out and entertain her aunt's friends. She visits Mr Shew, the dentist, three times, but does not tell us exactly what he did, though the results were satisfactory. *'I went to Mr Shew & returned much improved'* and *'He is more clever & much more reasonable than the last I consulted.'*

November 21st *'We went to the Arcade A covered Passage with Shops each side & Musick plays all the time.'* It seems this must have been a new idea for Charlotte to bother to describe it.

On the 23rd, *'We dined at Mrs B Helyars. Mr Hugh Helyar took me Prisoner after Dinner which afforded nice conversation for the old Ladies.'* Charlotte's age apparently does not make her feel immune from gossip. Hugh was one of William's brothers. When Charlotte first mentions him early in the diaries, she says he was very shy, so he must have recovered from this.

November 24th *'We left Bath, Arrived at Zeals just as my Aunt Chafin was seated at Dinner of which We were most happy to partake, very comfortable Fires in the old Mansion. My Aunt in A sad distress about her Servants.'*

Charlotte walks to Mere the next day and visits the women in the Lodge. I remember this lodge, if it is the same building, because it was occupied when I was young by Leigh Holman, the first husband of Vivienne Leigh, who she left for Lawrence Olivier. Leigh Holman, a charming old gentleman, employed me to photograph his three grandsons for his Christmas card.

November 25th *'I read to my Aunts the Newspaper nearly through & began the Novel my Aunt bought.'*

November 26th *'I read again & chatted by turns to my two Aunts. I can never do sufficient to express my gratitude to my Aunt P Grove for her kindness to me. I have promised should any unhappy Parylatic stroke happen to Her to take charge & see that She is well taken care of.'*

November 27th *'We went to Mere Church. Mr Casson gave Us A fine powerful Sermon on the Day of Judgement. A fine Organ there.'*

November 29th *'Mrs Charles Grove invited me to a Ball at Salisbury which I declined.'*

They return home the next day and life resumes its normal tenure. Donhead Hall has been sold to *'Mr C Wyndham'*. Charlotte goes with her parents to call on him and his wife. *'We are very much pleased with them.'* Susan Barter, who had the twins, *'is rather better'*. Mrs Grove has provided clothes for *'The eldest Girl & three eldest Boys'*. Charlotte starts to teach Bessy chess. *'Tom cannot bear the game. She is a very apt scholar.'* Mrs Shere has a daughter. The club blankets at Talbots are *'excellent'*. They cost 8s 6d. Charlotte gets a letter from Mrs Charles Jackson from Bombay, dated July, so it has taken five months to arrive. Waddington *'has thoughts of buying Upwood in the Chase if They ask A reasonable price'*. Harriet Lush has *'got quite well'*. Dr Grove and his family are staying. *'Henrietta is a very fine child.'*

December 7th *'I visited Mrs Shere & saw her very fine little Baby. Tom not very well pleased with his sister'*. This was little Tom Shere, much admired for his beauty.

The pony lent to Albert Helyar arrives from Coker. Charlotte meets the three boys, Tom Waddington and Masters Austen and Weld, when she goes to Berwick. *'The former delighted at the arrival of his poney.'*

For once she is cross with Tom and Bessy. *'They have behaved shabbily in deserting the Shaston Ball.'* However, some combination of the family went. *'It was extremely well attended & We all enjoyed it very much.'* There was, it seems, an obligation to support local events then – and now.

It is difficult to puzzle out who all the people are who Charlotte visits in Berwick, but on Christmas Day *'I met old Amy his sister & her Daughter coming up to Fern to dine.'* There was entertainment for servants past and present. This is where a lack of a comma can lead one into trouble. Oldy was not a sister of Amy; the party included Sarah Pinnock, who was. The next day, *'I danced two Country Dances with my nephew Tom Waddington in the Servants Hall.'*

At the end of the year, George again is so ill they send for John. *'He as usual with his excellent advice soon did him a great deal of good. William called having heard an account of his brothers illness.'* Charlotte makes some comments about George's health, which include the words *'has been of late years'*, but she has crossed them out. She also says that William returned home, which puzzled me because I thought he was living at Ferne, and if he was not, where was he living? William is the most confusing of the family, his sporting activities taking him everywhere.

The end paper for this year is worth quoting in full, remembering Fonthill Abbey had been sold by Beckford to Mr Farquhar.

December 21st *'Fonthill Abbey the Tower of it fell down being built of such very slight materials. Mr Farquhar eat his Dinner as contentedly as if it had not happened. It is A very great loss in the Front View from Fern – remaining as it is, it now looks like an old Barn with A Tower of A Church – Fortunate it was when such Crowds of People went to see it in 1824 & 1823 that it did not then fall down when many lives would have been lost.'*

1826

This year starts with a recipe for spruce beer. I had often come across references to it and had wondered if one had to gather pine needles, but no, to every three gallons of water, add *'one tablespoonful of Essence of Spruce'*. Otherwise, it contained treacle, powdered ginger and yeast. The contents are given for six gallons of water and as it was to be drunk *'about 4 or 5 days after bottling'*, you would need quite a gathering to consume it.

Tom Waddington is still on holiday. He exercises in the riding house and hunts with his grandfather and his uncles. He visits the Welds and takes *'a ride with Master Greenaway'*, staying to dine with the Welds. I have a vision of him rambling about our lanes and hills much as my own children did. Charlotte is trying to get a nursery place for Emma Weeks. Finding places for her various pupils is becoming an occupation. Aunt Grove cannot visit them because her maid Vashti is too unwell. Arrangements for the club continue.

January 8th *'William drove my Mother & Me to Church, Mr Weld did the duty for Mr Bingham, who is gone to Bath. Mr W reads extremely well & I should like often to have the pleasure of hearing Him.'*

John stays overnight. January 9th *'Dr Grove left Us. Wm walked with Him to the Cribbage Hut when his Gig overtook Him with Tom Waddington who walked back to Fern with his Uncle.'* I take it this was with prior arrangement, though Charlotte does not say so. Tom, in his twelfth year, is considered capable enough to drive his uncle John's horse along, what was then and is now, the main road. The Cribbage Hut was called thus when I arrived here in 1969 and is now the Lancers but certainly not the same building. It is on the left when you are going from Swallowcliffe to Fovant. The entry ends *'Our Evenings pass so very rapidly with Our delightful Readings.'*

January 11th *'I walked with Eliza to Talbots, on our return We met my Brother Tom. Mrs T Grove has the finest Blue & Silver Dress for the Fancy Ball at Salisbury that ever was seen. Dr Groves House has been A fire. But no lives lost.'* The next day, *'My kind Aunt P Grove has taken the Dr & his Family into her House.'*

On the 14th, *'Farmer Sharps youngest Daughter is dreadfully burnt & not expected to survive.'* This was the real hazard of the age so reliant on candles. She dies on March 17th.

January 19th *'My Brother has taken Holnest, Mr Davies Place, nr. Sherborne, for several Years.'* That settles a residence for Tom for a bit. The house was built by Mr Davis in 1802, according to one source, and rebuilt in the 1840s by the Drax family. One does wonder why, as it was only forty years old. It is now apartments and was badly burnt in 2010, so we can have no vision of how it was when Tom lived there.

January 20th *'A strange Story of A Person dressed up as A skeleton Ghost that walks the Streets of Salisbury & frightens the People. It springs some paces when followed.'*

Charlotte reports on Bessy making a large party for the *'Shaston Ball'*, so perhaps making up for missing the last one. William takes out his father's new horse *'& it went very quietly with him'*. Mr Grove is now sixty-eight, not considered young, though he goes on until eighty-four. I feel William checking the horse out on his behalf.

January 26th *'Fanny & Henry Jackson come to accompany Wm & myself, to the Shaston Ball – A great many people & very pleasant Parties from Pythouse & Wincombe.'* The next day, *'my Cousins staid with Us, & We had great pleasure in talking over the Ball – indeed I think these County*

Assemblies, very pleasant indeed.' Charlotte is just short of her forty-third birthday and content with local entertainment.

On February 4th, *'My dear brother Tom had a fall from his horse.'* She does not say in what way he was hurt. He is immediately bled, the great inexplicable cure-all. He is just about over it by the 12th.

February 5th they all go to Wincombe to take leave of Tom and his wife. *'Tom W. also of the party, with whom little Mary was much pleased.'* I am glad to think Tom Waddington is happy to play with the baby.

February 8th *'My nephew John Waddington arrived to pay Us a visit, before he joins the 6th.'* There was the equivalent of Sandhurst then, for the training of officers, but no compulsion to go there. They learnt the business on arrival. Charlotte then says, *'The foreign silk Trade is going to be encouraged. I hope it will not be detrimental to old England.'* I think of the children in the workhouse reeling of the silk from the cocoons and realise it must have been quite a local industry.

On the 9th, *'I was busily employed taking out of my Brothers Wardrobe the invaluable Presents my dear Sister Bessy has given me.'*

They enjoy John Waddington's company until the 18th, when his young brother Tom comes to dine *'& take leave of him'*. He goes by the mail to London to join his regiment.

The year goes on with its normal occupations, visiting, charitable and otherwise, Charlotte's pupils and Sunday school, in which there are up to thirty-three girls and eleven boys.

There is a ruction on the 21st. *'That little Urchin Cupid has made sad havock amongst the Female part of our Household. A thorough change is to be effected.'* The next day, *'My Mother very busy giving Warning to the Cook, Dairy Maid, & Housemaid.'* However, on the 23rd, *'There will not on Investigation be such A Change as was expected.'* I am sorry Charlotte does not enlarge on the matter.

George's health is still causing concern, though he has taken to singing *'the Heroine's Songs in a most pathetic style'*. What are these?

Fanny Jackson comes to stay. On March 2nd, *'Fanny & I looked over the Silver that was given Me & I hope to make trimmings for dresses.'* A lot of self-help went on. Charlotte had *'worked'* a dress for John's daughter Henrietta, I imagine embroidering it in some way. Aunt Grove gives money to S Barter, whom she had helped clothe her children, towards buying a cow.

March 5th *'I accompanied my Mother & Cousin to Church. I took a walk with the latter but it was rather A task being so very cold.'*

Henry Jackson joins them. *'The Gentlemen hunted. George equipped my Cousin Henry Jackson for the Occasion.'* The Jacksons leave on the 11th.

On the 13th, Charlotte goes to *'Mrs Lushes School. My nephew Tom W. met me there & heard the Children read. Complaints of Martha Bradley & Grace Chowne.'*

Tom and Bessy *'with their nice little girl'* arrive on the 21st, as does John Waddington. His father joins them the following day, and Tom Waddington *'came Home to meet his Father'*. Certainly Ferne was more home to this child than anywhere else. Charlotte now spends time playing with little Mary.

On March 23rd all the male Groves and Waddington dine with the tenants, the *'Ladies dined in the Library'*. It is apparent only the tenants came, not their wives.

On Easter Sunday, they go to church and *'received the Sacrament'*. This is something that has changed in the Church of England. Even ardent churchgoers like the Groves only celebrated Holy Communion on the most important days in the church calendar.

Waddington leaves and Charles and Eliza arrive.

March 28th *'Eliza accompanied Me in A Walk to Berwick. We called on the Miss Lushes, & were treated with some of their nice Easter Cake.'* What was traditional for an Easter cake then? *'George was very unwell.'* We hear this all the time but do not here more of William and the rheumatism. He goes off to the Salisbury ball with his nephew John.

On the last day of the month, *'Mrs Thos. Grove my Brothers with old Amy were hard at Work making A new Walk.'* The young Groves were up for a bit of manual labour and apparently Bessy was not too precious to join in. She seems robust, though I calculate she was about three months pregnant. If she and Tom had had a boy, Ferne would not have passed to John. The subsequent story would have been different.

April 4th *'I walked with Mrs Thos. Grove to Mr Welds – John Austin & my Nephew have tame Squirrels the formers, is kept in his Pocket.'* The grey squirrel was introduced in the 1870s from the U.S.A., so the boys had the red ones. Both boys take their Sunday dinners at Ferne on a regular basis.

April 7th *'My Father hunted. Henry I & JW – officiated as Whippers in & enjoyed it much.'* Henry refers to Henry Jackson. I think Mr Grove must have been taking out his harriers, which he would have done on foot. Charlotte then says, *'Granby is but A stupid Novel'* thus dismissing what was a new publication by T.H. Lister.

Charlotte's visiting at the moment includes William Wicks. *'He is very cheerful tho' so ill.'* He dies on the 13th, *'within the Hour after I left him'.* She duly goes to see him in his coffin two days later.

Their social life continues much the same, though Mr Gordon and his new wife are an addition, now living at Wincombe in place of Tom. *'Mr & Mrs Gordon & her Brother Mr Willoughby Brassey, dined here. A very deaf Trio.'*

On the 9th, young John Waddington goes off to Dorchester, where his regiment is stationed. He takes his breakfast on the way with his uncle Charles at Tarrant Hinton.

April 16th *'A letter received from Sir William Fraser with the good news that he has procured Henry Jackson A Cadetship. My Aunt Jackson has now four Sons in that line of Life.'* The family network is in action as usual. I assume these cadetships were in the East India Company.

April 18th *'Mrs Long has worked me A fashionable net cap & Aunt Grove paid for the trimming.'* Netting was an occupation down the knitting/crotchet line. It was often done to make purses. Wearing a cap was a mark of age for a woman. The famous portrait of Jane Austen, done by her sister, definitely features a cap.

April 19th *'I walked to Charlton, to see General Coffins new House. I waited some time before General & Mrs Coffin came accompanied by Mr & Mrs Charles Coffin: it is A most excellent planned House & pretty situation.'* I think this must be the second house along when you have turned left at the top of Ludwell Hill. Later she visits with her mother and refers to it as *'Charlton Lodge'*.

The following day, Charles arrives to *'enquire about the Living of Sedgehill which is to be sold'*. Two days later, William returns from staying with Tom and Bessy at Holnest Lodge. *'He does not give A favourable account of the situation.'*

April 23rd *'Edwards our late Butler, brought his Bride here. She is A very pretty young Woman. They keep the Lamb at Hindon.'* I do not recollect Charlotte mentioning the loss of Edwards or who replaced him. Perhaps it had to do with the ruction amongst the staff reported on March 21st.

Charles and Eliza have gone to London with Aunt Grove. Charles sends some drawings of the dresses, no doubt to keep his female relatives informed of the fashions.

Charlotte mentions Harriet having *'A grand Christening of her two youngest Children'*. So long as a child had been safely baptised, the Christening could take place several years later. Now we do not separate them out in the same way.

Old Sarah Maidment dies, who Charlotte describes as friend, underlining it. She is soon off to view the body and plead the cause of William Maidment with Mr Blackmore. Was he their landlord?

On May 4th, Charlotte and her parents go to Holnest to stay with Tom and Bessy. *'My Brother has A very nice House indeed.'* So Charlotte does not agree with William. She is soon taking *'A nice exploring walk'* and finds the country pretty.

They return on the 11th. There now commences a mystery about the Jacksons. *'I pity my Cousin F Jackson, as she is now in A most uncomfortable situation'*, and later, on the 22nd, *'I accompanied My Mother to Combe. I pity My dear cousins J very much. The best Arrangement is now made that they can Adopt we think.'* Had they run out of money?

May 17th *'I accompanied Mrs Bingham to Birdbush. We saw Mr Jones scholars, & heard Him preach in the Presbyterian Chapel.'* I really am surprised at Mrs Bingham and Charlotte doing this; I would have thought it totally against their principles. Francis thinks the chapel was at this end of the council houses at Birdbush. Charlotte goes on to say William has *'some extraordinary opinions'*. It is frustrating not knowing what these might be. The following day, she says, *'my gown arrived from Lewes's with A very pretty Muslin My Aunt has given Me.'* Those very light muslins we associate with Georgette Heyer and the Regency must have still been in vogue.

May 19th *'I walked to Donhead Hall & called upon Mrs C Wyndham… Mr C Wyndham shewed me his handsome Cows.'* However grand, practically everyone was involved in agriculture.

On May 24th, they hear that the Binghams *'were overturned from their Gig & too much hurt to return Home. Particulars we know not.'*

Mr Bingham has broken his arm *'& his head is much hurt'*. Mrs Bingham is badly bruised.

May 28th *'Our Friend the Rev. P Bingham died at two o'clock this Morning much regretted by his Parishioners and all his Acquaintance. We had prayers at home. Mrs Bingham is rather better. She does not yet know of her Husbands Death. I Wish We have as kind A Rector & his Wife to the Poor as Mr & Mrs Bingham have been.'* Mrs Bingham goes to her sister, Mrs Burlton.

There is further bad news the following day. *'We heard the sad News that Mr Keith Fraser was thrown from his Horse down a Precipice, & killed on the Spot.'* This was a brother of Jane, John's wife.

Fanny and Frederick Jackson come to stay. Fanny is often unwell, but Charlotte thinks it *'only nervous'*. We do not know exactly what went wrong for the Jacksons, but on June 6th, *'We received very comfortable accounts from my Aunt Jackson. Mr Walsh has been such a kind son in law.'*

I take this as a hint Arabella's husband has sorted things out, probably with financial help. Fanny, when well, spends much time with the Foots.

June 2nd *'Fanny Jackson very ill again. Frederick shot some rooks. I walked to see the little Reads. Beasts foot A good Herb for The Worms to take away the Hoof which is poisonous.'* I tried the Internet for an explanation for this confusing entry. Home cures seem alarming to us, but what else did they have? John Lane looked it up in *Culpeper's Complete Herbal*. Humans cannot get lungworm, but they can get roundworms in the lungs. The cure was coltsfoot, but it was also poisonous. It seems, from Charlotte's garbled statement, she knew which bit of the plant to remove in order not to poison anybody.

Mr Bingham is buried on the 4th. *'Mr C Bowles & Capt. Benett attended the Funeral.'* Who did or did not attend funerals and weddings is quite mysterious. Bowles was his brother-in-law and Benett married to his wife's niece, so that seems logical, but I would have expected Mr Grove to attend. Instead he sets off for Norfolk, where they had property, with William.

There was a general election in this month, but Charlotte does not mention it.

Dr Grove is attending on Mrs Bingham. On the 16th, he returns as far as Netherhampton with Mrs Grove *'& most lucky he did, as on their Arrival They found My dearest Father had been thrown out of the Phaeton, he had A Black Eye & cut his Arm But I trust nothing more Serious'*. Despite a horse or horses being slow in comparison to the motorcar, they seem to be just as dangerous.

June 21st *'Mr Hater tuned the Piano & took Home mine & my Mothers watches to repair. Charles and Eliza arrived & both very anxious about Sedgehill'*, and on the 23rd, *'Mr Chitty called with the delightful News that Charles has the Living of Sedgehill.'* Aunt Grove had said, on inheriting a fortune, she would buy Charles a living, so it is likely this was it. They are soon off to look at the Sedgehill Rectory. Mr Chitty must have been the agent. He is frequently mentioned at this juncture.

Charlotte is now regularly visiting *'Mrs P Bingham'*, Mrs Bingham's daughter-in-law, while she stays with her family at the Rectory. As a widow, Mrs Bingham would have to give up the Rectory almost immediately. The Berwick living belonged to New College, Oxford, so rather than it being sold, it would be conferred on a clergyman of the college's choosing.

July 2nd *'Mr Downes has been to see the Living, & if He is elected proposes to behave most liberally to his Predecessors widow.'* This was the 'dilapidations' that had to be paid for by the outgoing clergy if the Rectory was considered to have 'gone back'. Remember Charlotte complained of Mr Blackmore being ungenerous to Aunt Jackson when he took the living of Donhead St Mary. This is Charlotte's first mention of Mr Downes.

July 4th *'My brother & Sister CH Grove went to Sedgehill, are more pleased with the House & Environs.'*

On July 5th, *'Charles went to Sedgehill. Mr Macpherson has behaved in some little Articles in A close Scotch manner.'* Mr Macpherson must be the outgoing rector and not so liberal on the business of dilapidations: there was obviously much bargaining to be done.

July 10th *'General & Mrs Coffin dined here. My Aunt Grove arrived in the Evening – She is cutting two Understanding Teeth A wonderful thing at 69.'* So that was what wisdom teeth were called then.

They still see plenty of the Marklands. Captain Markland, who had some accident with his gun, *'has nearly recovered the use of his arm'*.

On Saturday the 15th of July, *'7 of my pupils came. S Wright has been beaten in the Face by her Mother.'* I look ahead to see if Charlotte follows this up, but there is no further mention of it. She goes off the following day with Fanny Jackson to see the alterations made to the *'Church & Parsonage'* in Lower Donhead. Tom Waddington goes to town to see his family and William drives Charles to Salisbury to see the Bishop. *'The latter has delayed giving him his Presentation.'*

George has been staying with Tom and returns *'looking so well & in such good spirits'*. The other person who has been causing concern is Caroline Waddington, mentioned as being poorly, slightly better or not.

On July 25th, whilst Charlotte is at Netherhampton, *'My Aunt received A letter from Waddington with the sad News of his Daughter Caroline having died the 23rd inst (most lovely Blossom returned untainted to her Maker).'* She was fourteen. The unshakable belief held in the Hereafter certainly helped Charlotte to reconcile herself to these events. She goes on to mention, *'We escaped A sad Accident the Reins of the Carriage Horses breaking.'*

Instead of going to the races, they *'went into the Field to see the Carriages &c pass'.*

Charlotte returns home on the 29th. She reports on the following day a man in Berwick named Blanchard Ludwell *'has had his House burnt down & all his Clothes lost & his effects'.*

In August, Waddingtons come and go. *'Emma talked to me of her dear departed sister.'* John Waddington goes by the mail to Dorchester, presumably to his regiment.

Charlotte goes to Holnest on August 5th. She has to put off her visit to Coker because Ellen has scarlet fever. She cannot visit the cottages at Holnest because of the typhus fever. They are joined at Holnest by Aunt Grove and Waddington and his son George, who goes off to Dorchester to see his brother. Nothing out of the way occurs until September 4th. *'I received from Miss Lake the sad News that little Emma Helyar was taken ill of the Scarlet Fever Wednesday & died Saturday.'* I have not found her birth date, but she must have been around four. Charlotte gets a letter from Harriet on the 10th. *'She bears her Affliction with Christian Fortitude.'*

However, on the 8th, *'We were called up at one O'clock & at five Mrs Thos Grove gave birth to A nice little Girl – Both Mother & Babe are quite well & She is to be named Charlotte in compliment to her Grandmama.'*

Being at Holnest gives Charlotte a whole lot of new walks to the surrounding villages, Glanville Wooton and Armitage, which she describes as pretty. She cannot go to Lyle *'as the Fever is there'*. They meet a glove-maker and commission some gloves at 1s 8d a pair. She is accompanied by Emma Partridge. Tom goes off to spend a day with his late wife's mother, old Mrs Farquharson, as it is her birthday. Charlotte says, *'Miss Fanny Grove & Mr Bullock called here in their way to Zeals where he was driving her in his Gig.'* According to Hawkins, Maria Caroline Grove married George Bullock of North Coker in 1826. Their son George Troyte Bullock inherited Zeals House, adopting the name of Chafin Grove. Certainly when I was young it was 'old Mrs Troyte Bullock' who lived at Zeals House. I am not sure how Caroline Maria turns in to Fanny, but he certainly would not have been driving around any girl but his fiancé in his gig.

September 15th *'Mr Farquharsons Hounds came cub hunting.'* This famous master of foxhounds certainly got about. The baby was baptised the same day.

On the 23rd, Bessy came down in the evening, and on the 24th, she ventures out in the carriage for an *'airing'*, having given birth on the 8th. My mother, giving birth in the 1940s, told me it was customary to be in bed for a month after a confinement, wrapped in hot towels, which seems extraordinary. I wish she was still with us to enlarge on the subject, as I cannot believe this was universal. In comparison, Bessy seems quite active.

Bessy is obviously fond of Charlotte. *'That dear Sister of mine desires Me to consider this as my other Home.'* This was more important than it sounds, because spinster sisters were not guaranteed a roof over their heads when their oldest brother married and inherited the property.

On the 27th, Tom drives Charlotte home in his phaeton.

September 28th *'Mr Downes the new Rector seems to be doing A great deal of good in the Village'* and on October 1st, *'I was introduced to our new Rector Mr Downes. He gave Us an excellent Sermon & We received the Sacrament.'* We now get tantalising glimpses of Mr Downes. He is immediately in attendance on the Sunday school and dines at Ferne on October 5th. He was forty-nine.

October 2nd *'I walked with Emma to Mrs Danseys. Her Children look delicate.'* Waddington has gone to stay a couple of nights at Pythouse in order to shoot.

The next day, Charlotte's mother, Emma and Frederick Jackson *'went to Fonthill to see the Ruins of that once noble Edifice'*. There really is no end to the Jackson male cousins, more than I can comprehend. Charlotte is teaching this one the chess moves. Charles' friend Mr Wallinger is staying, so there is more chess. Mr Downes attends Sunday school. He *'heard them their Catechism & questioned them'*. He does this again the following Sundays.

On the 5th, Charlotte sees Mrs Bingham for the first time since the accident. She is still with Mrs Burlton, her sister, in Donhead St Mary.

October 20th *'I accompanied My Mother & Eliza to Farnham Cottage. We saw Mr & the two Miss Marklands…A fine Family of Children. Lucy Markland quite A Beauty.'*

Aunt Grove gives ninety pounds for the three clubs, I suppose the Berwick one and the two Donheads, a really huge sum. Mr Downes puts *'13 pupils to Mrs Lush'*. I think this must mean he pays for them to go.

October 25th *'Miss Downes arrived yesterday & gave the Ringers 10s for ringing for her.'* It was customary to ring the church bells to welcome a new incumbent, and on this occasion it was extended to Mr Downes' sister, presumably coming to Berwick to keep house for him. Charlotte goes with Fanny Jackson to call on her on the 28th, and she goes again on November 2nd. Charlotte says absolutely nothing about her, not even 'pleasing' or otherwise, which is her normal. Mr Downes has gone to Oxford to be inducted to the *'Living of Berwick'*. Miss Downes dutifully returns the call on the 7th.

The whole proceeding for obtaining your 'living' was long winded. Mr Downes is *'instituted to the living of Berwick'* on the 19th but he still has to be *'inducted'* on December 1st, accompanied by Charles, who *'on his return the chill of the Church made him so ill He was obliged to go to Bed'*. On December 3rd, *'Mr Downes read in the 39 articles.'*

On November 13th, there is unexplained servant trouble. *'My Mother is obliged to part with Harris. Daniel acted as A trustworthy upper Servant.'* Did he spill the beans on Harris? She leaves a few days later. In the same entry, *'George amused Himself in making a Carriage go with the powers of Mgnetism.'* This is Charlotte's spelling, not mine.

Mr Downes, on the 14th, *'is obliged go to Town to attend the Bishop & cannot dine here Tomorrow'.*

November 15th *'Mr & Mrs C Wyndham & Miss Downes dined here. The latter slept at Fern.'*

November 16th *'I walked to Talbots with Miss Downes & then escorted Her home to Berwick. She shewed me the Parsonage…Miss D. gave me a French Almanack.'*

November 17th *'I am embroidering a Dress with the Beetles Wings.'* This form of decoration came from Asia. It was possible to do it yourself. The iridescent wing is very durable and can be seen on old textiles where the fabric has just about disintegrated. The art is still practised.

Fanny and Frederick Jackson seem to be more at Ferne than at home. Fanny helps Charlotte with the school, both of them teaching when *'H Amy'* was ill. I am confused as to whether this is the Lushes' school or not. They are reading *Pride and Prejudice* for the second time, as popular then as now.

November 27th *'Mr & Mrs C Wyndham are now settled in the purchase of Donhead Hall.'*

November 29th *'Mr Downes called here. My Mother being busy writing letters sent me down to receive Him'* and the following day, *'I walked by myself to Berwick met Mr Downes on my return who had called at Fern.'* Apart from being enthusiastic about his sermons and his general generosity, we learn nothing of him, yet Charlotte was to marry him the following year.

The erring Harris is replaced by Mrs Lampard as lady's maid to Mrs Grove. She was Daniel Lampard's wife. Henry Jackson *'is so silly'* to give up his cadetship. They hope to get it for Frederick instead. They receive *'Bride Cake'* from *'Mr & Mrs Bullock'*. Tom Waddington still spends his Sundays at Ferne, with or without *'Master Austen'*. At the start of the Christmas holiday, he goes in the phaeton to his uncle in

Salisbury to be put on the coach *'to Town where he is to meet his Father & Brother George'*.

December 5th *'Miss Pakington & my Aunt Grove came. We passed our evening in Conversation.'* I am interested Charlotte actually says this, making it clear it was a departure from their normal reading aloud.

December 7th *'I walked with Eliza & Fanny in the Corridor being so fine an exercise on A wet Day.'* I cannot see we would bother nowadays.

The business of the clubs goes on, but Sarah Pinnock, who was *'Club Collector'* does not seem to manage the job and is replaced by Martha West. Reading in the evening continues, both William and Frederick Jackson *'took their turns'*. Fanny Jackson is Charlotte's constant companion, though quite often *'feint'*.

On the 18th, *'We received the good news that Frederick Jackson is to succeed to the Cadetship of his brother Henry.'*

December 21st *'We called on Miss Downes. She walked back with Us & then I escorted her to the entrance of Berwick again.'* This does sound as though they had plenty to say to each other.

December 23rd *'I went with Fanny J. to Talbots paid £12 of my Berwick Penny Club Bill – 5 of my pupils came through the Xmas Holidays. Accusations against G Chowne.'*

December 24th *'Mr Downes has behaved very handsomely about the Penny Club.'*

Christmas comes and goes as usual, but on the 27th, *'I walked to Berwick alone Fanny J having sprained her leg. I taught Frederick the Quadrilles. Mr Bennet Miss Ethel & Mr & Mrs Phipps called'*.

On December 29th, *'very pleasant Shaston Ball. 5 Officers of the Lancers, & 76 People there. I accompanied my Cousins & Wm. He is appointed Steward next time.'*

December 30th *'I walked with Fanny. She called on Mrs Foot. 4 of my Pupils came. I have expelled G Chowne my School for L—'* Charlotte does not say what the L is for. It could be larceny, but it was probably lying.

*

Charlotte wrote extensive end papers for this year, mostly concerning the weather. She mentions the sale of Fonthill to Mr Bennet. *'Mr Benett is to take the inside of Fonthill Wall under A Valuation on every Tree Shrub – &c &c also the inside of the demolished Abbey.'*

She goes on to report William's account of the Salisbury fancy-dress ball on January 21st. It is quite amusing reading what costumes were chosen, but my eye was really caught by this: *'Mr W C Grove dressed like old Mr Helyar (with the plan of that House in his hand).'* This picture, by Thomas Beach, was sold at Christie's in 2015 for twenty thousand pounds, exceeding its estimate of five to eight thousand pounds. Thomas Beach was a pupil of Sir Joshua Reynolds and practised from Bath. He did fourteen portraits of the Helyar family. William Chafin Grove was therefore wearing an 18th-century embroidered blue coat and waistcoat, the coat with a red collar. You might suppose a Helyar would have worn this for himself, but the only Helyar mentioned is Mr C Helyar *'in A Velvet Suit of his Grandfathers'*. Charlotte's brothers Tom and William went in *'Mr Farquharsons Hunt Uniform'*, which smacks of cheating as they would have had it anyway, but Bessy went as Clari from the Italian opera of that name. Charlotte had admired her dress of *'the finest blue and silver'*. Peasants of all nations except British ones were a popular choice.

There is mention of Mrs Grove being upset because John Waddington was transferred from the *'14th Regiment under Col Keane'* to Lord Pembroke's Enniskillens. The 14th was a Bedfordshire foot regiment. Perhaps his grandmother thought this more appropriate for his station in life, but we will never know.

A note for July 16th: *'Mr Dansey has not improved our Pew in his Church, having stopped up our Window by building the Vestry against it.'* The Groves paid for a pew in Lower Donhead as well as Berwick, but Ferne does actually stand in the latter parish.

The December 7th marriage of Maria Grove to Mr Bullock is mentioned, so I am still wondering why he was driving out with *'Fanny'*. Otherwise, there is more talk of the weather and a list of books read including '*Diary & Correspondence of Samuel Pepys Esqr.*' I am assuming this was an expurgated version, but maybe not.

The diary for 1827 is missing. Charlotte's married life is continued in a second volume, *Charlotte as Mrs Downes*.

Printed in Great Britain
by Amazon